ORIGINAL
M G B
With MGC and MGB GT V8

ORIGINAL
M G B
With MGC and MGB GT V8

ANDERS DITLEV CLAUSAGER

PHOTOGRAPHY BY JOHN COLLEY
EDITED BY MARK HUGHES

FRONT COVER

Alan Osborn's Tartan Red roadster,
dating from 1964, shows the MGB in
its earliest form, with a chrome grille
and pull-out door handles.

HALF-TITLE PAGE

The bonnet bulge instantly identifies
George White's Dark British Racing Green
1968 roadster as an MGC. A total of 9002
of these six-cylinder cars were built
in roadster and GT versions.

TITLE PAGE

The other big-engined derivative, the
MGB GT V8, is also covered in detail
in this book. Owned by Bill Donaldson,
this 1974 'chrome-bumper' version is
painted in Mirage. Out of 2591
MGB GT V8s built, 1856 were
'chrome-bumper' models.

BACK COVER

John Heagren bought this 'rubber-bumper'
MGB GT V8, painted in Flamenco, new
in 1975 and has cared for it fastidiously ever since.
As a result it survives as an outstanding
record of original specification.

Published 1994 by Bay View Books Ltd
The Red House, 25-26 Bridgeland Street
Bideford, Devon EX39 2PZ

Reprinted 1996 (twice)

© Copyright 1994 Bay View Books Ltd
Typesetting and layout by Chris & Sarah Fayers

ISBN 1 870979 48 6
Printed in Hong Kong
by Paramount Printing Group

CONTENTS

INTRODUCTION

Since my publisher and my editor will not allow me to describe this book as 'the worst I have ever written', I have to settle for describing it as 'the most difficult I have ever had to write'. It was certainly long enough in coming while I struggled with an immense volume of data, so I thank Charles and Bridgid Herridge of Bay View Books for their patience. I hope the result was worth the wait – for them and for you.

We have certainly pushed the format of the *Original* series to its limit. This book contains more pages, more pictures and more words than any of its companion volumes. This turned out to be very necessary. The more I researched the MGB in detail, the more obvious it became that there was so much more information to be conveyed. Not surprising really, since the MGB was in production for 18 years and reached a total of more than 500,000 cars. To quote fellow authors Jonathan Wood and Lionel Burrell, whose *MGB – The Illustrated History* appeared quite a few years ago: 'There have been thousands of modifications made to the MGB throughout its production life and it is obviously impossible to list them all.' Well, I thought it was worth having a go at this obvious impossibility. The result is the pages that follow, in particular the list of production changes at the end of the book.

Much of the raw material for the book has come from the archives of the British Motor Industry Heritage Trust at the Heritage Motor Centre, Gaydon. This includes the 70-odd volumes of 'Modification Notes', the master file kept by the engineering department at Abingdon to record the changes that affected the MGB (and other models) over the production period. I doubt anyone has ever before gone through these in detail. When discussing this source with Don Hayter, one of the MGB's designers, he commented wryly that these notes indicated what *should* have happened. I think that mostly it *did* happen. Certainly in so far as it has been possible to correlate these notes with the parts lists, they tell the same story. The MGB parts lists themselves are regrettably unreliable, especially the hard copy versions published in the mid-1970s before everything went on to microfiche.

The other main primary source was the MGB production record ledgers. I managed to work my way through quite a few of these before running out of time but have every intention of returning to them in the future, to produce the final additions to the production figure tables. Although I may be in a slightly privileged position as archivist of the BMIHT, I must record my thanks to the Trust and to the Rover Group for preserving all of these records, and for giving public access to them.

It is rather unfair that the reading public normally only gives credit (or otherwise!) to the author whose name appears first on the cover and title page. In the

case of the *Original* series, the photographs are just as important as the text, and John Colley's work gracing these pages contributes enormously to telling the story of the MGBs and associated models. From his delightful overall studies of the cars and right down to the most trivial and insignificant-looking detail, his pictures have captured the essence of the MGBs. In addition, I must not forget that other pictures were also contributed by Graham Cox, Alan Osborn, Arthur Hall, Rinsey Mills, Tony Baker and even myself, while in the USA Dennis Trowbridge and Martin Bartlett provided us with crucial coverage of the different North American export versions. The other person whose input has been of overwhelming importance is our editor, Mark Hughes, who not only edited my text but also did a lot of legwork, finding the right cars to be photographed, organising the shoots and – together with long-suffering typesetters Chris and Sarah Fayers – producing this book.

You will gather that considerable teamwork lies behind a book like this. All of the owners of the cars which have been photographed were important team players, and their names appear in the adjacent panel. I would in particular like to mention my dear friends Frank and Anne Cangiano in New Hampshire. Frank sadly passed away in 1993, but we shall never forget his infectious enthusiasm for all things MG, and I am proud to have included some pictures of his amazing 1980 MGB roadster with 294 miles on the clock from new. Involved on the picture side were also Don Bishop and Phil Richer, who helped in finding the right cars for photography. In the USA, John Twist and Caroline Robinson of University Motors, both well-known MG luminaries, orchestrated the photography of most of the North American cars. Besides, they read the entire manuscript and offered

The 30 cars photographed in detail for this book range in age from a 1962 Iris Blue roadster that is the earliest known right-hand drive MGB in the world...

...to the 1980 LE GT that was the very last MGB built. Between them, the cars cover every significant permutation of MGB, MGC and MGB GT V8 specification.

cially appreciated because this had to be arranged at short notice. In the USA, apart from John and Caroline, the manuscript was read by two other leading MGB experts – Lloyd Faust and Orin Harding. I think they now both believe my production figure for the North American Limited Edition model! All these readers contributed very valuable points for which I am very grateful – any inaccuracies which may still remain are my responsibility alone.

I would like to thank my colleagues at Gaydon, especially Richard Brotherton, Paul Gilder, Fiona Tordoff and Ron Whitehead, who all assisted actively, but also everybody else for simply putting up with me, which I fear was not always easy when the going got tough and I was stuck worrying at some trivial bit of MGB lore!

I should point out that throughout this book, I have – mostly for the sake of convenience – used the description 'roadster' for the open MGB and MGC. I do not disagree that the correct nomenclature would be 'two-seater tourer' but I think that 'roadster' will be immediately understood on both sides of the Atlantic. I hope that American readers will tolerate the mostly British-English technical terminology, but I trust that most dyed-in-the-wool American MG enthusiasts will be familiar with the meaning of British expressions such as 'bonnet', 'wing', 'engine' and not least 'hood'. I have tried to use the expressions 'left-hand' and 'right-hand' so that they relate to a person sitting in the driver's seat, or looking at the car from the rear. If I have occasionally deviated from this convention, I hope I have remembered to include an explanatory note. I have also stuck to the traditional MG expression 'car number' except where it is necessary to explain that this is commonly still in the UK called a 'chassis number', or in the US a 'serial number', or in modern terminology a 'VIN' (Vehicle Identification Number).

My own first MGB experience came when, as a callow teenager with a brand-new driving licence, I was allowed to drive my slightly eccentric uncle's new MGB. He was a country GP (MD) who at the age of 70 bought the car for his rounds, and, unbelievably, later supplemented it with an automatic MGC GT! I only got my own – well, as a BL lease car – in 1981 when I managed to find a late model still sitting in a local dealer's stock. The next 18 months and 24,000 miles were the most enjoyable I have ever had in any company car. I hope that someone, somewhere, is still enjoying JVP 173W. That is the whole point of the MGB – it has given more people more pleasure than any other sports car. If this book reflects the pleasure and enjoyment of owning and driving an MGB, apart from possibly being at times useful to readers, I shall be well content.

many helpful comments, and supplied much of the information on US paint manufacturers' codes.

The manuscript was also read by the following MGB experts in the UK: Mike Akers (owner of the Coune Berlinette), Don Hayter (the MGB designer), David Knowles (the V8 expert whose own MGB V8 book is now available), Peter Morgan (owner of the 1973 Black Tulip GT), Geoff Simpson (of the MG Car Club register for MGB Limited Editions) and Danny Waters (owner of the 1977 green US roadster). Don, Peter and Danny were kind enough to attend a seminar to discuss many of the pictures, espe-

OWNERS OF FEATURED CARS

IN THE UK
Michael Willrich (1962 Iris Blue roadster, the oldest known surviving RHD car); Alan Osborn (1964 Tartan Red roadster); Mike Akers (1964 Coune Berlinette); Rinsey Mills (1965 Old English White roadster with hard top); Mark Green (1965 Sandy Beige GT); Barry Sidery-Smith (1965 works MGB); George White (1968 British Racing Green MGC roadster); BMIHT, Heritage Motor Centre (1967 sectioned GT; 1969 Tartan Red automatic MGC GT, donated by Michael Alderson; and the two 1980 last-off-line MGB LE roadster and GT models); Naylor Parts of Shipley (1969 Snowberry White roadster); Nick Akers (1971 Bedouin US roadster); John Honour (1971 Bronze Yellow roadster); Arthur Hall (1972 Harvest Gold GT); Colin Lanning (1973 Glacier White automatic GT); Peter Morgan (1973 Black Tulip GT, and Primrose Yellow roadster with hard top); Bill Donaldson (1974 Mirage GT V8); John Hall (1975 'Jubilee' GT); John Heagren (1975 Flamenco GT V8); Danny Waters (1977 Brooklands Green US roadster); Brian Keates (1980 Vermilion roadster); Heather Wood (1980 Brooklands Green GT)

IN THE USA
Geoff McCoach (1969 British Racing Green US roadster); Tuppin and O.D. Hauschild (1973 Black Tulip US roadster); Peter Robinson (1973 Green Mallard US roadster); Joel Tanis (1975 Tahiti Blue US roadster); Nancy Abbott and Tom Taber (1976 Damask Red US roadster); John Leese (1980 Black Limited Edition US roadster); Mary Jo Stievator (1980 Black Limited Edition US roadster); Frank Cangiano (in memoriam) and Anne Cangiano (1980 Brooklands Green US roadster)

Anders Ditlev Clausager
Birmingham, July 1994

PAST, PRESENT & FUTURE

When in 1962 the MGA came to the end of its resoundingly successful seven-year and 100,000-plus production run, its replacement was launched to almost universal acclaim. Introduced on 20 September 1962, the new model bore the cumbersome title of MG MGB 1800, soon shortened to just MGB. And despite the praise heaped on the new model and the frequent predictions that it would be a great success, no-one at the time dreamed that the MGB would have an 18-year run, or that more than 500,000 cars would be made, or that a derivative of the original design would make a comeback 30 years later.

To this day, the MGB remains the all-time best-selling sports car in the world. While claims for this title have been put forward on behalf of other long-time stalwarts such as the Chevrolet Corvette or the Datsun Z-series, they should be discounted because both of these have gone through far more radical metamorphoses than the MGB ever did.

As the car was introduced in 1962, it was a logical – if modest – development of the MGA. In place of the MGA's chassis was a unitary bodyshell. In place of the sweetly rounded curves of the predecessor was a handsomely proportioned assembly of straight lines and angles, with modish little tail fins, in the Italianate style so wholeheartedly embraced by BMC, MG's corporate parent. The engine was the same, if a little bigger and a little more powerful. Shorter and wider than the old model, the car was noticeably more roomy and more comfortable. It had put on a little weight in the process – don't we all? – so there was only a small improvement in performance despite the extra power. Traditional sports car features such as a rev counter and optional wire wheels were augmented by creature comforts such as winding windows and optional overdrive. And all this for a

Alan Osborn's 1964 roadster in Tartan Red, fitted with optional wire wheels but the standard pack-away hood, is to many people the classic MGB.

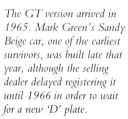

The GT version arrived in 1965. Mark Green's Sandy Beige car, one of the earliest survivors, was built late that year, although the selling dealer delayed registering it until 1966 in order to wait for a new 'D' plate.

From this angle the MGC is easily distinguished by its different bonnet, but it is not so obvious that the wheels – in this case optional chrome wires – are larger than on an MGB. This 1968 model is owned by George White.

modest 4 per cent price increase. Best of all, it was still an MG, a good-natured, charming and forgiving little car, not a hell-raising, hairy-chested brute...

The predicted success was not long in coming. Together with little brother Midget and adopted Austin-Healey siblings, the MGB soon pushed the old factory at Abingdon to capacity. Enthusiasts at home and abroad took to the newcomer. In a policy of continuous improvement, the introduction of the more robust five main bearing engine in 1964 was a major step forward, but there were countless other changes, each in its own way just as significant. In 1965 the pretty GT model offered the MGB enthusiast not only a roof over his or her head, but also kept the family together for a little longer because at least small children could fit into the rear seat.

MG and motor sport are almost synonymous – but let it be said that the career of the works MGBs was mostly for flag-waving and publicity. The car was always handicapped, by its 1800cc engine uncomfortably straddling two classes, and by the need to compete in hard top form in events where open cars were no longer allowed. *And* by the fact that it was just a workaday, mass-production, road-going pleasure machine, not some hugely expensive, scientifically engineered racing car. The MGB did modestly well in racing all the same.

A major development occurred in 1967 when the Mark II model arrived – not that any difference is noticeable by looking at the car. There was a new gearbox, belatedly introducing synchromesh on first gear. There was also the option of an automatic transmission. Catering to the Americans, they sneered. Not so – American MGB customers never received the auto. What they did have was a special MGB with numerous changes to meet the new US motor vehicle safety and emissions standards – the first steps in a never-ending process which would not only strangle

The 1969 model MGC GT from the BMIHT collection, here photographed at the Heritage Motor Centre at Gaydon, is unusual in being fitted with the optional automatic gearbox.

the poor car but which in later years would make life extremely difficult for the poor historian.

There was also the MGC. As a replacement for the lamented Austin-Healey 3000, it could not be taken entirely seriously. As simply an upgraded MGB with a six-cylinder engine it made more sense, but was still not totally satisfactory. The performance was there but the car was 'softer' and more of a touring model in character. The front suspension needed to be redesigned, which did not help. It was called a tractor, and although the model found Royal favour as the first car owned by HRH The Prince of Wales, it was not a great success and lasted only two years. By then the much more exciting and very special lightweight GT versions had come and gone, fleeing across the race tracks like two errant shooting stars, and leaving about as much impression. At least one had the idea that this time BMC was serious about it, but the lightweights were cut off in their prime.

The reason for that was the now infamous BMC-

The recessed grille and Rostyle wheels were hallmarks of the British Leyland version of the MGB, introduced in late 1969. Nick Akers' 1971 US specification car is in the unusual colour of Bedouin, and has the correct combination of exterior mirrors for this type.

Another 1971 car but this time a home market model. John Honour's roadster, in Bronze Yellow, is fitted with optional chrome Rostyle wheels and headrests.

market the V8 in the USA were shelved, and although the car persisted for three years in the home market, only some 2600 found buyers.

By 1974, ever-tightening American safety standards made it necessary for MG to fit large impact-resistant bumpers to its cars – the so-called rubber bumpers. They did not actually look *too* bad on an MGB, and would blend in nicely on a dark or black car. The 'rubber-bumper' cars were also modified in many other respects. One alteration was that their ride height was slightly increased, which played havoc with the handling, especially as until 1976 the front anti-roll bar was deleted from the roadster specification. The new cars compared unfavourably with earlier models. And in 1975 the first MGB fitted with a catalyst went on sale in California. Sounds almost like modern times, doesn't it?

With a final set of major revisions in 1976, the MGB soldiered on. And like an old soldier, it just faded away. The occasional 'Limited Edition' model along the way helped perhaps to create that little bit more interest and sell a few more cars, such as the 'Jubilee' GT of 1975. This was supposed to mark 50 years of MG cars, but in reality marked 50 years of the MG 'Old Number One' car – which was probably the first real MG sports car. In 1979 the Americans were given their own 'Limited Edition', but with 6682 cars made one questions the use of the word 'limited'.

Almost at the same time as MG and Abingdon celebrated their half-centenary together, it was – somewhat tactlessly, one feels – announced on 10 September 1979 ('Black Monday') that the MG sports car would go out of production and the Abingdon factory would be closed. The resulting storm of protest caused BL's then chairman Sir Michael Edwardes to note reflectively in his autobiography that, 'you mess with famous marque names at your peril' (*Back from the Brink*, 1983).

Leyland merger of 1968. Not only did this put a stop to further MG competition activities, but before long the 'Leylandised' MGB arrived – 1970 models had plastic instead of leather seats, Rostyle wheels and a horrid grille. But it did not stop the car from selling better than ever; annual production figures were never higher than in the early 1970s.

Excitement returned with a vengeance in 1973. One fortunate result of the Leyland merger was that the excellent Rover 3.5-litre V8 engine became available. It turned out to be a surprisingly easy fit in an MGB, although some historians maintain that MG had to be shown how to do it by the outsider Ken Costello. No matter, the factory-produced MGB GT V8 arrived in the summer of 1973 with a top speed of 125mph and a very reasonable price tag. The timing was not impeccable. Within a few months, the first oil crisis sent the cost of fuel sky-rocketing, with inflation in Britain hot on its heels. The market for large-engined sports cars all but dried up. Plans to

Peter Morgan's GT is a 1973 model, in the rare colour of Black Tulip, fitted with the black plastic grille that was introduced for this model year.

Introduced in August 1973, the MGB GT V8 was made for little more than one year in its original 'chrome-bumper' form. The alloy wheels and badges set it apart from four-cylinder cars. Bill Donaldson's car is painted another rare colour, the short-lived Mirage.

There were sound commercial reasons for discontinuing an ageing and unprofitable product, and for closing an antiquated factory – notwithstanding its fiercely loyal and highly productive workforce. But with proper investment and foresight from the pre-Edwardes generation of management, it need never have happened. Of the final production run of MGBs which stopped on 22 October 1980, 1000 cars were given a special paint job and extra equipment and were marketed in the UK in 1981 as 'LE' models. Some went straight into museum collections, including the last roadster and the last GT (the last of all MGBs) which went to BL's own Heritage Collection. And was this then goodbye MGB, farewell MG?

Luckily it was not. As things have turned out it was more in the nature of *Auf Wiedersehen*. From 1982

onwards the MG name returned on a range of Austin-based saloon cars. These fairly simple exercises in badge-engineering were not sports cars, but they were honest efforts and were appreciated by enthusiasts for that reason. They were also good cars for their time. In 1988, the Rover Group off-shoot, British Motor Heritage, introduced a remanufactured MGB roadster bodyshell, subsequently followed by the MGB GT shell, giving classic car restorers an alternative to the often Herculean task of welding up a badly-corroded body. It was a new idea and was warmly welcomed. Although there were those who were pessimistic about the prospects, in a booming classic car market the idea of reshelling a decrepit car caught on and Heritage bodies have sold strongly.

So successful, in fact, that when Rover Group

The rubber bumpers were introduced in September 1974. John Heagren's V8, painted in Flamenco, is quite a late car built towards the end of V8 production as it has the little GT badge at the top of the rear pillar. The sunroof was fitted when John bought his car new.

This immaculate roadster is a 1977 US specification car, a particularly well-known car in MGB circles owned since new by Danny Waters. Triple wipers and side-marker lamps are indicative of the North American specification.

finally decided to return to the sports car market, it developed an updated version of the classic MGB roadster, fitted with a 3.9-litre V8 engine in a subtly restyled bodyshell – which the company asked Heritage to build. The RV8 model was launched in 1992 and has created its own niche in the market. It has been a remarkable sales success in Japan, of all places, where 'retrocars' have a particular following and where MG cars of all sorts have always been admired. So, while the present book concerns the *original* MGB in more than one sense of the word, it should not be forgotten that at the time of writing an MGB derivative remains in production for the foreseeable future.

And even beyond that, the future may be brighter still. When Rover Group – and MG – came under new ownership in 1994, the idea of the last big British

car manufacturer being taken over by a foreign company did not please everyone. The fact, however, that BMW is a company with a proud sporting heritage of its own, and that its chairman often talks about British classic cars, augurs well for future MGs. The all-new MG of 1995 may just be the beginning, and the marque may even return to its once-biggest market in the USA.

The present and future history of MG may yet hope to reflect the lines from Arthur Hugh Clough's poem, also once quoted by Churchill:

And not by eastern windows only,
When daylight comes, comes in the light;
In front the sun climbs slow, how slowly!
But westward, look, the land is bright.

BODYSHELL

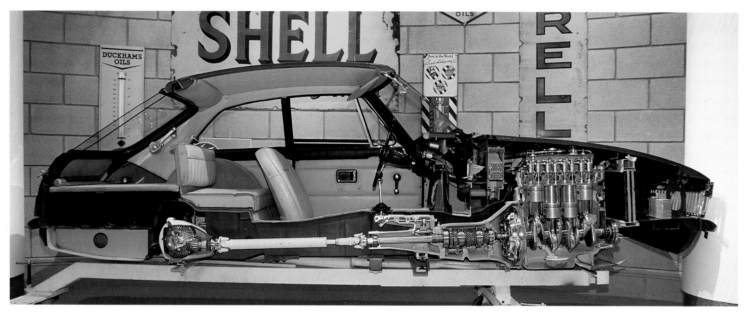

The basic design of the bodyshell changed very little over the years of MGB production. The body was a classic case of unitary construction, with its main strength deriving from built-in box section members which in effect took the place of a separate chassis. The bodyshell was made of steel, but the bonnet was aluminium until 1969.

From the front of the car, two front side members (commonly called chassis legs) ran back to a cross member behind the gearbox. They were linked at the front by the front suspension cross member which was bolted on. Further strength was added by the double-section sills which linked up with the rear side members. These swept over the rear axle and continued alongside the boot floor to the rear end of the car. The sills were linked transversely by the two main floor panels and the transmission tunnel. Transverse stability was ensured by the front bulkhead and dash assembly, the dash side panels and the A-posts (door hinge pillars). Inner front wheelarches forming the sides of the engine compartment linked the front side members with the bulkhead, and the front end sub-assembly was completed by the radiator duct panel and the bonnet locking platform. The power unit was suspended on three points, with engine mounts at either side of the engine at the front to the side members, and to a transverse rear engine mounting cross member below the rear of the gearbox.

The rear end sub-assembly was built up from the heelboard, the tonneau floor (with a common access hatch to the battery boxes below), two inner wheelarches with a transverse bulkhead between them, a boot opening support panel and the boot floor in three parts. The basic bodyshell was finished off with a front fairing (below the radiator grille and behind the bumper), a front shroud (the panel in front of the windscreen), the rear wings and inner quarter panels, the rear deck or tonneau panel (between cockpit and

boot lid), B-post panels (the door locking pillars) and the lower rear body or valance panel. The front wings were simply bolted on but still contributed to the structural strength of the bodyshell. All that needed to be added now were two doors, a boot lid and a bonnet - *et voilà*! A complete MGB roadster body.

The GT body differed little in principle, apart from the addition of a windscreen frame panel incorporating the front shroud panel, a roof panel with cant rails and a rear reinforcement panel to hang the tailgate from. On the GT model, the rear wings incorporated most of the C-posts and were called rear quarter panels. There were also additional inner C-post panels, and simple upper B-post sections hidden behind bright finishers. The GT had different front wings. The boot floor was the same as for the roadster, but had additional support members for the GT's boot board or spare wheel cover. The transverse rear bulkhead was missing on the GT, the doors were different at the top from the roadster doors, and the tailgate had two spring-loaded assisted lift units.

This sectioned MGB GT from the BMIHT collection at Gaydon is an early Mark II model and is thought to have been prepared for the 1967 Turin Motor Show – its combination of features is unique to the Italian export specification. It gives a good idea of the overall layout of the MGB as well as much of the interior detailing on the GT – disregarding the non-standard colour scheme.

An important difference on the MGC is the welded-in cross member which combines the functions of suspension and engine mounting. We are looking down into the right-hand side of the engine compartment (left when seen from the front). Also on view is the bracket intended for the second servo on the North American cars.

Although this is a late MGB with the forward-mounted radiator (right), the underside of the bonnet changed little and always had the reinforcing cross member halfway back, with separate pieces of felt front and rear. Note also the telescopic strut on the left-hand side of the car. The MGC bonnet (far right) had no strengthening cross member and the insulating felt was in one piece. On this 1968 car, the open bonnet is supported by a simple prop on the right-hand side of the car.

The V8 bonnet is the same as fitted on four-cylinder models but the insulating felt at the rear has two little circular cut-outs to clear the carburettor tops, and the front felt has a larger rectangular cut-out to clear the raised part of the radiator top tank with its prominent plug.

On the MGC models, the longer engine was allowed to expand forward, and in consequence these cars had much narrower radiator duct panels and a pierced bonnet locking platform mounted further forward. A very substantial welded-in U-shaped front cross member gave support to both engine and front suspension. The front side members were splayed out into shallow triangular boxes at their rear ends, and rear anchorage points were provided in the floor cross member for the front suspension torsion bars. The most obvious difference between MGB and MGC is the bonnet, with the MGC bonnet having a substantial bulge towards the front to clear the radiator and the front end of the six-cylinder engine. This bulge is decorated with a transverse stainless steel moulding. A smaller bulge further back on the left-hand side of the bonnet gives clearance to the front carburettor. The bonnet panel was originally in aluminium but was possibly changed to steel towards the

end of the MGC production run in 1969. Otherwise, from the A-posts backwards, the MGC bodyshells appeared identical to their MGB equivalents – but in fact the floor panels were different.

Differences between the later four-cylinder GT and the GT V8 were largely limited to the under-bonnet area, and even so the front side members, for instance, were commonised between the two models when the 'rubber-bumper' GT was introduced in 1974, while the front inner wheelarch panels remained different. From its introduction, the V8 had the radiator mounted somewhat further forward than the four-cylinder cars, but this configuration was adopted for the 1977 four-cylinder models, in June 1976 from car number 410001.

When the MGB roadster was introduced in 1962, individual panels were pressed by the still-independent Pressed Steel Company in its factories at Cowley and Swindon, but were then supplied to the old Morris Motors Bodies Branch in Coventry where the MGB bodies were put together, painted and trimmed, before being supplied to Abingdon for final assembly. The GT body, from 1965, was by contrast supplied complete by Pressed Steel, the shell being made at Swindon, but finished with paint and trim at Cowley. In 1966 Pressed Steel merged with BMC, and in 1969 production of the roadster body was moved south from Coventry. It seems that from then on basic shells were made at Swindon, but as Swindon did not have facilities for lead-loading this continued to be carried out in the Cowley body plant together with paint and trim, until lead-loading was discontinued in 1976. While it can be confusing to sort out which part of the work was carried out where at all times, it is important to realise that bodies supplied to Abingdon were fully trimmed throughout the production period. I remember seeing truckloads of completed bodies as they had arrived at Abingdon

All GT models had two of these 'assisted lift' spring-loaded units (far left).
The MGC bonnet bulge (left) was finished off with a stainless steel trim strip, and a smaller bulge was required to clear the front carburettor.

when I first visited in 1975, and in the case of roadsters they even had their hoods erected!

Some of the changes which affected the basic bodyshells were quoted by body number in the Parts Lists. As bodies were never used in the exact numerical sequence represented by body numbers, such changes are particularly difficult to pinpoint, especially as the factory gave up writing the body numbers in the production record ledgers in 1972.

Early on, in May 1963, the clip for the body-coloured bonnet prop on the right-hand side was replaced by a rubber stop, and around the same time stiffer aluminium was introduced for the bonnet panel. Body modifications were introduced in early 1965 to accommodate the larger fuel tank which was bolted to the boot floor and which may be found on some cars built as early as January, and on all cars from 22 March that year. In the following month, the doors were modified as the original pull-out handles were replaced by push-button handles. At the same time improved anti-burst door locks were fitted. In June/July 1966 there was a small modification to the inner rear wheelarches concerning the seat belt mounting points (which were found on all cars from the start of production). Reversing lamps were fitted as standard in 1967, necessitating a depression with a cut-out in each rear wing panel. This occurred on roadsters in March 1967 and on GTs in April.

More extensive changes were made to the bodyshells for the introduction of the Mark II and MGC models in late 1967. Most notable was a wider and more square-sectioned transmission tunnel, to accommodate the fully-synchronised gearbox or the automatic alternative. Mark II and MGC cars for the USA were given their own types of bodyshells with numerous smaller differences and unique body number sequences. These US-type bodyshells were introduced also on cars for Canada in August 1968.

Further changes were made to the North American type bodyshells for the 1969 model year, as side marker reflectors were added to the front and rear wings, and a new front shroud panel was introduced on roadsters with three windscreen wipers. All 1969 models had new front wings on which the combined indicator and side lamps were moved closer to the radiator grille. During the latter part of 1969 the bonnet was changed from aluminium to steel, but unfortunately it has not been possible to establish a specific change point.

For the 1970 model year there were further changes, and export cars for Sweden, Germany and (a little later) Norway were now built using North American type bodies, although such bodies were given their own sequences of body numbers. On all 1971 models, the bonnet prop was replaced by a telescopic strut on the left-hand side, and on the roadster the boot lid prop was replaced by a similar telescopic strut. Roadster door hinge pillars were now fitted with courtesy switches for an interior lamp (these switches had been found on the GT from the start of Mark II production in 1967). A boot lid or tailgate operated courtesy lamp switch was added on all cars. The introduction of the new standardised

The boot lid is similar on all roadsters. Points to note on this 1964 car are the multitude of individual fixings for the boot badge, the manual prop for supporting the boot lid, and the rubber seal mounted on the edge of the lid (in 1976 it was moved to the lip of the aperture).

One of those little differences it can be difficult to spot. The Iris Blue car is a 1964 model, the Tartan Red a 1969 model – note that the indicator lamp is closer to the radiator grille on the later car. The detailing of the bumper bolts and overriders can also be studied.

and an engine restraint tube was added between the engine and the gearbox cross member. On all 1973 models, the front fairing panel was given two rectangular air intake holes behind the number plate.

The changes to the bodies carried out in 1974, when the 'rubber-bumper' models were introduced, were so comprehensive that new series of body numbers were brought in for all four-cylinder models, with new prefixes. While there were obvious changes to front and rear wings to accommodate the new bumpers, the new front wings still had an aperture for the sidelamp although these were now bumper-mounted. These apertures were enlarged and now served to accommodate the bumper springs (or corner brackets). The old twin six-volt batteries were replaced by a single 12-volt battery, fitted in a new battery box on the right-hand side of the car, with changes to the tonneau floor and a new battery access panel. There were sundry other revisions to the bodyshells, some to do with the need to raise ride height (to meet US requirements for bumper height), such as changes to the front suspension cross member and lowered rear spring hangers. The rear valance panel was made wider and the rear wings narrower so their joints moved further outboard, and these joints were no longer lead-loaded. All LHD export cars were now manufactured with the North American type of bodyshell.

Front wheelarch reinforcements were added on 1976 models and the bonnet strut of LHD cars was re-positioned on the right-hand side to avoid fouling the servo. The front fairing and rear valance panel below the bumpers were now finished in satin black instead of body colour. The lead-loading of the joints between rear quarter pillars and the roof panel on the GT was discontinued approximately in March 1976, but this is another important modification for which the exact change point is not known. In June 1976, from the start of the 1977 model year, the under-bonnet layout of four-cylinder models was commonised with the about-to-be-discontinued V8, with the radiator being moved further forward and new inner wheelarch panels being used. Mounting points were added for the new rear anti-sway bar. Production of LHD GTs was now discontinued (the GT had already been dropped from the North American model range in December 1974) and LHD roadsters were built only to North American specification. A new front shroud panel was introduced in September 1977, when both roadster and GT models were fitted with new windscreen washer jets.

The final important change to the bodyshells occurred in late 1979 when it became necessary to re-tool the front suspension cross member, and the opportunity was taken to alter this so that it would allow fitting of BL's new O-series engine, which at that stage was still planned for the MGB in 1981 or thereabouts. As we now know, this did not happen...

Michelotti-designed folding hood on the roadster also necessitated small body changes on 1971 models.

North American roadsters from the start of Mark II production had been fitted with unique rear mounting points for static seat belts on the tonneau panel instead of the rear wheelarches, but these mounting points were moved back on the wheelarches when inertia reel belts were introduced on North American cars in December 1971. On other roadsters, the tonneau panel seat belt anchorages were found from January 1971 to May 1977. The 1973 models for North America were fitted with additional special anti-burst units fitted below the door locks, which meant further changes to doors and B-posts. These cars also had strengthening bars in the doors between the lock face and the hinge area. In February 1974, the engine mountings on North American cars were revised to comply with new US legislation,

BODY TRIM

The front end of 1962-69 models is characterised by a grille with vertical bars, all in bright finish, combined with all-chrome bumpers and overriders. The shield-shaped grille badge shows the combination of black and red colours. The rear of this 1964 car shows the original style of boot lid badging for the roadster, the standard non-locking fuel filler cap and the pre-1967 type of rear valance panel without reversing lamps.

The relative absence of decoration is undoubtedly one of the factors which makes the MGB such an attractive car. The changes made over the years contribute to creating four distinctively different MGBs in terms of exterior appearance: the Mark I and Mark II cars (including the MGC) of 1962-69, the 'Leylandised' model of 1969-72, the face-lift model of 1972-74 and the 'rubber-bumper' cars of 1974-80.

The first type of radiator grille was a clever modernisation of the traditional MG grille, with vertical bars and a thicker central divider, still featuring the classic 'false nosepiece' treatment, but lower and wider than any previous MG grille, to suit the MGB's contemporary proportions. The early cars until late 1964 had a multi-piece grille, with a total of 36 vertical stainless steel bars riveted to top and bottom fixing bars. Then a one-piece pressed grille of anodised aluminium was introduced (from car number 49502) with a total of 39 vertical bars, of which the two end ones and the centre one are invisible. Both types appear exactly the same to the casual observer, and both share the same centre bar and case (frame) which is chrome-plated. The false nosepiece on the centre bar bears the MG octagon in a shield shape. This is a one-piece plastic badge, with the letters and octagon in silver, a red background inside the octagon, and a black background to the shield.

The grille on MGB Mark II models, and on the MGC, was exactly the same.

The 1970 models adopted a frankly much less attractive style of grille, with the grille panel recessed into the air intake. The grille had a total of 37 verti-

The MGC has its unique bonnet with the large bulge finished off with a stainless steel trim strip and a smaller bulge over the carburettors, but the grille, bumper and lamps are exactly like the MGB of the same period. With this 1968 model MGC we have moved into the Mark II era but the only noticeable difference at the rear is the addition of reversing lamps, which in fact pre-dated the introduction of the Mark II by a good six months.

air intake at the front of the bonnet, front wings and front fairing. This lasted only three years, as 1973 models sported a more traditional grille, with an anodised aluminium case, centre bar and false nose-piece. The grille motif was provided by a matt black plastic cross-hatch which was 'handed', with the bars running down towards the centre being more prominent. The MG octagon was back in the pre-1970 type of shield, with red now the background colour for both octagon and shield, and again with silver letters and surround. The same grille was used on the V8, with the addition of a self-adhesive V8 badge on a screwed-on plinth on the right when seen from the front. This corporate BL V8 badge, borrowed from the Rover P6, was not found on the front of the 'rubber-bumper' model from 1974.

The 'rubber-bumper' cars did not have a grille as such, merely a simple wire mesh set some way back in the air intake formed by the bumper. The shape of the bumper, with two nostrils and a centre bar, still retained a suggestion of MG tradition. The MG badge was now located at the top of the centre bar of the combined bumper and grille. The colours were originally silver letters and surround with a red background, but for the 'Jubilee Year' of 1975 they were changed to gold on a black background. As well as being found on the limited edition GT Jubilee model, these colours also appeared on other cars manufac-

cal bars and was painted black. An MG octagon was fixed in the centre, with silver letters and surround and a red background. A thin stainless steel moulding was fixed to the actual grille panel, and another strip of anodised aluminium outlined the shape of the

The 1970 to 1972 model year cars featured a recessed grille (and revised badge), painted matt black, with a bright trim strip on the actual grille panel and other trim pieces surrounding the recess, on the front edge of the bonnet, front wings and lower valance panel. This 1971 car also has the rubber-faced overriders which were new that year on home market cars. The boot lid badge is the one-piece plastic type – still with the MGB letters above it – and the rear lamp lenses have been squared up to increase the area of the reflectors in particular.

tured during 1975. In January 1976, the badge changed to silver letters and surround with a black background. The final variation concerns only the home market 1980 LE models, which again had a red background to the octagon.

Other body ornamentation was limited to the chrome-plated air intake grille in front of the windscreen, and the slim polished stainless steel mouldings which ran along the flanks of the car, from headlamp to tail lamp, in three sections – front wing, door and rear wing. Neither the air intake nor the mouldings were changed during the entire production run, but the mouldings were painted body colour (Racing Green) on the 1975 GT Jubilee model. On the early GT models until February 1968, there was a small chrome-plated finisher at the top of each windscreen pillar, camouflaging the joints with the roof panel.

From the start of the 1970 model (GHN4/GHD4 series, car number 187170 in October 1969), a corporate style British Leyland badge was added to each front wing. This rectangular badge had the words 'British' and 'Leyland' above and below the so-called 'mangle-handle' (or 'plug-hole'!) symbol with a central L, the words and logo being silver on a dark blue background. The badge had two studs and was held by 'blind fixes' from inside the wing. An interesting variation concerns exports in the 1969-72 period to Arab countries (not many, one imagines),

where cars had MG badges on the wings with the logo in red on a silver background as British Leyland was *persona non grata* in the Arab world at this time.

In May 1972, at car number 282455, a simpler stick-on British Leyland badge was introduced, with light

The grille was different again on the 1973 and 1974 models, with black plastic mesh in an anodised aluminium frame. The shield-shape badge was back but was now all red. This 1974 V8 model has the additional V8 badge and twin exterior mirrors as standard. Note that the wipers are now matt black. The rear end shows the new style of GT rear badge, here in combination with the V8 badge on the left-hand side. This car also has the unusual number plate lamp mounting on the rear bumper bar, found only on 1974 non-North American models.

blue letters and logo on a silver background. From this point only one badge was fitted to each car, always on the wing on the passenger side (the Parts List quotes two badges for these later cars but this is incorrect, as will be born out by studying sales brochures

for 1973 and later models). There does not appear to have been an MG badge for Arab countries after May 1972. On the MGB GT V8, a V8 badge of the same type as originally found on the radiator grille was fitted in front of the British Leyland badge. The V8 motif on the wing was also gold during 1975 as opposed to the normal silver. The British Leyland front wing badge was deleted in December 1977.

The other main badges found on the cars were on the boot lid, or, in the case of GT models, on the tailgate. On 1962-69 cars, the classic slim chrome-plated MG was used, with separate pieces for the letters M and G and the octagon surround, the paint colour of the car forming the background. The logo was fixed with spire nuts on roadsters, but in 1966 (from car number 91380) these were changed to the push-on fixes found on all GTs. On roadsters, the motif sits in the middle of the boot lid, with a one-piece MGB legend above it, the three letters connected by a grained bar; this separate badge also had its fixings changed in 1966. On the GT, the MG octagon is at the lower right of the tailgate, with three separate letters MGB to the left, and two letters GT to the right. The only difference on the MGC models was that the letter B was obviously replaced by a C.

The rear badges were changed on the 1970 models. The roadster acquired a one-piece plastic MG badge with silver letters and surround on a black back-

From September 1974, all cars had one-piece rubber bumpers, the front one incorporating the air intake. The all-amber front indicators were now mounted in the bumper. The nose badge changed colour a few times but on this 1980 LE model is red. The chin spoiler under the bumper was found only on the limited edition cars, North American as well as home market models. At the rear, notice the fog guard lamps of the 1980 LE model, the black number plate lamps at either end of the number plate backing plate, the unleaded body seams inboard of the reversing lamps, and the one-piece metal MG badge on the boot lid. The black plastic-covered fuel filler cap was a Unipart accessory.

ground. In January 1975, the plastic badge was replaced by a metal badge, gold on black during 1975, then silver on black from January 1976 onwards. The gold version of the boot lid badge is apparently rare on American cars. The MGB legend was still found above the badge until it disappeared in a fit of penny-pinching in January 1975. The silver and black plastic badge was also found on the 1970 GT models, in the lower right-hand corner of the tailgate, and there was a new BGT badge in the lower left-hand corner. The B was separate and the GT joined up, all three letters being arranged on a downwards slant towards the centre of the car. The letters had raised silver outlines and black centres.

On 1973 models the GT badging was changed again, and a one-piece 'wing' metal badge was fitted in the right-hand corner of the tailgate. This had an octagon with embossed black letters and surround, augmented by a wing on the right-hand side with the letters BGT embossed in light blue (later black), all on a silver background. This type of badge continued to the end of production, again with a gold version during 1975. On the V8 it was supplemented by a V8 motif on the left of the tailgate, identical to those used elsewhere on the car, with silver or gold versions. On the home market LE models of 1980, the GT tailgate badge had the MG letters and the octagon in red.

The final badges were found only on late GT models from around March 1976, when it was decided to stop lead-loading the body seams. To cover up the otherwise unsightly joint where the C-posts meet the roof panel, a badge was fitted on each side in the manner of Mr Spock's ears (except they pointed backwards), with a silver arrow motif and silver GT letters on a black background.

The boot lid (or tailgate) lock assembly was a straight-forward affair, with a push-button (with inset key lock) and a small lifting handle, and was not changed during the production run. The boot key was originally the same as that used for the glovebox lock (although they may be different on some GT models), typically in the FS-series (FP-series on some early 1962 cars). On later cars with a steering lock the same key was used for the doors and the boot, with a third key for the glovebox. Some cars, notably the V8 models, have the same key operating everything except the steering lock.

Key-operated locks were fitted to both doors on all cars. They were originally operated by the FS-series ignition key (FP-series on very early cars), but later, when steering locks became universal, by the boot key. The most important change to the exterior door handles occurred early in the roadster production run, when the original pull-type door handle was replaced by the fixed push-button type in April 1965 from body number 57986 (around car number 58804). A simplified push-button was used on the Mark II model, and early in Mark II production a second stud was added for fixing the handle to the door. This final handle continued until the end of production.

Changes to the original chrome bumpers were mostly confined to the overriders. For home market models, overriders to the front bumper were originally quoted as an optional extra, and only became officially standard on roadsters in 1966 – but export cars and all GTs were always fitted with overriders as standard. It is extremely unusual, in fact, to find even an early home market car without overriders, and there are no notations in the production records to indicate whether or not cars had them. The original all-chrome front overriders were the same on both sides of the car. The front bumper was bolted to two bumper springs or bars, each with an inner bolt (which also secured the overrider) and a dome-headed, chrome-plated outer bolt. If overriders were not fitted, the inner bolts were also of the dome-headed type. In addition, the front bumper was attached to a steady bracket at each rear corner, with another dome-headed bolt used here. The overriders sat on 4in long black plastic mouldings.

The rear bumper was attached at either end to a spring bar which in turn was fixed to a cast bumper mounting bracket. There was a dome-headed bolt at each forward end of the bumper, and the second inner bolt from each spring bar also secured an overrider. The rear bumper was always fitted with overriders, as for most markets these held the chrome-plated housings for the rear number plate lamps. However, early cars for Japan and cars for Germany from 1965 (from car number 57028) had different number plate lamps and so had plain rear bumper overriders which were the same as the front overriders. From September 1970, standard rear number plate lamps – and thus overriders – appear to have been introduced for Germany and Japan. Small filler pieces were added to bridge the gaps between bumper and body below each corner of the boot lid. They were body coloured until January 1964, but from then on they were made of bright alloy and were slightly smaller.

Cars for the North American markets from the start of the 1970 model year received new front and rear overriders fitted with black rubber buffers. These front overriders were originally 'handed', but when rubber-buffer overriders appeared for other markets at the start of the 1971 model year (from car number 219001) they became identical. Number plate lamps continued to be fitted to rubber-buffer rear overriders until early 1974, when they were moved (from car number 339965) to the bumper bar below the number plate, except on North American cars – and

The pull door handle (right), with a little rubber buffer on the door at the front of the handle, was replaced in 1965 by the push-button fixed handle (far right), which remained identical in appearance to the end of production. Note also the slightly different styles of key-operated lock on these two cars.

at this point the rear overriders became identical to the front ones.

The rear bumper developed differently on North American cars. For the 1970 model year only (cars with numbers from 187170 to 218651), rear quarter bumpers were fitted, still with rubber-buffer overriders, but with the number plate lamps tucked inside the inner ends of the quarter bumpers. For the 1971 model year, North American cars reverted to the standard full-width rear bumper and had the number plate lamps in the overriders. In early 1974, quoted from roadster car number 339095 (but possibly earlier on cars for California) and GT car number 339472, North American cars acquired huge and hideous black rubber overriders (sometimes known as the 'Sabrina' overriders) front and rear as a first step towards coping with the new impact legislation. They had 5⁄16in thick spring blades and added a total of 6in to the overall length of the car, but were evidently no more than a stop-gap. On cars with these overriders, the number plate lamps were mounted on the rear number plate bracket and the rear bumper bar was modified. The rear overriders of this type were positioned further outboard than normal, to give better clearance to the fuel filler.

One of the most major changes ever to affect the MGB came when rubber bumpers replaced chrome bumpers for all markets in September 1974 at car number 360301. The term is actually misleading as these bumpers were made from polyurethane, with substantial steel armatures inside. They were an effective way of coping with the American 5mph impact requirement, and blended in fairly well with the lines of the car. Numerous minor changes to the bodyshell and wings were necessary to accommodate them. They were not designed to be painted – although at least one GT in 1978 had an experimental paint finish of metallic Denim Blue with dark blue bumpers in flexible paint – and were uniformly black, which makes them difficult to keep in pristine condition unless the devoted owner resorts to boot polish. They necessitated new arrangements for the rear number plate lamps, while at the front the bumper also took the place of the radiator grille and had apertures for revised flashing indicators. These bumpers were not subject to any change in appearance but their armatures were modified on several occasions, with front bumper springs or corner support brackets being deleted, re-introduced and deleted again.

All cars had backing plates for the front and rear number plates, unless dispensed with due to local regulations in some export markets. The front one was wide and shallow for most markets, except for North America where it was narrower and taller. The same difference applied at the rear of the car, but there were two additional types of rear number plate backing plate: one for Japan with mountings for placing a standard Lucas number plate lamp vertically at each side,

On this 1969 North American car, the side reflector behind the front wheelarch is particularly interesting. This car also has the odd – but correct – combination of a door mirror on the driver's side and a passenger side wing mirror, the all-amber sidelamp/indicator lens, chrome wire wheels with octagonal nuts and, just visible, the first type of headrest found only on the 1969 North American models.

The quarterlight frame was originally made from chrome-plated brass, later from brushed stainless steel, but neither this nor the windscreen frame changed much in appearance. The bright finish on the windscreen frame of this 1964 car was later replaced by a more matt finish.

and another for Germany (from car number 57028 in 1965) with two standard Lucas number plate lamps mounted horizontally on extensions at the top. Both of these types appear to have been discontinued in 1970. The 1974 North American cars with big overriders had a new type of rear backing plate with a number plate lamp on an ear at either end, and this was carried forward on North American 'rubber-bumper' cars. On non-North American 'rubber-bumper' cars the rear backing plate was lengthened and had slightly rounded ends, again to accommodate the rear number plate lamps. Bumpers and number plate backing plates on the MGC and V8

Most of the major bumper variations are illustrated in the overall front and rear view shots featured earlier in this book, but this one deserves a special mention – the unique black rubber overriders of the so-called 'Sabrina' type found only on 1974 model year cars for North America.

The rear overriders on North American 1974 model year cars were positioned further outboard than normal, to give clearance to the fuel filler.

brackets that went through the joints of the front wings with the shroud panel), a top rail and a bottom rail (with a rubber apron seal between it and the body). On early 1962 cars the apron seal goes over the bottom rail, but otherwise it goes under the rail. The windscreen glass was always laminated, and in March 1966 (from roadster body number 80091) a change was made to high impact-resistant glass on North American cars. This type of glass was fitted to roadsters for all markets from the start of Mark II production (car number 138401) in late 1967. The original glass supplier was Triplex, but in later years – particularly after Britain joined the EEC in 1973 – glass was sometimes supplied from other European sources, such as Sicursiv. An otherwise unspecified change to the roadster windscreen glass and rubber glazing strip in April 1977 is thought to concern the introduction of slightly thinner glass. A tie-rod on the inside of the windscreen frame originally served to hold the internal rear view mirror. Sun visor brackets were found on the top rail on roadsters for the USA from the start of Mark II and MGC models, for Canada from August 1968, and for Sweden and Germany for the 1970 model year – but they only appeared on home market cars from the start of the 1977 model year.

Like the roadster, GT models changed to high impact-resistant glass in March 1966, but this took immediate effect for all markets. The rubber glazing strip for the GT windscreen had anodised aluminium finishing strips, inserted in four pieces with four separate corner pieces. Triplex Sundym (or later Sicursiv Climaglass) tinted glass for the windscreen and other glass was introduced as standard on North American GTs from the start of the 1971 model year, and became optional on home market models a year later. Tinted glass was standard on the V8 and 1975 Jubilee GT models, and on all GTs from the start of the 1977 model year (car number 410001).

Loose sidescreens for open sports cars were fast becoming passé by 1962, so the MGB was fitted with winding windows in the doors. The door glasses were not changed at all during roadster production, but there were some changes to the glass channels and regulators in the early years. The front quarterlights (or ventilators) on the roadster partly existed to provide a channel for the door glass. The quarterlight frame was changed in 1965 (from car number 65865) to incorporate an extra front leg going down inside the door, and during Mark II production the original curved locking handles were changed to a flat type, first for the USA, then Canada, and soon after for all other markets. The entire construction of the quarterlight frames was changed from chrome-plated brass extrusions to brushed stainless steel in April 1972 (at car number 279340).

The GT door glasses were frameless and rather taller than on the roadster. The swivelling quarterlights and their frames were similar in principle to those on the

models were the same as on the four-cylinder cars.

One external addition was made on the Limited Edition cars of 1979-80, first for the North American market, then also on the home market LE models. This was a black hard rubber front spoiler of an aggressive shovel design, its leading edge jutting forward almost to the front of the bumper. These spoilers or air dams were manufactured in the USA and were only fitted on North American cars by the importers, with a batch of spoilers being shipped to England for the home market LE models.

The roadster windscreen was fitted in a cast aluminium frame comprising two side pillars (with

Bright-finish wipers (far left) were used until 1972. One of the two windscreen washer jets originally found on roadsters can be seen. On the GT (left), the wipers were longer as the screen was taller, and the spindles were closer together nearer the centre line of the car. This 1973 car was one of the first models to have black wipers. The GT originally had only one twin-nozzle washer jet.

From 1978 all cars had two black plastic nipple-type washer jets as seen here (far left). From the start of the 1969 model year, North American roadsters had triple wipers (left), originally in bright finish. This is also a good view of the chrome-plated air intake grille on the scuttle.

roadster, but again were taller. The most notable changes, to the locking handles and in frame construction, were shared with the roadster.

The GT's opening rear quarterlights were hinged at the front and fastened with an over-centre toggle catch at the rear. The original brass frames were replaced by stainless steel frames in May 1972 (from car number 286062). At the same time the original piano-type hinge was replaced by two small hinges, one each at top and bottom, and the original short toggle with two fixing screws was replaced by a longer catch with three screws for its bracket, permitting the window to open slightly further. All GTs had bright finishing strips below the side windows, on the centre pillar between door and rear quarterlight, and on the drip rail above the side windows. They were mostly anodised aluminium, except the centre pillar finisher which was chrome-plated until May 1972 and in stainless steel thereafter.

The rear window in the tailgate was set in a rubber glazing strip with a two-piece anodised aluminium finisher, split vertically at the centreline of the car with two joining clips. A Triplex Hotline electrically heated rear window became available as an optional extra in 1966. It became standard on home market cars in August 1972 (from car number 296001), although it was still omitted on some export models after this date.

A windscreen washer was always standard. This was originally a Tudor type with manual pump and a round bottle fitted in a blue-painted bracket at the

rear of the engine compartment, on the left-hand side on RHD cars and on the right-hand side on LHD cars to avoid conflict with the master cylinder box. The pump control on the facia changed places with the light switch in 1966. On roadster models there were two single jet nozzles on the shroud panel in front of the windscreen, while the GTs had a single nozzle with twin jets. From the start of production of the Mark II and MGC models, US export models had an electric windscreen washer with a Trico pump, activated by the column-mounted stalk switch which also operated the wipers. The electric washer spread to cars for Canada in August 1968, as well as some other export models subsequently. On the Mark II, the Tudor washer bottle was moved to the front right-hand corner of the engine compartment, just behind the radiator diaphragm panel, while the MGCs had a larger square reservoir in a similar position.

North American cars also changed to matt black wipers in 1972. This 1977 model year car still has the original type of washer jets.

This rather unusual door mirror was factory-fitted standard equipment on North American cars from 1968 to 1971, combined with a wing mirror on the passenger side. The later door-mounted mirrors are seen in many of the overall shots of cars featured in this book.

BOOT & TOOL KIT

A square bag-type windscreen washer reservoir was introduced on cars for Sweden in November 1968, fitted on the right-hand side of the engine compartment at the front, and it is thought that the bag variety also made its appearance on North American export models some time between 1968 and 1973, but it has not been possible to establish when. In January 1973, a larger rounded bag holding three pints was introduced on North American cars, apparently at this time replacing the original square bag. The rounded bag was fitted to all non-North American models from June 1973 onwards, and continued in use on home market and other RHD cars until 1980.

The V8 model had the electric washer from the start of production, and kept its water in a larger box container in the rear left-hand corner of the engine compartment. From September 1973, all cars with an electric washer were fitted with a Jideco pump instead of the Trico pump. From the start of 'rubber-bumper' production in 1974, all cars were fitted with the electric washer, and at the same time North American export models adopted the V8-type box water container, situated on these cars in the right-hand rear corner of the engine bay. The final change came in September 1977 when all cars adopted two plastic nipples on the front shroud panel in place of the earlier single or twin jet nozzles.

Single or paired wing mirrors were quoted as factory-fitted optional extras until 1965, when in line with revised BMC policy such fripperies became dealer-fit accessories. The preferred type was a Desmo Boomerang Continental mirror with trapezoidal head and convex glass, but other types were also available, at least as dealer fits. A driver's door mirror was standard on the Mark II model for the USA and in 1968 on Canadian cars. The 1968 MGC GT, and all 1969 model year North American cars, had the odd-looking combination of a door-mounted mirror on the driver's side and a wing mirror on the passenger side. Furthermore, the mirrors were of two different types. This North American arrangement persisted to the end of the 1971 model year, but two door mirrors were fitted on 1972 models and continued until the end of production. The first home market MGB to have two door-mounted mirrors as standard was the V8, but these also arrived for the four-cylinder models at the start of 'rubber-bumper' production a year later. These later door mirrors were originally chrome-plated but were changed to stainless steel in March 1976. A matt black version was fitted only on the 1975 GT Jubilee model. In 1977 the British Leyland bean-counters decided that British MGB owners did not take their cars abroad and took away the passenger door mirror. At the same time the flat glass in the driver's door mirror was replaced by convex glass, at least on RHD cars. The mirror on the passenger door made a brief comeback on the LE models in 1980.

In the boot of both roadster and GT models, the spare wheel was stowed on the boot floor, with a clamp – basically a bolt with a retaining plate – which reached through the centre of the spare wheel and was screwed into a bracket on the floor. The spare wheel was usually stored so that the outside faced upwards, except for the disc wheels (to 1969) and the V8-type cast alloy wheel. There were several different spare wheel clamps, broadly speaking one for each type of wheel – disc, wire, Rostyle and cast alloy. Wire-wheeled GTs also had a different spare wheel clamp from wire-wheeled roadsters, to ensure that the wheel would clear the boot board found on the closed model.

The original tool kit was confined to the barest essentials. The jack was a simple single-leg, side-lift type with a screw mechanism operated by a winding handle. There was a box spanner (with tommy bar) for the plugs. Disc-wheeled cars were supplied with

This immaculately presented boot is from a 1964 roadster, with the wire wheel correctly stored facing upwards and the toolbag stowed on the right-hand side in front of the fuel filler hose connection.

With the spare wheel removed from the same car, the simple bracket into which the spare wheel clamp screws can be seen. As this car has the early style of fuel tank, there are no visible fuel tank fixings on the boot floor. The small black rubber plugs – two at the front, one in the rear left-hand corner – fill the holes which allowed surplus primer to drain away after the first stage of the painting process.

On this very original disc-wheeled 1969 model, the spare wheel is stowed facing downwards (above left). This car has the straps for holding the bag for the pack-away hood frame in place, as well as the piece of foam originally fitted to avoid the stowed frame damaging the paintwork. With the spare wheel and tool bag removed (above right), the bolts for fixing the later type of fuel tank can be seen. The bungs in the drainage holes are now of translucent plastic and there is a T-shaped fuel pump breather on the ledge to the right of the bulge over the differential.

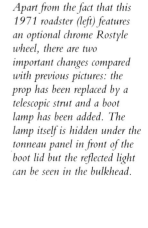

Apart from the fact that this 1971 roadster (left) features an optional chrome Rostyle wheel, there are two important changes compared with previous pictures: the prop has been replaced by a telescopic strut and a boot lamp has been added. The lamp itself is hidden under the tonneau panel in front of the boot lid but the reflected light can be seen in the bulkhead.

On this 1980 roadster, the boot lid sealing rubber is mounted to the lip of the aperture, and the fuel pump is now fitted inside the boot, under the black cover to the right of the spare wheel. Just visible on the bulkhead above the spare wheel is the bracket to which the tool bag was tied on North American models, to ensure that the tool bag did not damage the fuel pump in the event of a rear shunt.

When raised (below), the longer one-piece boot board used from 1973 reveals details at the front of the boot, including a central bracket with two screws in holes which were mounting points for rear seat belts. Note that on the V8 the alloy wheel was stored facing downwards. This owner carries a Unipart first aid box, one of the many accessories which were available at the time but which were not specific to the MGB.

When the wooden boot board of the GT is lifted, it will be seen that the spare wheel and tool bag are stowed in much the same way as on the roadster. The hole in the boot board, just visible at the top of the picture, gives additional clearance to the spare wheel clamp on wire-wheeled cars.

a lever for removing the hub cap and a spanner for the wheel nuts. Wire-wheeled cars were supplied with a copper-headed (or alloy-headed) hammer, and for cars with octagonal nuts rather than knock-ons there was also a special octagonal spanner to fit round the wheel nut. This was originally found only on some export cars, but was supplied with all wire-wheeled cars when octagonal nuts became standard. Everything was stored in a PVC-coated felt bag which closed with a flap, and could be rolled up and secured with two straps. A pump was not included in the tool kit, and a starting handle was never supplied.

For the 1970 models, on which disc wheels were replaced by Rostyles, the hub cap lever was deleted and a new wheel nut spanner introduced. Yet another wheel nut spanner was found on cars with cast-alloy wheels, although at least the same type of spanner was used for both V8 and LE wheels. The plug spanner

and tommy bar were deleted on the 1970 models. Although in principle the same tool bag (AHH 6540) was quoted throughout production, in the 1975-80 period an alternative plastic tool bag (BHH 1808) was found on most cars. The copper hammer for wire wheels was 11B 5166, later quoted as 88G 329 (a part number change only). Alternatively an alloy-headed hammer (AHH 6665) may be found, but probably only between July 1966 and approximately 1969.

The spare wheel clamps were different on the MGC, but the tool kit, tool bag and jack were shared with contemporary MGBs. Differences on the V8 amounted to the special clamp for the cast-alloy wheel, and also initially a different jack (BHA 5178) which was blue and was made by Metallifacture, although this was supplied with some four-cylinder cars as well.

The most important changes to the tool kit over

With the spare wheel and other contents removed (above) it will be seen that this V8 also had the fuel pump inside the boot, and the construction of the rear side member shows up very well.

From 1965 to October 1973, GT models had this type of wooden board (right) covering the spare wheel, with a narrow fixed strip adjacent to the rear seat. Note the square canvas patch covering the circular hole giving clearance to the spare wheel clamp on wire-wheeled cars. Later GTs had a one-piece board (far right) which was hinged at the bottom of the rear seat squab.

This tool kit and bag are from a 1964 car – but the plug spanner and tommy bar are missing. The red jack is the original King Dick type. This appears to be an alloy-head hammer which may not be the type originally supplied with this car. As the wire wheels on the car have knock-ons there was no need for an octagonal spanner.

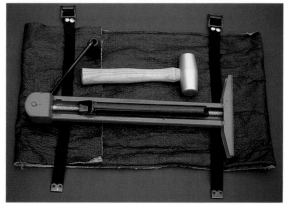

the years concerned the jack. The original red-painted King Dick jack (AHH 6538) was replaced in May 1973 by a stronger alternative (BHH 1264) from the same maker. A new black Metallifacture jack (BHH 5329), introduced in February 1974 and common to four-cylinder and V8 models, continued to the end of production. On later roadsters, probably from April 1978, there was a small bracket on the forward bulkhead of the boot. The tool bag on US cars was tied to this to avoid the jack in the tool bag damaging the fuel pump in a rear-end shunt.

On GT models, the spare wheel was covered by a wooden boot floorboard, hinged at the front and fastened with two quick-release screws, one in each rear corner. Originally in two pieces with a separate narrow strip at the front, it was redesigned in October 1973 as one piece and continued in this form to the end of production. This floorboard was normally painted black and was covered by a piece of carpet. A hole in the boot board, covered with a piece of canvas, gave additional clearance for the spare wheel clamp on wire-wheeled cars. The small pockets on each side of the rear wing on the GT were fitted with carpet liners. Mark II and later GTs had an interior lamp mounted on the rear header rail above the boot, originally operated by door-mounted courtesy switches. A boot lamp was added on 1971 model roadsters, and all cars from then on had a courtesy switch for the boot lamp operated by the boot lid or tailgate.

Apart from some earlier export cars which had the car number stamped in the floor of the boot, all cars from October 1979 had the VIN number (complete with prefix) stamped in the right-hand side member of the boot, and originally covered by a piece of transparent protective tape.

From a 1973 car on Rostyle wheels (right), this tool kit contains a later type of jack painted blue and the wheelnut spanner – and that is it. The bag is the same as the earlier car. The tool kit of the 1980 LE GT (far right) was stored in this unprepossessing plastic bag. The black jack is the final type of Metallifacture jack, and the spanner is the slightly different type used for the cast alloy wheels.

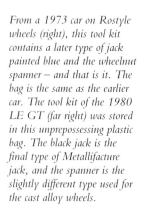

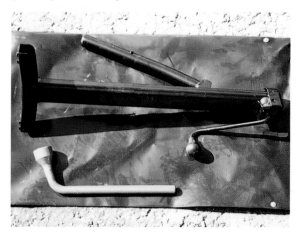

INTERIOR TRIM

The first MGB interior trim scheme was characterised by the use of contrast-colour piping for the leather seats and the trim panels, and the availability of three trim colours – black, red and blue. On the GT model of 1965, the interior trim scheme was almost the same, but with the addition of a leathercloth-covered rear seat and the use of slightly different door trim panels. The original trim scheme lasted until late 1968 and was also found on the first year's production of the MGC.

The trim was completely revised on 1969 models, with new seat patterns. The front seats were still upholstered in leather but had reclining seat backs, while headrests were fitted for the first time, initially only on North American cars. The most important trim colour was black, but a few GTs had Mushroom (beige) trim. Seat piping was now in the main trim colour. Although the new trim scheme was supposedly introduced from the start of the 1969 model year in November 1968, some cars built through December may still have had the old trim style, and Mushroom colour trim only appeared in production in March 1969.

It was again all change for the 1970 model year, with leather upholstery replaced by Ambla, which for the first year was offered only in black. A year later,

the additional trim colour of Autumn Leaf (light brown) was introduced. For the 1972 model year, black trim was replaced by Navy (a very dark blue), and GT models had their seat centre panels in brushed nylon. On 1973 models, GTs had all-nylon seat facings while both roadster and GT models had revised seat patterns with transverse pleating. For this one model year, Autumn Leaf was replaced by a lighter yellow/brown trim colour called Ochre, although at the end of the 1973 model year Navy and Ochre were replaced by black and Autumn Leaf again. Most of the early V8 models had the Navy and Autumn Leaf trim colours, and V8 trim was in all respects identical to that of the four-cylinder GT.

The final major revision occurred in June 1976, for the 1977 model year. At this point, different trim styles were introduced on RHD and LHD (North American) cars. The North American roadsters kept the Ambla seats in modified form, but all RHD cars were now fitted with brushed nylon seat facings in a striped 'deckchair' design in two colour combinations – orange and brown or silver and grey. All cars had new door trims. Also on 1977 models, full carpeting (instead of the original combination of carpet and rubber mats) was standardised on all cars, but the 1975 Jubilee GT had full carpeting before this. RHD

The seat style on the Mark I GT was exactly the same as on the roadster but the door trim was different, with an additional line of piping below the pull handle. The door waist rails were always black until 1970 regardless of the main trim colour. The steering wheel, a leather-rimmed Motalita, is not original.

cars were fitted with black headrests as standard. RHD roadsters were fitted with sun visors for the first time – these were previously found only on LHD roadsters and GT models. In this form, both styles of interior continued to the end of the production.

The 1962-68 front seats were upholstered in leather for the seat facings, the cushion having a front bolster, two side bolsters and a centre panel with five flutes, all outlined in contrast-colour piping. The squabs had two side bolsters running from top to bottom, a lower centre panel with five flutes, and a plain top centre panel, again outlined in contrast-colour piping, as was the rear edge of the seat squabs. The flutes in the centre panels ran lengthwise in the car. The squabs folded forward, but could be locked upright by a bolted-on bracket at the bottom rear. The bottom of the back of the squabs was covered in carpet. The tubular seat frames were painted black, and both seats could be adjusted lengthwise with a catch on the outside slide. The cushion was built up with a foam rubber pad over Pirelli webbing straps. The cushion foam was redesigned in April 1963 and a full base diaphragm was introduced, the seat piping was modified in February 1964, and a new base diaphragm was introduced in December 1964. These Mark I type seats were never available with reclining squabs but the rake could be adjusted by two bolts at the bottom of the squab.

The seat covers were modified on two occasions. First, a finer-grained leathercloth was introduced between June and August 1963, to commonise the

The design of the Mark I GT rear seat followed the pattern of the front seats, with similar pleating and contrast colour piping.

material with the Midget and Sprite models. Second, leather with HB grain replaced FG 1093 grain in September 1965. The leather was supplied by Connolly, whose reference numbers for the three original trim colours are: red 1454, blue 1805 and black 1560. The leathercloth was supplied by ICI, and the colour reference numbers are: red RE.138 and blue BL.341; black is referred to simply under the grain/finish reference number of 413/1028 (common to all colours). For customers who desired it, the MGB roadster could be supplied with a rear compartment cushion upholstered in leathercloth, in colours (and piping)

This curved quarterlight handle was used until 1967, when it was replaced by a straight version. On this early Iris Blue roadster, note the correct combination of pale blue piping behind the black door waist rail.

The rear bottoms of the seat squabs were covered in carpet until 1968. The two protruding bolts permitted a measure of rake adjustment. The black bracket in the middle of the bottom of the squab could be turned 180° to lock the squab into the lower seat frame when upright, as required by law in some export markets.

matching the front seat, with a front bolster and a full-width fluted panel.

The door trim panels on the early roadsters featured two horizontal flutes, with a length of contrast-colour piping immediately below the lower flute. This pattern was repeated on the rear quarter side liners. The black plastic door furniture, similar to the items used on the BMC 1100 range at the time, comprised an inside door handle in the front top corner, a window winder below the flutes at the front, a door pull centrally below the flutes, and an inside locking knob set at the rear of the flutes on the passenger door only. This locking knob, however, was discontinued in April 1965 when improved door locks with push-button exterior handles were introduced, and the inside door handles were fitted with an interior locking position on both doors – the door trim panels were modified to suit.

The waist rails at the top of the door casings were always black until 1970, regardless of trim colour, to match the facia crash roll. The first type of waist rail had a small 'tab' pointing downwards at the rear. In August 1965, a new design of waist rail was introduced, with a downwards 'step' just behind the rear frame of the quarterlights. The earlier type of waist rail had a separate trim roll. Contrast-colour piping behind the waist rail at the top continued into 1966 but was then replaced by black piping.

At the rear of the cockpit was a transverse bulkhead liner in the main trim colour, and the edge of the tonneau panel was finished off with a moulding,

always in black. At the front there was a scuttle side liner on each side, again in leathercloth in the main trim colour. If desired a map pocket could be fitted on the passenger side, with a chrome finisher at the top. The map pocket became a standard fitting on the GT and on North American roadsters from 1967. The toeboard liners, and the three liners around the air intake box above the transmission tunnel, were at first in leathercloth, but carpet was substituted in November 1962. On early cars, the cross-head screws and cup washers used to fit trim panels were chrome-plated, but in January 1963 this finish was replaced by a coating of Florentine bronze.

The most noticeable difference on the GT was that an extra line of contrast-colour piping was introduced on the door trim and rear quarter panels, below the door pull. Also on this model, black rear quarter waist rails were fitted below the rear quarterlights. The inside of the windscreen pillars and centre pillars were covered in black finishers, and two small panels in the main trim colour were fitted to the inside of the tail-gate below the rear window. The upper quarter liners behind the rear quarterlights continued below the level of the waist rail and were cut off at an angle at the lower rear. They were mostly grey, but could be beige on cars painted in beige colours. Similarly, the roof lining, the windscreen header rail finisher, the two cant rail finishers above the doors, the rear header rail finisher and the sun visors were usually grey, but again were beige on cars painted in beige colours.

The rear seat on the GT had a removeable cushion

The 1969 models, like this MGC GT, had all-new seats with reclining seat backs. On most cars, the trim colour was black and the seat piping was the same colour, while the door trim piping was discontinued altogether. The car shown has an incorrect type of door pull handle.

held in place by four 'lift-the-dot' fixings, and a folding rear squab which was hinged at the bottom to the boot board and held by catches to the inner rear wheelarches. The GT rear seat was upholstered in leathercloth, not leather, and had a front bolster to the cushion and a top bolster to the squab, but otherwise featured full-width panels with longitudinal fluting similar to the front seats. The rear seat also had contrast-colour piping, and the back of the squab was completely covered in carpet.

Floor coverings were a mixture of PVC-coated rubber mats and carpet glued to rubberised felt. The actual floor panels were covered in rubber mats, in two sections – front and rear – on each side of the transmission tunnel. The sills were also covered in rubber, and there was a rubber moulding acting as a footrest and cover for the starter motor on the tunnel in the right-hand footwell. A shaped one-piece carpet covered the tunnel, with cut-outs for the radio loudspeaker console and for the gear lever. The gear lever came through a black rubber gaiter, with a chrome-plated surround which was originally oval in shape but became circular on the Mark II and MGC models in 1967. The heelboard was covered by a single piece of carpet, and another piece was fitted on the shelf in the rear compartment (below the rear seat cushion on the GT). Specially shaped pieces of carpet were fitted over the inner rear wheelarches. The GT also had a piece of carpet covering the boot floorboard, and carpeting in the small pockets formed on either side of the boot behind the rear wheelarches.

The rear seat on the 1969 GT conforms to the style of the new front seats, with transverse pleating in two separate panels.

The 1969-style seat: the facings were still trimmed in leather, but these seats were used only for one year.

The colour of the carpets and mats always matched the main interior trim, so they could be black, red or blue. The front floor mats had a 'heelmat' pattern in both footwells – the heelmats were always black, regardless of trim colour. In June 1963, the front floor mats were modified to allow their removal with the seat runners in the maximum forward position. In December 1965, the shade of red for floor mats was changed. In December 1966, the boot floor carpet on the GT was modified in respect of the number and position of carpet fasteners. A small difference between the MGB and the MGC was that the two models had different grains to their rubber floor mats,

The sills were originally covered in ribbed rubber mats, found until 1976. On this 1968 car the door sills were yet to be fitted with tread plates, which appeared at the start of the 1970 model year. This bright trim strip was found only on GTs.

The tonneau area and rear wheelarches were always carpeted. The straps at the rear of the tonneau are there to hold the folding hood (removed here) in place when folded. These are the early type of static seat belts.

while the MGC front floor mats were a slightly different shape to accommodate the torsion bar anchorages under the floor. While the original supplier of carpet material was Rivington, in May 1968 a change was made to Dunlop's 'D' carpeting, although this type of carpet appears to have been fitted to MGC roadsters from the start of production. Floor underfelt was originally used under the rubber mats but was replaced in May 1966 by heat-fusible insulation pads.

An ashtray – basically a black box with a chrome-plated lid – could be fitted as an optional extra, on the transmission tunnel in front of the gear lever. In July 1966, a modified type of ashtray with concealed

screw fixings was introduced. From August 1968, the ashtray became a standard fitting on all export cars.

The interior rear view mirror on the roadster was originally fitted with a clamp to the central tie-rod inside the windscreen between the top and the bottom of the windscreen frame, so that the height of the mirror could be adjusted. The first type of roadster mirror was frameless, with a gold-painted metal backing plate. On the GT, the mirror was conventionally mounted on a stem above the windscreen, with a buffer to the windscreen glass. For North American markets on Mark II and MGC models, a break-away mirror was fitted to both body styles (in the case of the roadster this was now attached to the top bracket of the tie-rod), and this American-type GT mirror was soon standardised for all GTs. This type of mirror had a suction cup stabilising the stem against the windscreen. The early GT mirror had grey plastic backing and frame, similar to the North American Mark II mirrors, and mirrors on other roadsters from June/July 1968. All these early mirrors were non-dipping.

A number of other changes were implemented on the Mark II and MGC models in late 1967. The door furniture was new, with a new door pull, a window winder with a bigger knob, and a recessed black plastic door handle and locking catch combined in a rectangular chrome-plated casing (a style previously seen on the BMC 1800 range). The new door handle was set centrally in the door, just above the door pull. The door casings were modified with new trim panels fea-

These seats with centre panels in brushed nylon and side bolsters in vinyl were unique to the 1972 model year GT. The door pull of this simple type was used only for this one year. The chrome strips on the door trims were new on 1972 models, and so was the centre console with armrest and ashtray. This is the Navy blue trim colour, and this car has the inertia reel seat belts.

turing two contrast-colour strips of piping, above the door handle and below the door pull, and the trim panels were now plain, without flutes. On Mark II GTs, the original Vyweld headliner was replaced by a fibreglass headliner. A roof lamp was added to the rear header rail on the GT, activated at first by courtesy switches in the doors but from August 1970 by a switch in the tailgate. The new North American roadsters were fitted with internal sun visors.

Although seat belt mounting points had been built into all MGB bodyshells from the start of production, seat belts were as yet not a legal requirement in the car's major markets. BMC Service Limited offered seat belts for installation by dealers at point of sale. The belt available for the MGB in the early years of production was the static three-point type, which was originally supplied by Britax but a Kangol Magnet alternative was offered from February 1964. Front seat belts became compulsory on all new cars in the UK from 1 April 1967, but the practice of having them installed by dealers continued and they were still charged to customers as an extra. In North America, some early MGBs may have been fitted with locally-manufactured belts, probably of the lap type, but from 1967 Mark II and MGC cars to North American specification had static three-point belts fitted as standard by the factory. One peculiarity of the Mark II North American roadsters was that the upper rear mounting point was on top of the tonneau panel, with a quick-release mechanism for the seat belt, instead of in the normal position on the inner rear

The rear seat of the 1972 GT matched the front seats, with two brushed nylon panels.

wheelarch. These mounting points were also introduced on non-North American roadsters in January 1971; when inertia reel seat belts were standardised on roadsters (North American cars in December 1971, RHD cars in May 1977) the seat belt anchorages moved back on the wheelarch.

The first major revision to the interior trim scheme occurred after the first year's production of Mark II and MGC models, when the 1969 model year cars were given completely new seats. The seat covers now had a 'ladder' pattern, with transverse flutes to the centre panels of cushion and squab. The optional rear compartment cushion for the roadster, and the GT rear seat, were redesigned to match, with two panels

For the 1973 model year, the GT was given all-nylon seat facings, although the seat edges, the headrests and the rear of the squabs continued in vinyl. The door pulls were more substantial. The seat pattern with transverse feature lines was also found on the roadster model, although the open car continued with Ambla trim. This trim colour is the short-lived Ochre.

Similarly, the 1973 GT rear seat was completely covered in brushed nylon. The characteristic cord-like background pattern shows up well here. Note the handle for adjusting the rake of the front seat squab, on the inner edge of each squab. By now the waist rails below the windows and the cover for the centre pillar were in the main trim colour.

with transverse flutes. The front seat facings were still in leather, and seat piping was now in the main trim colour rather than a contrasting colour. Separate piping on door and rear quarter liners was discontinued. The seat frames were modified and adjustable reclining seat backs were introduced for the first time, activated by a chrome-plated handle on the inside edge of the seat squab. A proper seat lock-down mechanism was fitted, with a black knob release handle on the outside of the seat. Headrests also became available for the first time, but only on North American models. They were fitted on twin poles and could be adjusted for height in friction bushes.

Red and blue trim colours disappeared for these

1969 model year cars (but in any case blue trim had been virtually discontinued on roadsters at the end of 1966, except for a few MGC roadsters in the optional extra paint finish of metallic blue), so the new trim style was at first available only in black, although between March and September 1969 small numbers of GT models finished in Sandy Beige paint had the rarely-seen optional trim colour of Mushroom (beige). It is not certain whether any cars were actually produced in the colour scheme of Metallic Golden Beige with Mushroom trim, as the metallic colours seem to have been discontinued before the Mushroom trim became available, but the combination was theoretically available for a short period.

The colours of individual trim parts followed the pattern of the earlier models, with liners and trim panels in the seat colour, and black carpets and mats on cars with black trim. On cars with Mushroom trim, panels and liners were also Mushroom, but carpets and mats were brown. The rooflining and other parts on GT models were now grey on all cars – beige was no longer available. Other important changes on the 1969 models were that the rubber mats were of an improved quality and carpets were now made from Firth's loop-pile material.

With the introduction of the GHN5/GHD5 series MGBs for the 1970 model year, the interior was changed again. The seat covers were an all-new design, with knit-backed expanded vinyl (Ambla) for the seat facings. Both cushion and squab had plain side bolsters flanking full-length centre panels, with

Although this picture shows a 1977 US model roadster, this type of Ambla seat was used from the 1973 model year onwards, the only difference being that 1973-76 models had the basketweave background pattern only on the centre panels, the side bolsters having a simpler grain. In fact this style with basketweave pattern on the side bolsters was found only on North American cars of the 1977-80 model years. The trim colour here is Autumn Leaf. Note that the North American type of headrests also have the basketweave pattern.

nine flutes and a perforated basketweave background pattern to the centre panels. A new style of single-pole D-shaped headrest was fitted on North American cars, the headrest also featuring plain side bolsters and a centre panel with a basketweave pattern similar to the seats. On the GT, the rear seat was redesigned along the same lines, with two fluted panels. The optional rear compartment cushion for the roadster was withdrawn. Vertical flutes were added to the bottom panel on the door trims, which now had heat-formed feature lines. All cars were now fitted with a

dipping interior mirror, and all roadsters now had the mirror fitted on a bracket on the top windscreen frame. Sill tread plates were fitted in the base of the door openings.

Smaller changes introduced during the 1970 model year included the fitting of an ashtray as standard on home market cars in December 1969, and around the same time GTs and North American roadsters received a new, standardised grain for their sun visor covers. In April 1970 headrests became available as an optional extra in the home market, and headrest

Introduced only on right-hand drive cars in 1976, this striped nylon seat style, here in silver and grey, continued to the end of production (above left). The seat edges, headrests and door trims are all in black vynide. The rear seat design on late GTs (above) again matches the front seat but with in effect two 'centre' panels.

On this late model GT, the nylon seat facings are in the orange and brown colourway. If you compare this with the view of a silver and grey interior on page 38, you will notice a subtle difference in the layout of the stripes.

This view (above) shows the GT rear seat folded down. The grey colour of the rooflining and rear pillar liner continues below the level of the waist on the rear pillar. On this very late GT model (above right) the rear pillar liner is still of the same shape and still continues below the waistline, but the lower part is now black.

fittings were commonised with other Austin-Morris models. The seat frames were altered to cater for modified seat belt mounting points, while in August the carpets and mats were revised for the same reason, and North American cars were fitted with a new type of static seat belt.

Black had been the only trim colour offered during the 1970 model year, but on 1971 models an alternative trim colour was introduced. It was described as Autumn Leaf, but those who are less romantically inclined would simply call it light brown. Door waist

rails were now the same colour as the door trim, and on the GT the centre pillar cover, rear quarter waist rail and quarterlight seal were also in the main trim colour. A vinyl gaiter was added round the gear lever, shrouding it almost completely up to the knob. The map pocket became a standard fitting on roadsters for Germany and Sweden with the North American style facia, and headrests became available as an optional extra in all markets where they were not fitted as standard.

From 1 January 1971, all home market cars were

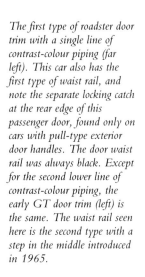

The first type of roadster door trim with a single line of contrast-colour piping (far left). This car also has the first type of waist rail, and note the separate locking catch at the rear edge of this passenger door, found only on cars with pull-type exterior door handles. The door waist rail was always black. Except for the second lower line of contrast-colour piping, the early GT door trim (left) is the same. The waist rail seen here is the second type with a step in the middle introduced in 1965.

The 1968 model Mark II door trim, seen on an MGC (far left), shows the new recessed safety-type door handle (à la BMC 1800) and also the two lines of contrast piping, now found on both roadster and GT models. For 1969 the piping was deleted, and instead the edges of the upper and lower vinyl panels were simply turned under and sewn. Introduced for the 1970 model year, this trim (left) had heat-formed feature lines outlining a centre panel, and vertical fluting at the bottom.

fitted with Kangol static seat belts in the factory as standard equipment, and at the same time inertia reel seat belts became available as an optional extra on the GT. By a quirk of the law, cars supplied to the Channel Islands were still delivered without seat belts. From December 1971, North American cars had inertia reel belts as standard, and on North American roadsters the seat belt mounting point was relocated from the tonneau panel back onto the wheelarch.

In general on 1972 models, black trim was replaced by Navy (dark blue). On the GT, the centre panels on the front seats and the two panels on the rear seat were changed from vinyl to brushed nylon, but the side bolsters remained vinyl. The roadster continued with the all-vinyl seat covers.

The headrests were modified with a plainer grain to their centre panels and continued in this form until 1976, always matching the seat colour and always covered in vinyl, even on GTs with nylon seat facings. The door casings were fitted with two bright chrome-finish trim strips, while the earlier hinged door pull gave way to a simple fixed door pull which was colour-matched to the trim. The transmission tunnel was covered by a console which linked up with the centre

console below the facia. This included a shelf round the gear lever, a new matt black – and inconveniently small – ashtray behind the gear lever, and an armrest between the seats. The padded armrest was covered in black vinyl and was hinged at the rear, lifting up to reveal a rather impractical cubbyhole. It is important to point out that the console and armrest were always black, regardless of trim colour. The carpet material was changed from Firth's loop-pile to the same manufacturer's cut-pile. On cars fitted with sun visors, a vanity mirror was added on the back of the passenger one. From May 1972, home market cars were fitted with a new type of Kangol static seat belt which allowed one-handed operation.

For the 1973 model year, the Autumn Leaf trim colour was replaced by a yellow/brown colour called Ochre. This was not a happy choice and Ochre never became popular, surviving less than a year in production before it was displaced by Autumn Leaf again. Also at the end of the 1973 model year, Navy was deleted and black re-introduced. The seat cover patterns were new on 1973 models, with narrower side bolsters and transverse fluting running across the bolsters and centre panel. The roadster still had vinyl seat

This 1973 model door trim (right) features the two chrome-finish trim strips and also the new armrest-type door pull. By this time the waist rail was in the main trim colour. The final type of door trim (far right) was found from the start of the 1977 model year. The Autumn Leaf trim colour, later replaced by Beige, was used on these door trims only on American vehicles – all RHD cars from June 1976 had black door trims. The door-mounted loudspeakers seen here were fitted to American cars from 1976, but on RHD cars only from the start of the 1979 model year. This American-spec car has the additional anti-burst units fitted below the main door locks.

facings, with a basketweave pattern to the centre panels and graining on the side bolsters, while the GT now had full-width brushed nylon seat facings, with a ribbed cord background pattern apart from the transverse flutes.

The gear lever gaiter was modified and there was a new door pull, still a corporate Austin-Morris design but one which now at least looked like a proper armrest. There was thicker carpet, and in general all trim material specifications were changed – and sometimes upgraded – to ensure that trim met US regulations for inflammability. In early 1973, a new type of optional extra inertia reel seat belt became available on the GT model. Inertia reel seat belts were standardised on the new GT V8, which was then just coming into production. The V8 was also fitted with headrests as standard but otherwise its interior did not differ from the four-cylinder GT. Only a handful of

V8s had Ochre trim and most of the early cars had Navy trim, but these colours were soon superseded by Autumn Leaf and Black, the standard trim colours on the 1974 models. The interior trim was hardly changed on the 1974 models, except that the GT acquired a new one-piece boot floorboard, and North American cars had a new type of inertia reel seat belt. Soon after the introduction of the V8, four-cylinder GTs for the home market also acquired inertia reel seat belts as standard. On home market cars in October 1974, seat belts were at long last included in the list price.

For the first couple of years of 'rubber-bumper' production, from 1974 to 1976, there were very few changes to the interior trim. The limited edition 'Jubilee' GT models for the home market in April 1975 were fitted with headrests as standard, and were also the first MGBs to receive full carpeting instead of the combination of rubber mats and carpets. At the end of 1975, the gear lever surround and gaiter retainer was changed from chrome-plating to a matt black epoxy finish.

Only in June 1976, from the start of the 1977 model year, was the interior given a major final overhaul. All RHD cars, both roadsters and GTs, were given new brushed nylon seat facings. These came in two different colour combinations, either silver and grey or orange and brown. They were patterned with longitudinal stripes, and in each case the darker colour was used for the centre stripe. The result was certainly striking, if a little loud. A similar fabric was used on some Minis of the period. The GT rear seat was also covered in this so-called 'deckchair' material, with two stripes in the darker colour. The nylon fabric was used only on the seat facings, with the edges and the backs of the squabs in black vinyl. There was a new, simpler design of headrest, now standard on all cars, and on RHD cars the headrests were always covered in black vinyl. Generally speaking, the vinyl grain was changed to a finer, less leather-like pattern.

To go with the new seats were new door liners,

The original type of roadster rear view mirror, used until 1968, had a gold-painted metal backing plate and no visible frame around the edge of the mirror. Note that the mirror was clamped to the windscreen centre brace, allowing height adjustment.

Used in 1968 and 1969, this roadster mirror with a grey plastic backing plate and frame was still fitted to the windscreen centre brace but was otherwise similar to the mirror found on contemporary GTs, and even on Mark I GTs from 1965.

The dipping interior mirror with black backing, now fitted to the upper windscreen frame on all roadsters, was introduced for the 1970 model year and remained to the end of production. The dipping mirror on GTs was very similar.

always in black on RHD cars. They had a circular feature round the window winder, rectangles in front of and behind the door handle, and a horizontal feature line below the door pull. The actual door furniture was not changed. The door liner design was the same on RHD and LHD cars, except that at first only North American cars had loudspeakers in the doors. These were only added on UK cars for the 1979 model year, from May 1978.

The North American LHD roadsters retained the vinyl or Ambla seat facings until the end of production, the design and pattern of these seat covers being basically the same as it had been on the pre-1977 model year cars but with the basketweave pattern extended to the side bolsters. North American headrests were similar in shape to those on RHD cars but had covers with the basketweave pattern. North American customers were still given the choice between black and Autumn Leaf trim until October 1977, when Autumn Leaf was replaced by the new trim colour of beige. On these late North American cars, the door liners and other trim parts continued to match the seat colour, whether black, Autumn Leaf or beige, whereas all the parts on RHD cars which had previously been colour-coded to match the seats now became black.

Full carpeting was introduced on all 1977 model year cars, covering the floor panels and sills as well the tunnel, heelboard and rear shelf. The carpets on RHD cars were always black from now on, as they were on LHD cars with black trim. On LHD roadsters with Autumn Leaf or beige trim, however, the carpet in the front compartment of the car was black, but the carpeting on the heelboard and rear shelf was Autumn Leaf (on cars with Autumn Leaf trim) or Chestnut (on cars with beige trim). In October 1977, at the same time that the Chestnut carpet colour was introduced, the specified carpet quality was changed temporarily to Astrakhan, but reverted to Firth's cut-pile after about a year.

Other smaller changes on the 1977 model year cars included the provision for the first time of sun visors on RHD roadsters. On all cars the driver's sun visor now had a document pocket on the back, and there was a vanity mirror on the passenger sun visor. On the GT, the rear quarter upper liner was modified so that the grey colour finished at a horizontal line following the line of the waist rail, and the bottom part of the liner became black. In February 1977, improved Kangol inertia reel seat belts were fitted, series 13 on LHD roadsters and series 12 on RHD GTs. In May 1977, RHD roadsters were also equipped with the series 13 inertia reel seat belts, while in April-May 1978 dual-sensitive belts of a common type were fitted to all MGB cars. In March 1980, in one of the last modifications to the car, the seat belts were altered to ensure that they met both North American and EEC requirements.

This style of tonneau panel seat belt mounting point arrived on North American Mark II models, and was used on UK and other cars with static seat belts from the 1971 model year through to 1977. They were rather impractical as it was necessary to detach the seat belts every time the folding hood or tonneau cover was used.

When this GT was built in 1973, inertia reel seat belts were still an optional extra in the UK. These belts were made by Kangol. The reel was mounted on the top of the rear wheelarch. This photo also shows the detailing of one of the two simple catches which lock the rear seat squab in place in the upright position.

From 1977, all roadsters also had inertia reel seat belts, with the reels mounted at the bottom of the rear wheelarches in the tonneau area. The short flexible seat belt buckle arms on the transmission tunnel are evident, and so is the third seat belt mounting point on the inner sill.

The final type of seat belt reel for the dual-sensitive Kangol belts which were fitted to all cars from 1978.

This shows the seat belt tongue being parked on its stowing hook on the rear inner quarter panel of a 1980 North American roadster. This view also shows the late North American trim colours of Beige (on the liners) and Chestnut (on the carpet), and even how the sill (and floor) carpets are black while the rear carpets are Chestnut.

FACIA & INSTRUMENTS

The original facia style stayed largely unchanged on non-North American cars through to 1971. Points to observe on this 1964 car include the three identical toggle switches below the radio, the washer push above the dual gauge and the shape of the loudspeaker box at the bottom where it meets the stepped transmission tunnel. The main instruments are marked British Jaeger while the radio (marked 'British Motor Corporation') is, oddly, most likely to be an American-made after-market item.

The original type of MGB facia was fitted on all Mark I cars until late 1967, and on home market cars as well as some export models until the end of the 1971 model year. It was also found on MGC cars, except those for North America. A totally different style of padded facia (known as 'the Abingdon pillow') with a centre console was adopted for MGB and MGC export models to the USA from the start of production of the MGB Mark II in November 1967 (and thus from the start of MGC production as such), but was only fitted to cars for Canada from August 1968. The US-type facia was found on cars for Sweden and Germany from the start of the 1970 model year (GHN5/GHD5 series) as well as on later cars for Norway.

Both the standard and the US-type facia were modified for the 1972 model year, the most obvious addition being the fresh-air vents in the centre of the facia, while North American cars gained a glovebox and a redesigned centre console, now linked with a console between the seats. The new style console was also introduced on non-North American cars. The facia was slightly modified on the MGB GT V8 model,

and these modifications were also found on four-cylinder RHD cars from the start of 'rubber-bumper' production in September 1974. All LHD 'rubber-bumper' cars, regardless of market, had the North American facia. The final update came with the 1977 models, with all-new facia panels and instruments being fitted to RHD cars and LHD North American cars from June 1976.

Starting with the early facia as introduced in 1962, this was a simple metal panel curving away across the car and turned under at the bottom, and finished in the semi-matt black crackle paint which became an MGB trademark. At the top of the facia was a padded crash roll covered in black vynide, and the scuttle panel behind the windscreen was covered in black Novon plastic. A hood surrounded the two main instruments on either side of the steering column. On the early 1962-63 cars, this had a chrome bead on the inside. The layout of the facia on LHD cars was an exact mirror image of that found on RHD cars, with the following sequence of instruments and controls, starting from the *left* on a *left*-hand drive car, or from the *right* on a *right*-hand drive car:

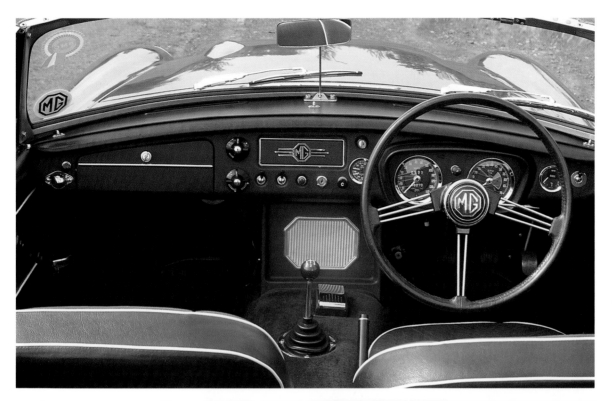

The Mark II facia on this 1968 model is almost identical to the original, but the washer push is now third in the row of controls below the radio panel, there is a beefier light switch with an appropriate symbol above the dual gauge, and the transmission tunnel is the later bulkier type (and so the bottom line of the loudspeaker box is quite different). As the car shown is an MGC, the speedo reads to 140mph and the rev counter has the red line at 5500rpm instead of 6000rpm. The instruments are now marked Smiths. The radio panel is the correct type for all pre-1977 models. Note the overdrive switch on the far right. The steering wheel is the same as on the MGB but has a sewn-on leather cover.

North American Mark II cars had this safety-type facia with what has become known as the 'Abingdon pillow' in front of the passenger. This car is actually a 1971 model, as evidenced by the steering wheel style. The gear knob is not original but may be a contemporary US accessory – but neither the fire extinguisher nor the roll of mints are!

Overdrive switch (if fitted)
Fuel gauge
Rev counter (tachometer), 4in diameter
Two direction indicator warning lamps, with the panel light rheostat switch centrally below them
Speedometer, with total and trip mileage recorders, 4in diameter
Windscreen washer push (above)
Oil pressure and coolant temperature gauge (below)

Radio aperture panel or radio (above)
Minor controls below radio panel, as follows: choke knob; ignition lock, with built-in starter switch; toggle switches for lighting, wipers and heater blower fan
Two rotary heater controls, for temperature (upper) and air distribution (lower)
Glovebox
Map light switch and map light

The radio panel, finished in crackle black to match the main panel, had a chrome trim strip round the edge and a winged chrome-and-black MG logo in the centre. The glovebox lid had a key-only operated locking catch (typically sharing the boot key but later often with its own FT-series key), and a chrome trim strip. Below the facia panel itself was a radio speaker panel set into a console filling the gap between facia and gearbox tunnel, with an aluminium mesh panel for the speaker, of rectangular shape with the corners nipped off to form a symbolic octagon. The shape at the bottom of the console was altered in 1967 for the new transmission tunnel. The ignition key was a Wilmot Breeden Union FS-series (some very early cars had an FP-series key), which also unlocked the doors. The black-and-chrome plastic heater controls were shared with the BMC Farina saloons of the time. Of the minor controls, only the choke knob and panel light switch were marked, with 'C' and 'P' respectively, while the three toggle switches were left unmarked. All of these knobs and switches were made out of black plastic.

Controls not found on the facia included the self-cancelling indicator stalk switch on the steering column (on the left on LHD cars, the right on RHD cars). This switch also controlled the headlamp flasher, which was originally an option but became standard on all cars (except North American models) from October 1965. The horn push was fitted to the centre of the steering wheel. The headlamp dipswitch was on the floor on all Mark I models, and on non-North American cars to the end of the 1969 model year. The bonnet release pull with a large knob marked 'B'

was always under the facia, on the left-hand side. Later the release pull was changed to a T-shape with a bonnet-open symbol, probably from the start of the 'rubber-bumper' models. Also under the facia, to the left of the radio speaker panel, was a lever which controlled the opening of the fresh-air vent built into the dash panel under the scuttle, with three different stages of opening.

Modifications to this style of facia were very few. The chrome finisher inside the instrument hood was deleted in May 1963. In April 1965, on cars equipped with overdrive, the original toggle switch was replaced by a larger cranked 'shepherd's crook' switch. In May-June 1966, the positions of the windscreen washer push and the lighting switch were swapped, and the lighting switch became a more substantial knob with a headlamp symbol. Two-speed wipers with a two-stage toggle switch were fitted from the start of the Mark II and MGC models in 1967.

On North American Mark II models and on 1970 non-North American models, the foot dipswitch was deleted and its purpose integrated into a multi-function steering column stalk controlling the direction indicators, the headlamp flasher and dip, and the horns (which were operated by pushing the end of the stalk). This was unpopular and for 1971 models the horn push returned to the centre of the steering wheel. Also in 1970, the original choke pull knob, marked 'C', was replaced by a new corporate knob with a fan symbol.

From the start of production in 1962 a steering lock was fitted for some export markets, notably Germany and Sweden, later also Finland, Austria and France. When a combined steering and ignition lock was fitted, the redundant ignition lock hole in the facia was covered with a chrome-plated blanking plug. Apart from North American cars, which commonly had a steering lock from late 1967, steering locks were fitted to all home market and other export cars from December 1970, and these models also for a time had the blanking plug until the basic facia pressing was amended to omit the ignition lock hole.

The instruments were always made by Smiths, although they were initially marked British Jaeger, with a small 'British' above a larger 'Jaeger'. The Smiths name was put on the dials in October 1964, coinciding with the introduction of the five main bearing 18GB engine and the replacement of the original mechanical rev counter with an electronic tachometer. Both types of rev counter read to 7000rpm, with an amber sector from 5000rpm and a red sector from 6000rpm, and incorporated a red ignition and charging warning light at the bottom of the dial. The speedometer read to 120mph in 10mph increments (200kph in 20kph increments on export models where required), and was fitted with a three-figure plus decimal trip mileage recorder above centre, and a five-figure total mileage recorder below centre.

This car is a 1973 North American model. It has the revised style of facia with centrally-mounted fresh-air vents and the glovebox introduced a year earlier, but the Ochre-coloured seats with transverse feature lines and the steering wheel design confirm that this is a 1973 model. Note also the steering column lock of the side-entry type.

Looking straight ahead at another 1973 North American model facia, the new heater controls are worth noting, together with the T-shaped choke handle. Although this car has the 1973 trim colour of Ochre, the seat style seems perversely to be of the 1972 type! This steering wheel style with tapered slots in the spokes was used only between August 1972 and June 1973.

The trip reset button was behind the lower edge of the facia. A blue headlamp main beam warning lamp was incorporated at the bottom of the dial.

The fuel gauge had simple E-½-F markings. The dual gauge recorded oil pressure up to 100lb/sq in in the upper half, and coolant temperature in the lower half. Originally either Fahrenheit or Centigrade gauges were offered depending on market, but in October 1968 both were replaced by the simpler C-N-H markings for all markets. All of the instruments had been changed a year before this, to suit the new

negative earth electrical system introduced from the start of the Mark II models. The green indicator warning lamps found between the main dials were each shaped like an arrow pointing in the appropriate direction.

The most important differences on the MGC concerned the rev counter, which had its amber sector starting at 5000rpm and its red sector at 5500rpm, while the speedometer read to 140mph (or 220kph). Also on this model, the Fahrenheit or Centigrade temperature gauges were replaced by a gauge marked

On this 1973 home market GT the fresh-air vents fill the space previously reserved for the radio. This has now migrated down into the new centre console, in turn displacing the loudspeaker (so this car has loudspeakers on the scuttle side liners). The switches are now generally of the rocker type and the second rocker switch from the left is for the optional fog lamp(s), a switch usually only found on some GT models.

The fresh-air vents in close-up. This particular car has a different style washer push – possibly not original – and lacks the fog lamp switch. Note the new console-mounted interior lamp.

C-N-H from October 1968. For the last model year of the original facia style, 1971, the map light on non-North American cars was also operated by courtesy switches in the doors.

The facia found on US export Mark II models from late 1967, as well as on cars for Canada from August 1968, and Sweden and Germany from the start of the 1970 model year, was of the padded safety type, covered in black vinyl. There was no glovebox because of the heavy padding in front of the passenger, so all these cars had the map pocket fitted to the

scuttle liner on the side of the passenger footwell (otherwise an optional extra on roadsters but standard on all GTs). The US-style or safety facia also had additional switches on a centre console above the transmission tunnel. The sequence of instruments and controls was as follows, starting from the left:

Brake pressure and circuit failure warning lamp, with test switch (above)
Main lighting switch, rocker type (below)
Fuel gauge (above)
Rotary heater temperature control (below)
Left-hand direction indicator warning lamp (green arrow)
Rev counter (80mm)
Ignition warning lamp (red)
Square oil pressure gauge
Headlamp high beam warning lamp (blue)
Speedometer, with total and trip mileage recorders (80mm)
Right-hand direction indicator warning lamp (green arrow)
Coolant temperature gauge (above)
Rotary heater air distribution control (below)
Choke pull (above)
Heater blower fan switch, rocker type (below)

In addition to the main facia, US cars now had a centre console which accommodated the radio aperture and extra switches. Above the radio (or blanking panel) was the map light, operated by a rocker switch on the right below the radio. On the left below the radio was a rocker switch for the hazard lights,

with a warning lamp adjacent to it. The cigar lighter, now standard, was mounted in the centre below the radio. On GT models an alternative console could be found, with a total of four rocker switches below the radio. The switch on the extreme left was for a fog or spot lamp if one was fitted, while between the cigar lighter and the map light switch was a switch for the heated rear window, with a warning lamp positioned to the left of it.

Other controls were found on the steering column. A stalk switch on the left controlled direction indicators, headlamp dip/flasher and horns; a stalk switch on the right controlled two-speed wipers, electric washer, and overdrive (if fitted). The panel lights were controlled by a small switch on the left of the column, and the combined ignition lock and starter switch was mounted on the right, the key being inserted from the side through the cowling. This was combined with a steering lock on most US-type cars, although it appears that the lock did not become a universal fitting on US cars until the 1969 model year, and on 1970 models a warning buzzer was also fitted as a reminder to drivers who left the key in the lock and opened the driver's door.

Further changes occurred on later US models. The choke knob was replaced by a T-shaped handle for the 1970 model year, while on 1971 models the panel light switch on the steering column was replaced by a rheostat switch fitted to the right of the temperature gauge. The 1971 cars also had a new interior lamp on the console, with a switch on the lamp body itself, making the rocker switch on the lower right of

the console redundant. On both roadster and GT models, this lamp was also activated by door-mounted courtesy switches. The horns were now again operated by a push in the centre of the steering wheel.

More drastic changes were in store for the 1972 model year. North American type cars now regained the lockable glovebox in front of the passenger, while a pair of fresh-air ventilation vents were fitted in the centre of the facia. The console below the facia was remodelled, with the lower switch panel being angled and meeting up with the new transmission tunnel console. The layout of the switches on the console panel was now as follows: hazard light switch; warning lamp for hazard lights; warning lamp for heated rear window; switch for heated rear window; blank for switch for fog or spot lamp; and cigar lighter.

Soon after the start of the 1972 model year, a rectangular 'fasten seat belt' warning lamp (combined with a buzzer) was fitted below the two round warning lamps for hazard lights and heated rear window. In December 1971, on all cars for the USA most symbols on controls and instruments were replaced by words, but cars for Canada (and other markets with the US-style facia) continued with international symbols. A further re-arrangement of the console switch panel occurred for the 1973 model year when the sequence became as follows, again from the left: fog/spot lamp switch; hazard lights warning lamp above seat belt warning lamp; hazard lights switch; switch for heated rear window, now with built-in warning lamp; and cigar lighter.

All 1975 cars for North America (from December

The V8 facia is identifiable by the smaller 80mm main instruments with a 140mph speedo and the rev counter red-lined at 5000rpm. Also noteworthy are the new stalk switches and the wider column shroud, while this 1974 model should probably have the earlier-style choke knob instead of the T-handle. This panel light switch was previously found only on American models. This car's owner has fitted a St Christopher medallion below the air vents. This was the first type of solid-spoke steering wheel, with a red MG badge in the centre.

The 140mph speedo of the V8 in close-up. Also visible is part of the 1975-type steering wheel with the background of the MG badge in 'gold'.

1974) with the new single carburettor engine had an automatic choke, so the choke handle now disappeared. The fog/spot lamp switch was now deleted on North American cars, as was the heated rear window switch (only found on GT models, which were no longer offered in the USA or Canada), but an extra rectangular warning lamp was added below the cigar lighter. This came on at 25,000-mile intervals, to indicate that the Exhaust Gas Recirculation valve needed servicing, hence the lamp was marked EGR. On some 1975 cars for California, and on all cars for the USA (but not Canada) for the 1976 model year, the lamp was marked EGR Catalyst, indicating that the catalytic converter also needed renewing after 25,000 miles. This warning lamp was discontinued at the end of the 1976 model year and was not found on later North American MGBs.

On the UK-type facia, the major change occurred from the start of the 1972 model year when a pair of fresh-air vents were fitted in place of the original radio aperture. The radio location was moved to a new centre console which took the place of the original loudspeaker box, and the old toggle switches were replaced by rocker switches. The map light to the left of the glovebox was discontinued and was replaced by a North American-style courtesy lamp above the radio aperture on the console, with a switch on the lamp as well as the door-mounted courtesy switches. The sequence of switches below the air vents on the main facia was, from left: rocker switch for the heater blower fan; rocker switch for the optional fog or spot lamp (deleted for the 1973 model year); push for

windscreen washer; rocker switch for wipers; and choke pull. The main lighting switch, also of the rocker type, was still above the dual gauge. Below the radio aperture on the console were, from left: a switch blank and a warning lamp blank; the cigar lighter, if fitted, in the centre; and a warning lamp and a rocker switch for the heated rear window on the GT, if fitted. Otherwise the facia layout still conformed to the original pre-1972 pattern.

The cigar lighter was standardised on the GT during the 1972 model year, and on 1973 models of the roadster. The heated rear window was standardised on 1974 model GTs, and hazard warning lights became available as an option, with a rocker switch occupying the previous blank on the console.

The MGB GT V8 was new for the 1974 model year. The V8 facia was broadly similar in layout to the four-cylinder models, but with some important differences. On the V8, new steering column stalk switches were introduced: the left-hand stalk switch operated the wipers, electric washer and (standard) overdrive; the right-hand stalk the direction indicators, headlamp dip and flasher. There was a new steering column lock with the key inserted from the right-hand side of the column, through a new shroud. Because of the new column controls, the shroud was wider and intruded on the space available for the instruments, so the V8 had smaller main dials of 80mm diameter, the same size as found on North American MGB four-cylinder models, and with the ignition and main beam warning lights moved below the instruments. The V8 speedometer read to 140mph (a kph version was not offered).

There were no wiper or washer controls on the V8 facia. The hazard warning lights were standard on this model, and their switch was soon moved to the right side of the centre console, swapping places with the switch and warning lamp for the heated rear window. Another innovation on the V8 model was the introduction of a new rheostat switch for the panel lights. 'Rubber-bumper' V8 models had the choke knob replaced by a T-shaped handle.

When the 'rubber-bumper' models were introduced in the autumn of 1974, four-cylinder RHD cars adopted the V8 facia layout, with the smaller main instruments, stalk-type controls and new steering lock – and hazard warning lights were now standard on all cars. In this form the UK-type facia continued to the end of the 1976 model year.

For the 1977 models, which went into production in June 1976, completely new facia styles were adopted for both RHD cars (roadster and four-cylinder GT, now mainly for the home market) and for LHD cars (roadsters, by now built exclusively to North American specification). The facia on RHD cars was covered in a dark grey grained plastic material supplied by the Trinite company, and new instruments of a style shared with the Triumph Spitfire were

The virtually all-new facia as fitted to RHD cars from 1976 to 1980, with Triumph Spitfire style instruments and dark grey Trimite covering. On this 1980 roadster, the switch furthest to the left below the air vents is for the rear fog guard lamps. The speedo and oil pressure gauge both have additional metric markings. The steering wheel is of the type common to both American and RHD cars from 1976.

fitted. The steering column stalk switches were modified, and most switches and controls were relocated. The sequence of instruments was, from left:

Oil pressure gauge (with additional kg/sq cm markings)
Speedometer (with additional kph markings), reading to 120mph and incorporating total and trip mileage recorders
Left-hand direction indicator warning lamp (green arrow, above)
Ignition warning lamp (red, below)
Fuel gauge
Right-hand direction indicator warning lamp (green arrow, above)
Headlamp main beam warning lamp (blue, below)
Rev counter, reading to 7000rpm (amber zone from 5500rpm, red zone from 6000rpm)
Coolant temperature gauge, marked simply C and H

Below the face-level air vents in the centre of the facia was a panel with room for up to five illuminated rocker switches. The first space on the left was blank on all roadsters, and on GTs until December 1977. From December 1977 until the start of the 1980 model year, GTs had the heated rear window warning lamp here, and on 1980 model year GTs the switch for the heated rear window with a built-in warning lamp was in this location. The second space was blank on roadsters until the 1980 model year. GTs until this

The revised centre console on post-1976 RHD cars, with illuminated heater controls flanking an electric clock, and the new round interior lamp between the cigar lighter and the choke handle. The white plastic knob on the fresh-air intake regulating handle to the left shows up well.

time had the heated rear window switch in this location, until December 1977 with a built-in warning lamp, from December 1977 to the start of the 1980 model year without a warning lamp. For the 1980 model year, both roadsters and GTs had a switch for the rear fog guard lamps in this position. The remaining three spaces were used on all cars for the switches for the facia-mounted courtesy lamp, hazard warning lights and two-speed heater blower fan.

In a recess below the switch panel were the illumi-

nated cigar lighter, a new design of round courtesy lamp, and the T-handle for the choke. The panel light rheostat switch was on the edge of the facia below the speedometer. The left-hand steering column stalk controlled wipers and washer, and now included a single-wipe facility. The right-hand stalk controlled the direction indicators, headlamp dip and flasher, and horns. Also on the right-hand side of the column were the main lighting switch and the steering lock. The overdrive switch was now fitted in the gear knob.

The radio aperture blanking plate in the centre console was a new type, of plastic with an embossed MG logo. Below this were re-styled illuminated heater controls, temperature on the left and air distribution on the right, with an electric clock between them. At the very bottom of the console were two warning lights, both red, the one on the left indicating brake circuit failure or handbrake operation, the one on the right serving as a 'fasten seat belt' reminder. On the RHD facia from 1976, the speedometer and rev counter were still of 80mm diameter. In October 1978, these instruments were changed so that the figures were found inside the scale markings rather than outside, and the speedometer now read 10/30/50 etc instead of 10/20/30/40 etc. On all 1976-80 cars, the glovebox had a press-button catch, still incorporating a key-operated lock.

The final style of facia found on LHD roadsters to North American specification (including cars exported to Japan) for the 1977 to 1980 model years also incorporated new-style instruments, but the layout was different, with the main instrument panel in front of the driver arranged as follows, from left:

Panel light rheostat switch
Switch blank (above)
Hazard warning light switch, illuminated rocker type (below)
Fuel gauge, for USA marked 'unleaded fuel only' (above)
Oil pressure gauge (below)
Left-hand direction indicator warning lamp (green arrow)
Rev counter (4in)
Bank of four rectangular warning lamps, from top: headlamp main beam (blue), ignition (red), hazard warning lights (red), brake circuit failure and hand brake reminder (red)
Speedometer (4in)
Right-hand direction indicator warning lamp (green arrow)
Electric clock (above)
Coolant temperature gauge (below)
Switch blank (above)
Heater blower fan switch, illuminated rocker type (below)

The centre of the facia was occupied as before by the air vents, with a slim rectangular courtesy lamp with a switch built into the rocking lens below them.

These instruments (far left) are from a 1977 US spec car – hence the fuel gauge is marked 'unleaded fuel only'. The typography of these later instruments is in a style common to the contemporary Triumph Spitfire. The facia from this 1980 model US specification car (left) is included to show the final type of speedometer reading only to 80mph and fitted with a six-figure odometer. Can you read the mileage? It was exactly 294 at the time this 13-year-old car was photographed.

The radio aperture was in the centre console below this, and at the bottom of the console were the rotary heater controls flanking the cigar lighter (all being illuminated) and the seat belt warning lamp. On the left of the steering column was the stalk for direction indicators, headlamp dip and flasher, and horns, while the main lighting switch was on the column below the stalk. On the right of the column was the steering and ignition lock, as well as the stalk for wipers and the washer. The overdrive switch, if fitted, was in the gear knob.

Subsequent changes on North American models were minimal. One difference that still persisted

between US cars and Canadian/Japanese models was that instrument and control labelling was in words on US cars, whereas non-US cars used the internationally recognised ISO-approved symbols. From the start of the 1978 model year, cars for Canada were fitted with a kph speedometer, also found on cars exported to Japan. The 1980 model year cars for the USA had a speedometer which read only to 85mph and had a six-figure total mileage recorder. This six-figure odometer was also found on Canadian and Japanese 1980 cars. The 1979-80 North American Limited Edition models had a plaque on the lid of the glovebox confirming the LE identity.

A detail shot of the console on a 1977 American car (above left), with the cigar lighter between the heater controls and a Motorola radio cassette. Another little detail from the late North American car – the inside of the glovebox (above) with a tyre pressure instruction label on the lid. Also just visible is the map pocket fitted to the inside of the passenger side scuttle liner on the outside of the footwell.

WEATHER EQUIPMENT

This is what you are faced with on an early car with a pack-away hood (right): a hockey-stick shaped felt bag which contains the two halves of the do-it-yourself hood frame. When erected in the sockets (far right) on the rear quarter liners, the hood frame should look like this. Note the light grey colour, correct on all hood frames until the end of the 1970 model year.

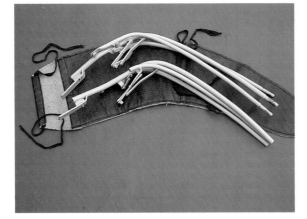

We've only just begun: the fun goes on as you take the hood cover out of its bag (right). The result of your labours should look like this (far right): an original grey pack-away hood neatly stretched over its frame. Reputedly this particular hood had never been fitted to the car between 1965 and the summer's day 27 years later when the photographer arrived!

From the inside (right), this pack-away hood cover displays the authentic grey backing material – but this example is a reproduction hood cover, with the wrong shape to the rear window and quarterlights, and exaggeratedly narrow strips between the Vybak panels. An original pack-away hood (far right), has nicely rounded corners to the Vybak panels and the 'Vybak Plastics AS6' script in red.

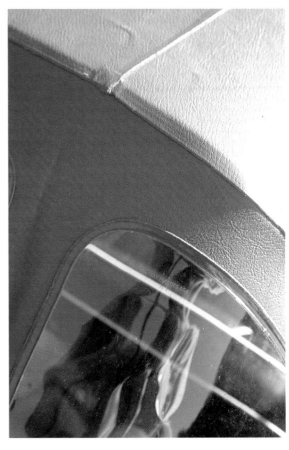

Until August 1970, all MGB and MGC roadster models were offered with a choice of a simple standard hood – known as the 'pack-away' type as it had to be completely dismantled and stowed in the boot in its individual parts – or the more convenient, permanently-attached folding hood which was an optional extra. Throughout this period, both types of hood were available in all markets, except that Belgian-assembled cars always had the folding hood, Irish-assembled cars to 1970 always had the pack-away hood, and Australian-assembled cars had a locally-supplied hood normally of the pack-away type until 1970.

At a glance indistinguishable, this is the folding hood which until 1970 was optional equipment, here fitted to a 1968 MGC roadster.

One may quibble at the fact that this black hood also has black backing material, but the light grey frame is correct and the rather different type of frame for the folding hood can be seen, with the double folding scissor links to the header rail and the strap holding the cover fabric to the frame.

The folding hood (far left) has been taken down, although the retaining straps at the rear of the tonneau have yet to be fitted round it. The transverse tonneau rail which supports the so-called short tonneau cover (properly called the hood stowage cover) has been fitted in the sockets also used for the pack-away hood frame. And here (left) is the hood stowage cover in place, fitting to the same fixing points used both for the hood and the long tonneau cover.

The pack-away hood was discontinued in 1970, and an improved type of folding hood, designed by Michelotti, then became standard on all roadsters until the end of production, the only significant modification being that from 1976 it was fitted with a zip-out rear window. All hoods are of superficially similar design, with three hoodsticks or bows to the main frame, a front header rail which is latched to the windscreen frame, a rear anchor plate which slips into a sewn pocket at the lower rear edge of the canopy and which is attached to the hood retaining plates on the rear tonneau panel, and a canopy with a rectangular rear window and two triangular rear quarterlights, all made from transparent Vybak.

Originally only coloured hoods were available, in red, blue or grey. The hood material was Everflex leathercloth which was grey-backed, and the colour reference numbers were: red RD.24/G/F1, blue BL.57/G/F1 and grey GY.2/G/F1. Red hoods may also be of ICI Vynide leathercloth, colour reference RE.362, grain VT.1356. Between August 1963 and August 1964, black hoods were gradually introduced for all colour schemes as an alternative to the coloured hoods, and in December 1966 coloured hoods were discontinued altogether. From then until 1980 all roadsters were only available with black hoods. So far as evidence is available, it is likely that most, if not all, CKD cars before December 1966 had black rather than coloured hoods. The hood frames for both the early types of hood were painted grey.

The standard pack-away hood consisted of two major assemblies: the frame, which split in the middle for more convenient stowage; and the canopy assembly, which incorporated the header rail and the rear anchor plate. The frame was not connected to the header rail. When erecting the hood, the frame had to be located in two sockets, one on either side of the rear compartment just behind the doors. The canopy was then spread over the frame, fastened with two over-centre catches to the windscreen frame, to the retaining plates on the rear tonneau panel as well as four 'lift-the-dot' fasteners on either side, and to a special socket on each rear wing just behind the door. For stowing the hood in the boot, a hockey-stick shaped bag was provided for the hood frame and a narrow rectangular bag for the hood canopy. Two straps were provided on the boot floor for the hood canopy bag, which should be stowed at an angle above the spare wheel towards the front of the boot, while the hood frame bag was stowed to the right and at the front of the spare wheel. Contemporary accounts allege that the world record for erecting an MGB pack-away hood from scratch was less than 60sec!

The folding hood was more convenient and easier to use. The frame was permanently attached to the rear inner quarter panels in the positions where the sockets for the pack-away hood frame were found.

This 1971 model was one of the first cars to have the new standardised folding hood, redesigned by Michelotti. All hoods were now black and would remain so.

The three-bow frame was connected to the header rail by a hinged over-centre link on either side. When the hood was collapsed it took up a fair amount of space in the rear compartment, and to cover it a separate hood stowage cover was provided, sometimes also referred to as the 'short tonneau cover'. The hood cover was attached to the various hood fasteners at the rear, and to two 'lift-the-dot' fasteners on each side inside the rear compartment. To give proper shape to the hood cover when installed, it was stretched over a tonneau rail which split in the middle for easy stowage. A bag shaped like a hockey-stick was provided for stowing the tonneau rail in the boot, and an almost square envelope for stowing the hood cover. The same envelope was used for stowing the optional full tonneau cover if supplied. The collapsed folding hood was held in place by two straps under the front edge of the rear tonneau panel. The most important change affecting the folding hood prior to 1970 was that the canopy, frame and header rail were extensively changed to improve fit in August 1963.

The improved folding hood introduced in August 1970 was a much more sensible design, its stouter frame, now painted black, having proper scissor links between the front header rail and the three bows towards the rear. Generally the fit of the hood and the hood fasteners were improved, and the result was a hood that was easier to handle and more weatherproof. Otherwise, in terms of attachment, fasteners and stowage, this hood was similar to the original type of folding hood. A hood stowage cover with tonneau rail and bags was also provided. Different types of hood stowage covers were quoted, depending on whether or not the car had seat belt mounting points on the rear tonneau panel. The most important

From the inside, the much-changed hood frame is evident. The frame was now painted black rather than light grey.

change to this type of hood was that the canopy was modified in June 1976 to incorporate a zip-out rear window, a feature particularly appreciated in the USA, where it gave additional ventilation without reducing protection from the sun. Some cars for Germany to 1976 were supplied with special crash pads to be fitted over the scissor links when the hood was erected.

The tonneau cover was originally an optional extra but became standard on home market cars for the 1973 model year, and on North American export models from December 1977. Prior to this, tonneau cover fasteners had been fitted to the heelboard as standard on all roadsters from March 1969, and similarly to the shroud panel behind the windscreen on all cars from September 1970. All tonneau covers had a central zip (so they could be fitted over the passen-

When folded, the 1971-type hood looks much the same as the original folding hood.

On the same 1971 model year car, the tonneau cover has been fitted. Note the additional pockets for the headrests and the absence of a transverse zip at the rear of the door – and the hole for the seat belt fixing in front of the rearmost 'lift-the-dot' fixing.

This is the inconvenient aspect of these early 1970s roadsters, with the seat belts having to be re-fitted to the rear mounting points every time the tonneau cover is even partly folded.

ger seat alone), a steering wheel pocket and headrest pockets where appropriate. At the back, the tonneau cover used the hood fasteners on the tonneau panel. When the tonneau cover was left in place but folded back to the tonneau rail behind either or both seats, flaps on the tonneau cover were fastened to the heel-board to hold it securely in place. Zips in the tonneau cover on either side behind the seat permitted the use of seat belts when the cover was in this position. Alternatively, the tonneau cover and tonneau rail could be removed and stored in the boot in their bags.

The tonneau and hood covers were originally available in red, blue or black, but in 1966 the blue and red versions were discontinued. It is important to realise that on 1962-66 cars the tonneau cover and the hood cover did not always match the colour of the hood, but were instead colour-matched to the interior trim. There were very many different tonneau covers over the years, for RHD and LHD cars, cars without or with headrests, and for cars with different types of seat belts.

The hard top was always an optional extra, introduced in June 1963 and officially listed until 1976 in home market brochures. It was still quoted in parts lists as an optional extra to the end of production, and while it may mainly have been sold as a spare part through Unipart from 1976 onwards, research in the production records has revealed that small numbers of cars did leave Abingdon with factory-fitted hard tops almost to the end of production in 1980, and that almost without exception these cars were exported to Canada.

The final type of hood, introduced in 1976, looks much like the previous type but has a zip-out centre rear window, the zip being camouflaged from the outside by an overlapping lip of the hood cover around the centre rear window.

From the inside the frame is the same and the black zip for the rear window is unfortunately invisible. Note that at long last even the RHD roadsters were fitted with internal sun visors!

Basically the hard top design was unchanged over the production period. It was made from fibreglass and incorporated a toughened glass rear window, as well as two fixed Perspex rear quarterlights in aluminium frames and with aluminium trim around the door window openings. Two locating brackets below the rear window latched under the hood retaining plates on the tonneau panel, the hard top was then fastened with over-centre toggle catches to the hood header rail brackets on the windscreen frame, and was bolted to a locating bracket on each rear quarter inner panel, just behind the doors. The original hard top colours were red, blue, black, Old English White and grey, and for most colour schemes there was a choice of up to four of these 'approved' hard top colours. However, all coloured hard tops were discontinued at the end of 1966, and thereafter the hard top was always painted black if factory-fitted, although it was frequently supplied in primer if sold as a spare part. From July 1976, however, spare hard tops were always sold in black.

Numerous non-factory hard tops were available, especially in the early years of MGB production. Some, such as the Bermuda, were a little strange in design, while others, like the Ashley, attempted to convert the MGB roadster into a fastback coupé, *à la*

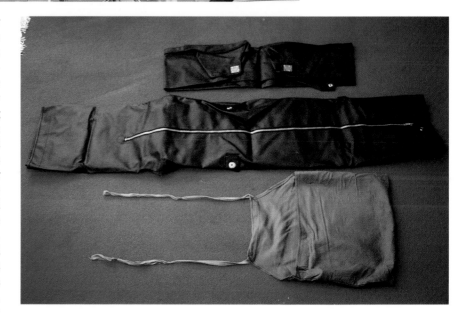

MGB GT but usually with less success. A rather neat hard top without rear quarterlights was offered in Australia, probably locally sourced and possibly supplied by BMC Australia as its original equipment hard top. In other countries, especially the USA, locally-made hard tops were also at times available.

From a 1980 American roadster, these are (from top) the hood stowage cover (short tonneau cover), the proper tonneau cover, and the grey canvas storage bag.

MGB ENGINE

The MGB was originally designed around BMC's planned new 2-litre V4 engine, but when this was cancelled the new model was instead fitted with a version of the well-tried B-series engine, which in different forms had powered the MGA models since 1955.

To give the MGB an advantage in performance over its predecessor, the B-series was bored out yet again, to 80.26mm (from 76.2mm on the last 1622cc MGA), while the stroke of 88.9mm remained the same: the resulting capacity was 1798cc. The MGB was the first car to use the 1800 B-series engine which subsequently was also fitted in BMC's Austin/Morris/Wolseley 1800 range, their Princess successors, the Marina 1.8 and early Sherpa commercial vehicles. The MGB also became the last model to use any B-series engine: by the time MGB production ceased in 1980, the Princess, Marina and Sherpa ranges had all been converted to the new O-series engine, which was only fitted to a small number of experimental MGBs in the 1977-80 period.

The basic architecture of the MGB engine was a classic piece of Austin or BMC design, with a deep cast-iron cylinder block and crankcase extending below the crankshaft axis, and a cast-iron cylinder head featuring Weslake-designed, heart-shaped com-

bustion chambers. The inlet and exhaust manifolds were both on the left-hand side of the engine, with all of the electrical ancillaries on the right-hand side. The camshaft was low in the block on the left-hand side and driven by chain from the front of the crankshaft. The overhead valves were activated by tappets,

18G ENGINES (1962-71)

Prefix	Engine numbers	Car numbers	Dates	Notes
18G-(R)U-H/L	101-31121	101-31793	May 62 – Feb 64	Three-bearing crankshaft, overdrive optional, low compression optional
18GA-(R)U-H/L	101-17500	31794-48766[1]	Feb 64 – Oct 64	As above, but with closed circuit breathing
18GB-(R)U-H/L	101-91175	48767-138400[2]	Oct 64 – Nov 67	Five-bearing crankshaft, closed circuit breathing, overdrive optional, low compression optional
18GD-(R)We-H/L	101-6945	138401-158230	Nov 67 – Oct 68	As above, with fully synchronised gearbox and alternator; home/export (not USA; Canada to Aug 68); overdrive optional, low compression optional
18GD-Rc-H/L	101-240	138401-158230	Nov 67 – Oct 68	As 18GD, but with automatic gearbox
18GF-(R)We-H	101-13647	138401-158230	Nov 67 – Oct 68	As 18GD manual type, for USA (1968 models) and Canada (from Aug 68), air pump and injectors, overdrive optional
18GG-(R)We-H/L	101-29642	158231-256646	Oct 68 – Aug 71	As 18GD type, but with carburettor ventilation instead of closed circuit breathing; home/export (not North America); overdrive optional; low compression optional
18GG-Rc-H/L	101-955	158231-256646	Oct 68 – Aug 71	As 18GG, but fitted with automatic gearbox
18GH-(R)We-H	101-43548[3]	158231-218651	Oct 68 – Aug 70	As 18GF type, but with carburettor ventilation instead of closed circuit breathing; North American export, overdrive optional
18GJ-(R)We-H	22647-43548[3]	187701-218651	Oct 69 – Aug 70	As 18GH type, but with fuel evaporative loss control equipment, for cars for California
18GK-(R)We-H	101-26226	219001-256646	Aug 70 – Aug 71	North American export, 1971 model year, all cars fitted with evaporative loss control, overdrive optional

Engine prefix codes: **U** manual gearbox, centre gearchange, first gear not synchronised **We** manual gearbox, centre gearchange, first gear fitted with synchromesh **R** Laycock de Normanville overdrive (optional), R found in front of either U or We **Rc** Borg Warner 35 automatic gearbox (optional from 1967/68) **H** high compression, 8.8:1 **L** low compression, 8:1

Notes
[1] Also intermittently from 28587; [2] Also intermittently from 47112; [3] 18GH and 18GJ number sequences shared from 22647

pushrods and rockers. The valves were vertical and sat in line in the cylinder head. The pressed steel sump was set towards the rear of the engine and contained the Hobourn-Eaton type oil pump, which was driven by gear from the camshaft. The lubrication system incorporated an oil filter mounted externally on the right-hand side of the crankcase.

The 1798cc B-series engine can be distinguished from other variations of the design by having the legend '1800' cast in the crankcase, on the left-hand side towards the front. As fitted in the MGB between 1962-71, the engines were painted dark red or maroon. The MGB engines were manufactured together with other B-series engines in the Austin factory at Longbridge. They were typically fitted with most ancillaries – including gearbox – at Longbridge, where they were also painted, sometimes in a rather slapdash manner! On the rocker cover was an MG name plate on the left-hand side and a patent number plate listing BMC and Weslake patents on the right-hand side. These plates were originally fitted with rivets but became self-adhesive in 1965. The Weslake plate disappeared in 1967 or soon after.

While many of the basic engine features remained unchanged throughout production, MGB engines were periodically updated and most major changes were usually marked by a new engine number prefix code, with the series of engine numbers starting again with 101. Sometimes the changes to the actual engine were only slight, with many of the new prefix codes being simply indicative of changes to ancillary equipment. This was particularly true from 1967 onwards, when it also became necessary to develop specially adapted engines for the North American markets, to comply with the new emissions control regulations. The accompanying table gives details of all MGB engine prefixes and number series, and a list of change points by engine numbers starts on page 140.

The first type of MGB engine in 1962 was series 18G, featuring a crankshaft with three main bearings. The bearing journals were 2.1262-2.127in (54.01-54.02mm) in diameter and had steel-backed copper-lead thin wall bearings which were 1.125in (28.575mm) long. The 18G engine featured a simple crankcase ventilation system with an inverted J-shaped pipe venting the front cylinder block side cover (tappet cover) to atmosphere, and a pipe from an outlet on the rocker cover venting into the front air filter. The metal oil filler cap was embossed with the names of recommended lubricants.

In 1964, this became the 18GA series, which still had the three-bearing crankshaft but now featured

The 18GA engine introduced in early 1964, complete with the positive crankcase ventilation system breather which is fitted next to the rocker cover between the carburettors. Otherwise there is no great difference in appearance, and the engine bay layout would stay the same also on later Mark I models with the five main bearing 18GB series engine. Common features for all Mark I cars are the radiator with the filler cap off-set at the back, and the position of the washer bottle in the rear corner opposite the master cylinder. From the ignition side the red-painted dynamo and the position of the ignition coil can be seen. The plug leads are numbered. The engine number plate is fitted at the top of the cylinder block between plugs number two and number three. The wire clips for the radiator hoses are correct.

positive crankcase ventilation of the closed circuit breathing type. The front side cover on the cylinder block now incorporated an oil separator, connected to a mushroom-shaped closed circuit breather control valve fitted on the balance pipe of the inlet manifold. The rocker cover was modified without a pipe con-

nection and the oil filler cap became the plastic type with a built-in air vent. Both the 18G and the 18GA engines had mechanical drive for the rev counter, taken from a gear at the rear of the camshaft.

The 18GA series lasted only a matter of months in production, being replaced in October 1964 by the 18GB series, which was a major re-design. The new engine had a crankshaft with five main bearings, also found on the then new Austin 1800. The diameter of the crankshaft journals was the same and the existing front, centre and rear bearings were of the same length as before, but the additional two intermediate bearings were .875in (22.225mm) long. Another change introduced on the 18GB series was that the gudgeon pins, previously of the semi-floating type held in split con rod small ends by a clamp bolt, now became fully floating with two circlips for location. The rev counter drivegear was deleted, as the MGB was now fitted with an electronic rev counter. Other engine changes in the period up to 1967 were mostly of a minor nature and parts were typically interchangeable. Fuller details will be found in the list of changes by engine number (see page 140), which also contains power unit and gearbox changes in general. It would appear, incidentally, that batches of engine numbers were set aside for engines with low com-

The sectioned engine from the display car at Gaydon is in an early Mark II and is therefore likely to be an 18GD series, but the internal layout is the same on all five-bearing 18G series engines from 1965 to 1971. The gearbox here is of the all-synchromesh type.

The Weslake patent plate was riveted on until September 1965, then became self-adhesive and was discontinued in 1967 on North American cars, a little later on others. This plate, together with the MG plate opposite and the oil filler cap, was often subject to a bit of overspray if engines were inadequately masked before painting…

pression (8:1 rather than the normal 8.8:1), or engines with overdrive gearboxes – hence the need in the list of changes to quote several different engine numbers for the same modification.

The change in November 1967 to engine series 18GD (not USA) or 18GF (USA) coincided with the introduction of the new MGB Mark II model. Linked to the new engines was a fully-synchronised gearbox, while the Borg-Warner type 35 automatic gearbox became available as an optional extra. The original dynamo was replaced by an alternator and the electrical system now became negative earth, while a pre-engaged starter motor was also introduced. A new inverted Tecalemit oil filter was fitted. The 18GF engine had a special cylinder head fitted with air injector tubes on the right-hand side, feeding into the exhaust valve ports. They were fed by an air pump through a special manifold. A special combined MG name plate and instruction plate was fitted on the rocker cover of the 18GF and subsequent North American engines until around 1970. Originally fitted only to cars for the USA, the 18GF series engine was also used in cars for Canada after August 1968. In March 1968, new valves with different valve stems and collets were introduced on the 18GD and 18GF series engines.

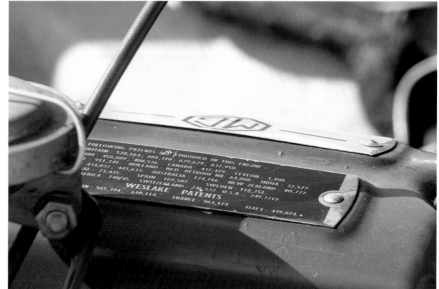

For the 1969 models, engines were modified again and became the 18GG series (not for North America) or 18GH series (for North America). The only change to the engine itself was to the dipstick and dipstick tube, but the closed circuit breathing system was now deleted, the oil separator instead being con-

This 1969 car is fitted with an 18GG series engine on which the closed circuit breathing system was replaced by carburettor crankcase ventilation, hence the black rubber tubes leading from the side cover to both carburettors. On all Mark II cars from 1967, the radiator was redesigned with a central filler cap at the front, and note the strip of foam filling the gap between header tank and radiator panel – this is often missing nowadays. The washer bottle has moved to the front of the engine bay. Viewed from the other side, the alternator is visible and the ignition coil has been moved to allow greater clearance to the alternator, which is fatter than the dynamo. The inverted Tecalemit oil filter, also new on Mark II engines, and its cover painted the same red as the engine can be seen directly behind the alternator.

nected by a Y-pipe to the carburettors. A year later, in October 1969, Californian requirements made it necessary to introduce an evaporative loss control system on cars for this state. Californian cars were now fitted with engines designated 18GJ, which had a non-vented oil filler cap. In March 1970, the MG

nameplate on the rocker cover was replaced by a British Leyland sticker, with some later North American engines having red British Leyland stickers. At around the same time, a new oil filter of the non-drainable cartridge type was introduced. New con rods of a tapered shape with solid small ends and the big ends split horizontally rather than at an angle were fitted from June 1970.

The evaporative loss control system was introduced on all North American cars for the 1971 model year, and the North American type engine therefore became the 18GK series in August 1970, without any other fundamental change. For all other cars, the 18GG series engine continued. On both 18GG and 18GK engines, new pistons with three rings rather than four and press-fit instead of fully floating gudgeon pins were introduced in March 1971.

In August 1971, from car number 258001 (which marks the start of the 1972 model year), a new system of engine designation was introduced. From now on all MGB engines had prefixes starting with 18V, which simply indicates an 1800cc B-series 'vertical' engine – meaning that it is an in-line engine for a rear-wheel drive car, installed vertically as opposed to being canted over for underfloor installation. The alternative code on an 1800cc B-series engine was

18V ENGINES (1971-74)

Prefix	Engine numbers	Car numbers	Dates	Notes
18V-581-F-H	101-5302	258001-336400[1]	Aug 71 – Nov 73	Home market, two SU HS4 carburettors, without overdrive
18V-581-Y-H/L	101-5302	258001-336400[1]	Aug 71 – Nov 73	Export (not North America), two SU HIF4 carburettors, low compression optional, without overdrive
18V-582-F-H	101-22341	258001-336650[1]	Aug 71 – Nov 73	Home market, two HS4 carburettors, with overdrive
18V-582-Y-H/L	101-22341	258001-336650[1]	Aug 71 – Nov 73	Export (not North America), two HIF4 carburettors, low compression optional, with overdrive
18V-583-F-H	101-870	258001-327990	Aug 71 – Aug 73	Home market, two HS4 carburettors, automatic gearbox
18V-583-Y-H	101-870	258001-327990	Aug 71 – Aug 73	Export (not North America), two HIF4 carburettors, automatic gearbox
18V-584-Z-L	101-19491	258001-294250	Aug 71 – Aug 72	North American export, two HIF4 carburettors, 1972 model year, without overdrive (to car number 294987 on 1972 GT models)
18V-585-Z-L	101-2751	258001-294250	Aug 71 – Aug 72	As above, but with overdrive
18V-672-Z-L	101-38094	294251-360069	Aug 72 – Sep 74	North American export, two HIF4 carburettors, 1973 and 1974 model years, without overdrive
18V-673-Z-L	101-6550	294251-360069	Aug 72 – Sep 74	As above, but with overdrive
18V-779-F-H	101-535	336500[1]-360069	Nov 73 – Sep 74	Home/export (not North America), HIF4 carburettors, high compression only, without overdrive
18V-780-F-H	101-7224	332000[1]-360069	Nov 73 – Sep 74	As above, but with overdrive

Engine prefix codes: **F** two carburettors, home and export except North America **Y** 'alternative' carburettors, export except North America **Z** two carburettors and emission control, North America only **H** high compression, 9:1 **L** low compression, 8:1

Note
[1] Approximate number

18V ENGINES (1974-80)

Prefix	Engine numbers	Car numbers	Dates	Notes
18V-836-Z-L	101-5401	360301-367818	Sep 74 – Dec 74	North American export, '1974½' model year, two HIF4 carburettors, without overdrive
18V-837-Z-L	101-1504	360301-367818	Sep 74 – Dec 74	As above, but with overdrive
18V-846-F-H	101-914	360301-409400	Sep 74 – Jun 76	Home/export (not North America), without overdrive
18V-847-F-H	101-40188	360301-523002	Sep 74 – Oct 80	As above, but with overdrive (overdrive became standard on these cars in 1976)
18V-797-AE-L	101-9361[1]	367901-386267	Dec 74 – Aug 75	North American export, 1975 model year, single Stromberg carburettor, less overdrive
18V-797-AE-L	To 10357	386601-409400	Aug 75 – Jun 76	1976 model year, continued for Canada only
18V-798-AE-L	101-1694[1]	367901-386267	Dec 74 – Aug 75	North American export, 1975 model year, single Stromberg carburettor, with overdrive
18V-798-AE-L	To 2007	386601-409400	Aug 75 – Jun 76	1976 model year, continued for Canada only
18V-801-AE-L	101-14801	382135-409400	Jun 75 – Jun 76	USA, single carburettor, catalyst exhaust, without overdrive; at first for California only, from start of 1976 model year (386601) on all USA cars
18V-802-AE-L	101-3509	382135-409400	Jun 75 – Jun 76	As above, but with overdrive
18V-883-AE-L	101-50984	410001-523002	Jun 76 – Oct 80	USA (not California), catalyst, without overdrive
18V-884-AE-L	101-10425	410001-523002	Jun 76 – Oct 80	As above, but with overdrive
18V-890-AE-L	101-12059	410001-500904	Jun 76 – Dec 79	California, catalyst, without overdrive
18V-891-AE-L	101-4584	410001-500904	Jun 76 – Dec 79	As above, but with overdrive
18V-891-AE-L	To 5389	517591-523002	Jun 80 – Oct 80	As above, continued for Japan
18V-892-AE-L	101-3559	414629-523002	Aug 76 – Oct 80	Canada, no catalyst, without overdrive
18V-893-AE-L	101-1277	414629-523002	Aug 76 – Oct 80	As above, but with overdrive

Engine prefix codes: **F** two carburettors, home and export except North America **Z** two carburettors and emission control, North America only **AE** single carburettor and emission control, North America only **H** high compression, 9:1 **L** low compression, 8:1

Note
[1] Approximate number

Black replaced red as the engine colour from the start of the 18V type engines in 1971. This 1972 model also has a British Leyland sticker on the engine instead of the MG label. The oil filter is now a Unipart type. The original prop for the bonnet has been replaced by a telescopic strut, at the top of the picture.

The 1973 engine bay is largely identical, but the air filters now have Unipart instead of Cooper labels.

18H, found on engines installed transversely in a front-wheel drive car. Prefixes starting 18V may also be found on Marina or Sherpa engines, so the only safe way of distinguishing an MGB engine from one of its relatives is by referring to the three-figure code number which comes after the 18V prefix (see the tables on the facing page).

All 18V series engines were painted black, and had a boss on the front left-hand side of the crankcase with a hole for the mechanical fuel pump found on Marinas or Sherpas – this was covered by a blanking plate on the MGB. The high compression ratio was increased to 9:1 and larger inlet valves were fitted. Bucket-type tappets were now used with longer pushrods, and single valve springs were introduced. On North American engines, the low compression ratio of 8:1 was standardised. It remained optional for other export markets, except on engines fitted with the automatic gearbox. North American engine equipment (carburettors and distributor) was changed after only one year, in August 1972. All engines were modified in October 1972 when the original duplex timing chain was replaced by a single chain. In November 1973 non-North American engines were also modified, and the low compression option was now discontinued on these engines. By now the automatic gearbox option, which was so rarely specified (see page 86), had been discontinued.

A substantial redesign was undertaken for the next generation of engines, introduced in September 1974 at the start of the 'rubber-bumper' model (car number 360301) for the '1974½' model year. The most important modification was that a new cylinder head was introduced with smaller inlet valves, which in fact reverted to the size found on the 18G series engines. As will be apparent from the list of change points, there is some confusion over which features were introduced on which engines and when, but it would be safe to state that from December 1974, when North American engines were changed yet again for the 1975 model year, these engines also had the smaller inlet valves, in a new cylinder head which was

Moving on to 1975, we have reached the 18V-847 series engine and the first of the 'rubber-bumper' cars – in this case a 'Jubilee' GT model. The radiator is still in the original position, but the washer bottle has disappeared and the now standard-fit brake servo has appeared at the rear of the engine bay, on the right edge of the picture. Looking across from the ignition side, we discover that the washer bottle has now become a bag suspended on the side of the engine bay, just visible behind the front air filter. This car has the seven-blade plastic fan common to all cars from March 1974, while the black alternator may not be correct – it would more typically have been left in natural metal finish.

tolerant of lead-free petrol. The revised 1975 model year North American engines also had an all-new inlet manifold as they were now fitted with only a single carburettor.

In July 1975, the first catalytic converter was fitted to an MGB, at first only for California but soon after for all cars for the USA. Cars for Canada, by contrast, continued to the end of production in 1980 without catalysts. The introduction of the catalyst created problems for American customers who wished to take delivery of their new MG cars in Britain for subsequent personal export, as in those days unleaded petrol was not available in the UK. The compromise solution was to supply PED (Personal Export Delivery) cars without the catalyst fitted, but with a box in the boot containing a neat conversion kit (including the catalyst) for installation when the car arrived in the USA!

For the later engine modifications, the official MGB parts list is not particularly helpful, but it does seem that fairly extensive modifications were made from the start of the 1977 model year (car number 410001 in June 1976), at least to the North American engines, which were given new prefix codes. It is to be expected that most of these modifications were also introduced on the non-North American

engine series 18V-847. The most obvious change was that the mechanical radiator fan was discontinued. As the radiator was moved forward, a thermostatically-controlled electric fan was introduced, two such fans being fitted to cars bound for the North American and Japanese markets.

The under-bonnet differences are much more striking on post-1976 cars. The radiator has been moved forward and there is a separate expansion tank just behind it. A cardboard mud shield fills the gap between radiator and engine. The mechanical fan has been replaced by an electric fan in front of the radiator, under a protective wire mesh. Behind the engine is the new direct-acting servo, introduced on RHD cars together with dual-circuit brakes in 1977. From the ignition side, note how the bottom radiator hose disappears through a cut-out at the side of the mud shield. These air cleaners have their intakes curved in towards the engine and exhaust manifold.

Very few changes are recorded after 1976, but one final cosmetic change should be mentioned. The British Leyland sticker on the rocker cover was deleted in approximately 1978, and in 1980 it was replaced by a sticker with the blue wing logo, the new corporate symbol of Austin Morris.

Exchange engines Non-original engines in MGBs fall, broadly speaking, into two categories. First, the factory reconditioned replacement engines that were supplied by BMC Service, later Unipart, frequently under the 'Gold Seal' label. Second, engines which have been taken from other vehicles using basically similar 1800cc B-series engines.

The Gold Seal replacement B-series engines can be distinguished by the special engine number prefixes which mostly start with 48G, later with BHM. These prefixes are in fact the part numbers for the stripped engine units. There are many different types, each tailored to suit a particular MGB engine type and application. The factory service parts lists are a little confusing in that they refer to exchange engines for engine types that did not actually exist in production. The accompanying table is a list of the most important variations for engines which were used in production vehicles.

There is one unsolved puzzle concerning MGB replacement engines. A number of very early 1962-63 cars have been reported in the USA featuring engines with the prefix 18S, and in at least one well-documented instance this engine is known to have been in the car since it was new. The only reference that we have to 18S prefixes in the BMC records sug-

This 1977 American car shares its forward radiator with contemporary RHD models but these cars had twin electric fans. This car is fitted with the single Zenith-Stromberg carburettor. In common with most 1975 and later American models, the car has no oil cooler so there are no oil pipes passing the radiator expansion tank. To clear the direct-acting servo on late LHD cars, the bonnet strut moved to the right-hand side. Just behind the strut is the box-shaped water container for the windscreen washer. By now even the air pump filter had a Unipart label, but the MG label on the rocker cover is most likely not original.

gests that S indicates a 'general service engine'. The theory has been advanced that some early cars were found to suffer from a design fault – possibly to do with the pistons – in the engine, and that such cars held in dealer stocks in the USA had their engines replaced with these 18S engines. Equally mysterious is the case recently reported where a later home market MGB model is said to have an engine prefix commencing 18SV, rather than the normal V, and followed by one of the usual MGB code numbers.

Turning now to 1800cc B-series engines which have come from other vehicles, it is fairly common in the UK to find MGBs with 18AMW-prefixed engine numbers. This indicates that the cylinder block (if not much else) has come from an Austin/Morris 1800 or Wolseley 18/85 – the transverse-engined front-wheel drive saloons of 1964 onwards. An engine prefix starting with 18H would indicate that the paternity belonged to a later 1800 or a Princess.

Of the later 18V type engines, units from Marinas as well as Sherpas have ended up in MGBs. If an 18V engine is found in an MGB with a three-digit code number *not* listed in this book, it will be from either a Marina or a Sherpa. Where an MGB engine number normally on home market models has a letter F in

the prefix for two carburettors, Marina or Sherpa single carburettor engines will have the letter E (but a Marina 1.8TC engine will, of course, have an F). If a prefix has the combination of letters E and L, it may be assumed to be a Sherpa low compression engine. Similar pitfalls await anyone looking at a

An early stage in the divergence of North American engine specification. On this 1971 engine, the air pump with its own air filter and associated piping is mounted above the alternator, while the gulp valve is in front of the front carburettor.

At the back of the engine bay on North American cars – this is a 1974 model – is the charcoal adsorption canister (on the left of the picture), and on the other side is the larger brake fluid reservoir typical of the early non-servo dual circuit braking system.

A late-model American engine removed from the car (top) but still complete with most of its ancillaries, including air pump, starter motor, distributor, oil filter (with a US-sourced replacement canister) and alternator. The combined bell-housing and gearbox casing is left unpainted. The remote control unit is bolted to the gearbox rear extension, and no overdrive is fitted.

On the induction side of the same engine (above) with the single carburettor and its rather complicated air filter – note the foam inside the fresh-air intake shaped like a tennis racket. Although barely visible, the detachable gearbox side cover bears the legend 'MOWOG' which was the old Nuffield Organisation and later BMC parts trademark standing for Morris, Wolseley, MG.

EXCHANGE ENGINES

Engine type	Compression	Gearbox	Replacement engine prefix code
18G	High	Manual	48G 279, later 48G 343
18G	Low	Manual	48G 280
18GA	High	Manual	48G 343
18GA	Low	Manual	48G 344
18GB	High	Manual	48G 392; later 48G 528, 48G 739
18GB	Low	Manual	48G 393
18GD/GG	Low	Manual	48G 527; later 48G 736
18GD/GG	High	Manual	48G 528; later 48G 702, 48G 755
18GD/GG	Low	Auto	48G 529; later 48G 736
18GD/GG	High	Auto	48G 530; later 48G 755
18GF/GH[1]	High	Manual	48G 539; later 48G 704
18GJ/GK[1]	High	Manual	48G 704
18V581/582/583	High	Manual/Auto	48G 733
18V779/780	High	Manual	48G 733
18V581/582/583	Low	Manual/Auto	48G 736
18V584/585[1]	Low	Manual	48G 737
18V672/673[1]	Low	Manual	48G 737
18V836/837[1]	Low	Manual	BHM 1074
18V797/798[1]	Low	Manual	BHM 1105[2]
18V801/802[1]	Low	Manual	BHM 1105[2]
18V846/847	High	Manual	BHM 1111

Notes
[1] Indicates North American specification engines; [2] Thought to apply also to later North American specification engines including 18V883/884, 18V890/891 and 18V892/893.

North American model MGB, some of which have ended up with engines from the short-lived North American specification Austin Marina.

It should hopefully be obvious if an MGB has been fitted with a totally non-original type of engine. Known conversions include cars fitted with BL O-series engines (predominantly ex-Marina/Ital, Rover SD1 or Sherpa), Rover 800 M16 engines (as supplied for rear-wheel drive installation to Morgan) and the ubiquitous all-alloy Rover V8 engine. There may also still be a few cars around fitted with the Daimler 2½-litre V8 engine.

MGC ENGINE

A six-cylinder MG sports car had been proposed by Syd Enever's team at Abingdon in the late 1950s, before the actual MGB design had been finalised, and there is little doubt that the possibility of fitting a six-cylinder engine was in the minds of the MGB designers all along. For the time being, however, the Austin-Healey 3000 kept its place at the top of BMC's sports car hierarchy, and only when the time came to phase out this model was the notion of a six-cylinder MG revived. It was not a particularly simple matter to install an engine which was half as large again, and the inevitably-named MGC featured extensive changes to the front end of the bodyshell as well as all-new front suspension. Nor was the engine for this car simply a Healey 3000 engine, appearances notwithstanding.

The original BMC C-series engine developed by Morris Engines had been based on the existing Austin B-series four-cylinder engine, and went into production in 1954 in 2.6-litre form, eventually powering Austin, Morris, Riley and Wolseley saloon cars, as well as the Austin-Healey 100-Six. In 1959, the engine was enlarged to 2912cc for the Austin-Healey

3000 as well as new Farina-styled Austin, Wolseley and Vanden Plas saloons. During the 1960s, BMC Australia developed its own first engine, a 2.4-litre six also based on B-series design. This engine was known as the 'Blue Streak' and was fitted with a seven main bearing crankshaft, whereas the British C-series still had only four main bearings. The 'Blue Streak' was fitted in the relatively unsuccessful Australian Austin Freeway and Wolseley 24/80 saloons.

The engine that was to power the MGC, as well as the new Austin 3-litre saloon which was launched at the same time in 1967, was a synthesis of features from the earlier C-series and the 'Blue Streak'. It used the seven bearing crankshaft with the C-series bore and stroke of 83.36mm and 88.9mm, producing a capacity of 2912cc. In terms of basic layout there was nothing that would be unfamiliar to a student of BMC engine design. The main difference compared to a B-series was that the camshaft and valve gear were on the right-hand side of the engine, thereby having the advantage of freeing up space in the cylinder head to allow separate ports for all 12 valves (the MGB engine had siamesed ports). It was a bulky engine – although

This engine compartment is from a 1968 model MGC still fitted with the positive crankcase ventilation system, but it is a particularly early car with the rocker cover painted in the unusual – but authentic – finish of crackle black. A small detail worth noting is that this car also has the early MGC heater with the water valve mounted on the heater box rather than the engine.

By contrast, on the 1969 model MGC the positive crankcase breather has disappeared and the carburettor crankcase ventilation system has been introduced. The rocker cover is now finished in the same silver-green paint as the engine, and the heater water valve is mounted on the far side of the cylinder head, just visible behind the oil filler cap.

2in shorter than the old Healey 3000 unit – and a heavy one, at 650–700lb depending on specification, compared to the 360lb of an MGB engine. With power of 145bhp compared to the MGB's 95bhp, output per litre was less than the smaller engine – and the last Austin-Healey 3000 had developed 150bhp.

There were fewer variations of the MGC engine than of the MGB. All MGC engines had a compression ratio of 9:1, and a low compression version was never available. The basic engine was type 29G (29 for capacity, G for MG), and the emissions control engine for North America was type 29GA. Then there was type 29GB, an under-bored 2850cc engine for France intended to fit below the 15CV threshold in the French car taxation system. These type designations were used in the engine number prefixes and were then followed by U on cars with standard gearbox, RU on cars with an overdrive or Rc on cars with automatic gearbox. All prefixes ended with the letter H for high compression. All three engines ran throughout the two-year production period of the MGC, with one series of engine numbers for each

MGC ENGINES

Prefix	Engine numbers	Exchange engine	Notes
29G-U/RU/Rc-H	101–4969	68G 347 (manual gearbox) 68G 355 (automatic gearbox)	Standard 2912cc
29GA-U/RU/Rc-H	101–4425	68G 366 (manual gearbox) 68G 367 (automatic gearbox)	Emissions control 2912cc (North America)
29GB-U/RU/Rc-H	101–344	68G 380 (manual gearbox) 68G 382 (automatic gearbox)	Standard 2850cc (France)

V8 ENGINE

type (including engines with automatic gearboxes). The accompanying table summarises the engine types, number series and exchange engine types.

The MGC engines were finished in a pale silver-grey-green, which was the traditional Austin-Healey engine colour. However, on very early cars – it is thought only the first 100 or so MGCs – the rocker cover was finished in crackle black, similar to the facia. The pale green colour extended to most of the engine-mounted ancillaries, including the prominent vertical oil filter housing and the starter motor. There were two self-adhesive labels on the rocker cover, in line and normally mounted to be read from the left-hand side – the front one with the MG badge, the rear one with Weslake patent numbers.

The closest relative of the MGC engine was the 29AA-type engine fitted in the Austin 3-litre, but this engine had its oil pump and sump at the front instead of the rear. The Austin engine was also equipped with a special crankshaft pulley and brackets for the engine-driven power steering and suspension levelling pumps fitted to this car – and there were other differences. The Austin engine is almost as rare as the MGC unit – only 10,000 3-litres were built – but it is more common in the UK, and undoubtedly engines (and parts from them) sourced from scrapped Austins have found new applications in MGCs.

There were very few changes to the MGC engine, or other changes quoted by the engine numbers. All starter motors were the Lucas M418G pre-engaged type, but from engine numbers 29G/624 or 29GA/127 the starter motor was modified with a new type of solenoid and other changes. The revised type was fitted on 29GB from the start of this series. A new oil pressure release valve was fitted from engine numbers 29G/2756, 29GA/357 and 29GB/171. Because of the way in which MGC cars were manufactured, it is difficult to relate these changes to specific dates or car numbers. From August 1968 onwards, cars for Canada, hitherto fitted with the standard 29G engine, received the USA-type emissions control 29GA engine.

The 1969 models were introduced with a number of changes to the power units in October-November 1968, from car number 4236 and engine numbers 29G/3201 and 29GA/1401 (the change point was not quoted for 29GB engines). At this point, the original closed circuit breathing system was replaced by a carburettor crankcase ventilation system. On the 29G series, the front air cleaner mounting plate and the throttle relay shaft bracket were commonised with the 29GA engine. The original 16AC alternator with a separate control box was replaced by a 16ACR alternator with a built-in regulator. There were new carburettor specifications. On cars without overdrive, the higher gearbox ratios from overdrive cars were introduced, and all cars had a modification to the reverse detent mechanism in the gearbox.

The story behind the Rover V8 engine was rather unusual. During a visit to the Mercury marine engine manufacturers in the USA in 1963, Rover's then managing director, William Martin-Hurst, literally stumbled over a small all-aluminium V8 engine lying on the floor. Learning that it was a Buick engine which had recently gone out of production, he approached GM for a licence to make it, seeing this engine as a solution to Rover's problem of how to improve the power and performance of its existing 3-litre car.

The first result was the 3.5-litre model launched in 1967. Subsequently the engine was also fitted in the 3500 (P6B), the Range Rover, the SD1, the Land Rover and the Discovery, apart from MG and Triumph models and countless non-Rover products. In 1994, the basic design was still in production. While the Buick parentage of this engine is well known, it is intriguing to speculate that the American designers might have found inspiration for their engine in the only previous all-aluminium V8 engine, manufactured in small numbers since 1954 by BMW. And so, 40 years later, did this particular wheel come full circle...

With the merger of BMC and Leyland in 1968, MG and Rover became part of the same group. At that time MG had just introduced the MGC: although this model was discontinued in 1969, the idea of a high-performance derivative of the MGB lived on. Some work was done on a project to fit the Daimler 2.5-litre V8 engine in the MGB. Then fate took a hand in the form of Ken Costello, who put a Rover P6B V8 engine in an MGB in 1970, and started small-scale production of such conversions. One of his cars was demonstrated to British Leyland in 1971, and another was given a rave review by *Autocar* magazine in May 1972. By that time, the design team at Abingdon had its own version of the Costello car well under way, as project ADO.75, to be known as the MGB GT V8 when it was launched in August 1973.

There was nothing particularly unusual in the design of the Rover V8 engine. The crankshaft ran in five main bearings, and the single centrally-mounted camshaft was driven by a short duplex chain from the crankshaft immediately below it. The hydraulic tappets were unusual in Britain at the time. Conventional pushrods and rockers activated the overhead valves, which were set in line in the cylinder heads, with inlet ports on the inside of the 'V' and exhaust ports on the outside. The oil pump and distributor drive were right at the front of the crankshaft, ahead of the camshaft drive.

The cylinder block was sand-cast in aluminium, with cast-iron dry cylinder liners. The cylinder heads were die-cast aluminium, with iron valve guides and valve seat insets. The combustion chambers in the cylinder head were relatively small, and the pistons had concave tops. The engine was oversquare, with

The oil filter on the MGC was painted the same silver-green colour as the engine, and in this instance bears the correct Tecalemit instruction label.

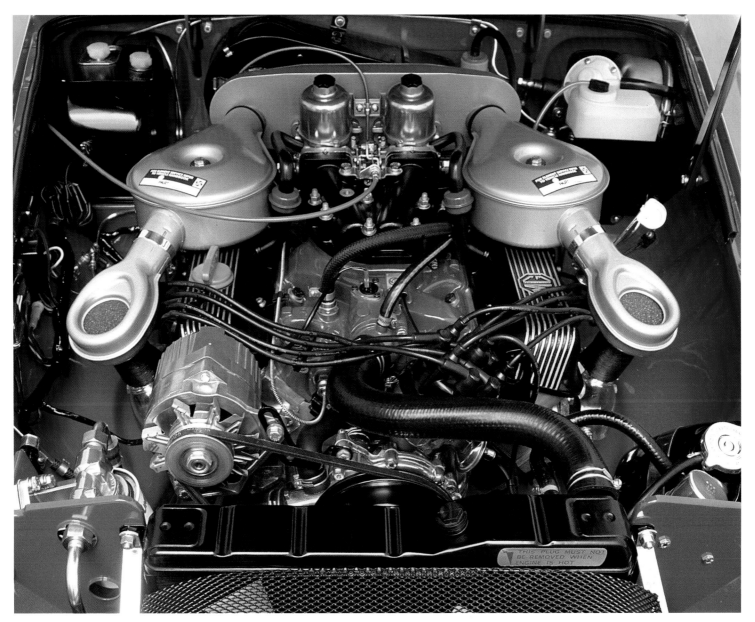

There was very little change to the under-bonnet appearance of the V8, so although this picture shows a 'rubber-bumper' model it will also serve as a guide to the 'chrome-bumper' cars. On this model the forward-mounted radiator with separate expansion tank (to the right in the picture) was introduced three years earlier than on the four-cylinder cars and always had two electric fans. Notable are also the rear-mounted carburettors on the black-painted inlet manifold extension and the complicated air intakes and filters. The oil filter is mounted remote from the engine, in the front corner of the engine bay next to the prominent AC-Delco alternator.

88.9mm bore and 71.1mm stroke for a capacity of 3528cc. As installed in the MGB GT V8, it had a low compression of 8.25:1 – similar to the contemporary Range Rover engine – and developed 137bhp (DIN) at 5000rpm. The weight of the engine was quoted as 40lb *less* than the four-cylinder MGB engine – in other words around 320lb.

The V8 engine had to be somewhat modified for installation in the MGB. The most important difference was that a new two-piece inlet manifold was developed to permit the carburettors to be installed at the rear of the engine, to avoid the need for an MGC-style bulge in the bonnet. There were also new exhaust manifolds, and the cast-alloy rocker covers were unique to the MG engine, with cast-in MG logos. Less obvious is the fact that pistons and bearings were also unique for the MG application. A remote oil filter was located at the front of the engine bay, on the left when seen from the front.

The engine numbers of the V8 follow the Rover numbering system rather than the BMC system. They are all-figure numbers without any letter prefix, but in common with other Rover engines the first three (or four) figures define the specification and model application. MGB GT V8 engines have eight-figure numbers which start with 4860. The only variation concerns the handful of pre-production cars which were built to North American specification and have engine numbers starting with 4900. Again in common with Rover practice, the engine number may have a letter suffix to distinguish major modifications, but as there were no major changes to the MG V8 engine the letter suffix should always be A. The main engine number series ran from 48600001 to 48602596. The engine number is stamped on a plate found at the back of the cylinder block on the left-hand side, near the bellhousing.

There are no change points quoted by engine number in the Parts List. The only change worth noting here is that the oil cooler installation was modified from the start of 'rubber-bumper' production in 1974, at car number 2101. Other changes affecting the power unit were minimal, and details of such changes quoted by car number are found in the general list of production changes at the end of this book, starting on page 140.

EMISSIONS EQUIPMENT

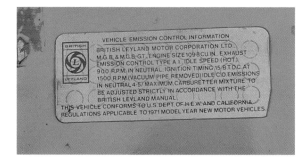

The new emissions control legislation which came into force in the USA on 1 January 1968 meant that special engines and ancillaries had to be developed to allow the MGB and the new MGC to continue being sold in the important American market. As will be clear from the tables of engine types found on pages 60, 64 and 71, these engines are readily identifiable not only by their special equipment but also by the engine number prefixes. The following is a summary of the various devices that were eventually installed on MGB (and MGC) engines for North America in the period from 1967 to 1980, by model year. Reference should also be made to the chapters on engine, exhaust system, ignition system, and carburettors and fuel system.

1968 model year (MGB Mark II, and MGC). Engine types for the USA: 18GF (MGB) and 29GA (MGC); these engines were only fitted to cars for Canada from August 1968. Cylinder head fitted with air injectors feeding air into the exhaust valve ports, supplied through an air manifold from an air pump, and fitted with a check valve on the manifold to prevent exhaust gases from blowing back into the air pump. The air injectors and the manifold were fitted on the right-hand side of the cylinder head. On the MGB, the air pump was fitted on the right-hand side of the engine and was driven by belt from the fan pulley. A separate air filter was mounted at the rear of the pump. On the MGC, the air pump was mounted on the left of the engine, with belt drive from the crankshaft pulley, and the air filter above the pump. The air pump also delivered air to a gulp valve on the inlet manifold to ensure that a leaner mixture was supplied during deceleration or on the overrun. Both models were also fitted with the positive crankcase ventilation system where fumes from the oil separator were fed through the breather control

valve fitted above the inlet manifold, and had an air filter in the oil filler cap.

1969 model year (MGB, MGC). Engine types for North America: 18GH (MGB) and 29GA (MGC). As for 1968, except that the crankcase ventilation control breather valve was now deleted, and the oil separator was now connected by a Y-pipe directly to the carburettors themselves. The carburettors were fitted with spring-loaded needles.

1970 model year (MGB only, series GHN5/GHD5). Engine types for North America: 18GH (Canada and USA, except California), 18GJ (California only). No change to Canadian and Federal cars. Californian cars were fitted with evaporative loss control equipment to collect fuel vapours and prevent loss of fuel caused by expansion due to increases in air temperature. This system comprised a sealed non-venting fuel filler cap, a fuel line filter, a separation tank for liquid fuel mounted to the right-hand side of the boot, and a charcoal adsorption canister fitted in the right-hand rear corner of the engine compartment. This was also connected by a purge line with a purge restrictor to the rocker cover of the engine. The oil filler cap was of the sealed non-venting type. The fuel tank had a built-in expansion chamber which limited its usable capacity to 10 imperial gallons (12 US gallons or 45 litres).

1971 model year. Engine type for all North American cars: 18GK. All North American cars were now fitted with the evaporative loss control system.

1972 model year. Engine types for North America: 18V-584-Z-L without overdrive, 18V-585-Z-L with overdrive. Compression ratio reduced to 8:1, and SU carburettors of type HIF4 fitted. Other systems as in previous years.

1973 model year. Engine types for North America: 18V-672-Z-L without overdrive, 18V-673-Z-L with

The air pump (above on a 1977 car) is connected by a tube running in front of the rocker cover to the gulp valve (polished on this car) and has another tube running backwards to the actual air manifold and the injectors in the cylinder head. As American emission control laws became stricter it was necessary to fit ever-larger and more complicated labels to the cars (above left), describing tuning procedures and confirming compliance with US laws. The upper label is from a 1971 model, the lower from a 1974 car.

Just to make the point, this label was fitted by the fuel filler, and the fuel gauge was similarly marked.

Catalyst-equipped cars had this warning on the driver's sun visor (top left). The text was copied from a similar warning on a Cadillac! What's good for GM was obviously also good for MG. This separation or catch tank for liquid fuel (above left) was fitted to all North American cars with evaporative loss equipment. It was always located inside the right-hand rear wing. On cars fitted with the full fuel integrity system, from August 1976, it was supplemented by a loop of fuel hose running round the boot and connecting the two sides of the fuel tank to ensure that fuel was safely contained in the event of the car rolling over. Found at first on Californian cars but from the start of the 1976 model year on all US models, this is the catalytic converter (above right), attached virtually directly to the exhaust outlet of the combined manifold.

overdrive. Anti run-on control valve added to the systems previously described.

1974 model year. No change from 1973.

'1974½' model year (the first 'rubber-bumper' cars, built between September and December 1974). Engine types for North America: 18V-836-Z-L without overdrive, 18V-837-Z-L with overdrive. No change to emissions control systems. These engines probably had the smaller inlet valves (compare list of engine change points).

1975 model year (cars built between December 1974 and August 1975). Engine types for North America: 18V-797-AE-L without overdrive, 18V-798-AE-L with overdrive. Fitted with a single Zenith-Stromberg 175CD5T carburettor with an automatic choke device and an induction heater for the inlet manifold. Air filter fitted with hot and cold air intake controlled by a bi-metal valve. Exhaust gas recirculation valve added to existing system. This valve was situated on the exhaust manifold and allowed a controlled quantity of exhaust gas to recirculate. To monitor the 25,000 mile service interval requirement for the EGR valve, a warning lamp was fitted on the facia console, and a service interval counter in the engine compartment. It should be noted that these engines were the first to feature the lead-free tolerant cylinder head design, and that the 1975 model year cars could not be sold in California unless fitted with a catalyst (see below).

1975 model year, cars for California only, built July/August 1975. Engine types: 18V-801-AE-L without overdrive, 18V-802-AE-L with overdrive. Introduced belatedly to meet the 1975 calendar year Californian emissions requirements, these were the first MGB engines to be fitted with a catalytic converter, and so in consequence had to run on unleaded fuel. The fuel tank filler neck was designed to accept

only the special dispenser nozzles used for unleaded fuel and had a trap door in the filler neck. The EGR warning lamp and service interval counter served also as a reminder when the converter should be renewed. Special labels were found at the fuel filler and on the fuel gauge. An electronic ignition system with a new distributor was fitted.

1976 model year. All cars for the USA were fitted with the 18V-801/802 engines and catalyst, while cars for Canada continued with engine types 18V-797/798. On Canadian cars, the service interval counter was deleted, otherwise the systems previously described continued without change.

1977 to 1980 model years inclusive. Engine types for USA: except California (Federal specification) 18V-883/884-AE-L, for California 18V-890/891-AE-L, and for Canada 18V-892/893-AE-L (in all cases without/with overdrive). Canadian cars continued through to 1980 without a catalyst. Cars for the USA (but not for Canada) were fitted with a fuel cut-off valve at the rear of the engine compartment. Fuel filter relocated to bulkhead adjacent to heater. EGR/catalyst warning lamp and service interval counter deleted. From August 1976 full fuel integrity system fitted, with additional roll-sensitive fuel cut-off valve; tank capacity increased to 11 gallons (50 litres). A fuel pipe loop was fitted in the boot to balance tank contents in a roll-over. From late 1976, a transmission-controlled spark advance system was fitted, to prevent engine revs surging when the clutch was operated. On 1978 models, the single charcoal adsorption canister was replaced by a primary and a secondary canister. The Californian model was discontinued at the end of 1979 calendar year, although the Californian engine with overdrive was subsequently fitted to cars for Japan. The Federal and Canadian versions continued until October 1980.

EXHAUST SYSTEM

Four-cylinder MGBs had a dual exhaust manifold, with the exhaust from cylinders one and four being taken into a Y-shaped manifold leading to the front of two downpipes, and the siamesed exhaust port from cylinders two and three feeding a joint single pipe in the centre, leading to the rear downpipe. Later exhaust manifolds fitted to the 18V type engines from 1971 onwards incorporated a hot-spot facility for the carburettors. Only the late North American cars with a single carburettor had a different exhaust manifold, cast together in a unit with the inlet manifold and with only one downpipe, attached at the front of the manifold.

The twin downpipes joined in front of the first of two silencers. The front silencer was originally of a flattened oval section but was changed to a crimped box on North American Mark II cars and also on cars for Sweden. This type of silencer was introduced also on other cars from the start of 'rubber-bumper' production in 1974. The rear silencer was always a simple cylindrical type. The tailpipe emerged on the left-hand side of the car and was originally cut off at an angle of 45°, but on later cars it curved towards the ground and was then cut at a right angle. The curved tailpipe was introduced at first on North American models, probably from the start of Mark II production, but eventually spread to all cars.

Other changes to the exhaust system over the years were mostly introduced either to increase the life of the system or to make the car quieter. A twin perforated tube front silencer was introduced in July 1965, and silencers with double end plates were fitted from March 1966. The material specification was improved in 1968, and a stainless steel tailpipe was fitted in October 1969. A special local noise level regulation had to be catered for on cars for Switzerland from October 1974, and a general EEC noise level regulation of maximum 82dB was met by the introduction of a three-pass exhaust in September 1977.

North American cars with a single carburettor (from December 1974) had only a single downpipe, and some of these cars had both silencers of the crimped box type. In 1975 cars for California – and soon after all of the USA – were fitted with a catalytic converter, of a simple cylindrical shape and located at the front of the exhaust pipe between the exhaust manifold outlet and the exhaust pipe proper. An improved catalyst was fitted from June 1977. Because catalysed exhaust systems tend to generate more heat, an exhaust heatshield was fitted to the underside of the gearbox tunnel from April 1977, and also added to non-catalyst cars.

On the MGC there were two separate exhaust manifolds, for the two groups of three cylinders. On North American cars with the 29GA engine, the exhaust manifolds had hot-spots for the inlet manifolds. Two downpipes merged in front of the front silencer, and the joined-up pipe incorporated a flex-

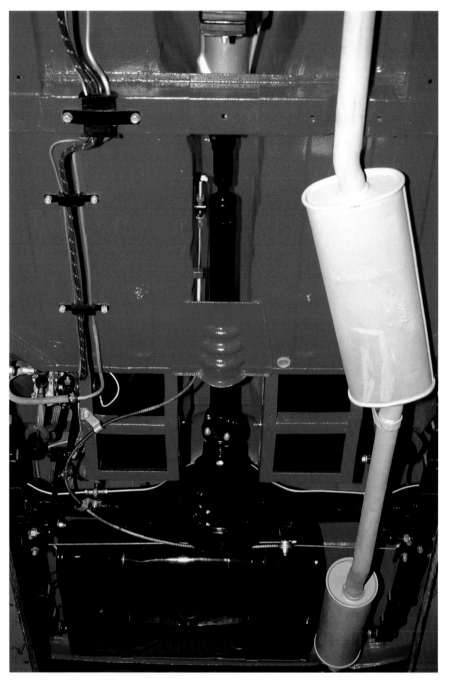

ible section. Both silencers were of the crimped type and were the same for all markets. The tailpipe was straight and cut off at an angle. No changes are recorded for the exhaust system on this model.

The MGB GT V8 had separate exhaust ports for all cylinders, but the exhaust manifolds on each side of the engine were quite simple, joining the exhaust ports and featuring only one downpipe on either side. The downpipes were joined immediately behind the engine, and the system incorporated two crimped silencers. The V8 exhaust system was revised in detail from the start of 'rubber-bumper' production but was not subject to any other important change. There were no regional variations for this model.

All MGB exhaust systems had twin silencers, this flattened oval front silencer being typical of Mark I cars as well as non-North American models through to 1974. North American cars had a crimped-box type silencer from 1967, and this was fitted to all 'rubber-bumper' models. The rear silencer was typically cylindrical, as seen here.

IGNITION SYSTEM

A conventional coil and distributor system was fitted to all models. On the MGB and MGC, the plugs and the distributor were located on the right-hand side of the engine. On MGB Mark I cars (1962-1967), the ignition coil was located on a bracket fitted to the right-hand front engine mounting. On later MGB cars and on the MGC, the coil was simply fixed to the inner wing valance on the right-hand side of the engine compartment.

A Lucas 25D4 distributor was used on MGBs between 1962-74, with minor variations to suit different engine specifications for various models and markets. Originally the distributor cap was of the side-entry type, but from the start of the Mark II model the cap was changed to the top-entry type, which necessitated fitting plug leads that were on average 4in longer than previously. Special suppressed cables to minimise radio interference were fitted to Mark I models for France and Canada, and from the start of Mark II production all cars had them. Another regional variation was that cars for Canada had special waterproof sparking plug caps and plug lead sleeves.

From November 1973, the distributor, distributor cap and plug leads on cars with the 18V-779 and 780 engines were changed to comply with the European ECE.10 standard for ignition suppression. With the exception of later North American models, 'rubber-bumper' cars normally used a Lucas 45D4 distributor, but some late cars in the 1978-80 period used an alternative Ducellier distributor. The contact breaker (or points) gap was always .014-.016in (.35-.40mm), but the dwell angle and vacuum advance curve differ depending on distributor type and specification (for this information reference should be made to the Workshop Manuals for each engine type).

From 1975, an electronic ignition system was fitted on North American export models with a catalyst exhaust. On these cars the distributor was either a Lucas 45DE4 or 45DM4. On the 45DE4, a combined amplifier and vacuum unit was attached to the body of the distributor, while the 45DM4 had a separate amplifier mounted remotely on the side of the engine compartment. It seems that all 1980 models had the 45DM4 type, but it may also have been used on some earlier cars. From January 1980 an improved amplifier (Lucas type AB14) was fitted. For these later models, distributor specification varied depending on whether the vehicle was to the 49-state Federal specification or to the Californian specification.

Until 1974, a Lucas HA12 ignition coil was the standard fitting, but this may have been replaced by a higher-performance coil on cars supplied to cold climates. On 'rubber-bumper' cars a coil with a ballast resistor was introduced, type 15C6 on non-North American vehicles or type 16C6 on North American vehicles, replaced in January 1980 by a 32C5 coil on the last cars for North America.

When introduced in 1962, the MGB was fitted with

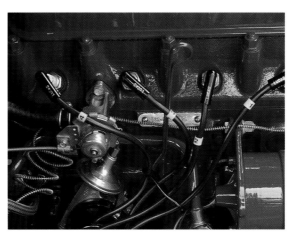

A dynamo was fitted on most cars – except Police specials – from 1962 to 1967. The ignition system can also be studied on this 1964 car.

Champion N5 sparking plugs, but they were quickly superseded in early 1963 by the equivalent N9Y type. The plug gap was quoted variously as .024-.026in (.625-660mm) or, more simply, as .025in (.640mm). The N9Y plugs were quoted also for North American cars after 1967. The plug gap was increased in 1976 to .035in (.89mm), and some of the final MGBs may have used RN9Y plugs. The firing order was 1-3-4-2. On all cars to 1967 and on non-North American cars with 18G type engines to 1971, static ignition timing was 10° BTDC on high compression engines, 8° BTDC on low compression engines, and stroboscopic timing at 600rpm was 14° (high compression) or 12° (low compression). For North American engines from 1967 and the later 18V engines of 1971-80, there were considerable variations, and it is again recommended that the Workshop Manual is consulted for this information. The ignition timing marks were a notch on the crankshaft front pulley and a pointer on the timing case.

On the MGC a Lucas 25D6 distributor was used, with a contact breaker gap of .014-.016in, an HA12 coil and N9Y plugs with a .025in plug gap. The firing order for the six-cylinder engine was 1-5-3-6-2-4, static ignition timing was 8° BTDC and stroboscopic timing was 20° BTDC at 1000rpm.

The MGB GT V8 had a Lucas 35D8 distributor driven from the front of the camshaft and mounted at a slight angle to the left. The contact breaker gap was again .014-.016in. A Lucas 16C6 ballasted coil was mounted on the radiator diaphragm panel on the left-hand side, in the corner by the expansion tank. Champion L92Y plugs with a plug gap of .035in were fitted, to the outside of each cylinder head. The firing order was 1-8-4-3-6-5-7-2, odd numbers being the left-hand cylinders and even numbers the right-hand cylinders, with numbers 1 and 2 at the front. Stroboscopic ignition timing was 8° BTDC at 1000rpm. There was a pointer on the timing case and degree markings on the crankshaft pulley. To protect the V8 plug leads, heatshields were added to the leads for the four middle cylinders in September 1974, and also to the two front plug leads in February 1975.

COOLING SYSTEM

The thermo-siphon cooling system used a pressurised water radiator, assisted by pump and fan, with regulation by a thermostat. Until 1976, the radiator on MGBs was the conventional type where the hot water from the engine entered the radiator at the top. The radiator was mounted in a diaphragm panel spanning the width of the engine bay, and was finished in semi-matt black paint, including the header tank. The top and bottom hoses were identical and were fastened with wire clips. The three-blade metal fan, painted yellow, was mounted on the water pump spindle, and both were driven by belt from the crankshaft pulley. Only very early cars had an MGA-type six-blade fan, also painted yellow. The standard thermostat was set to open at 82°C (180°F). The radiator cap relief valve opened at 10lb/sq in pressure and the cap was mounted on an elbow pipe at the back of the radiator, on the engine side of the diaphragm panel. On the top edge of the diaphragm was a rubber seal against the bonnet.

In addition to the standard thermostat, alternative thermostats rated at 74°C (165°F) for hot climates and 88°C (190°F) for cold climates were introduced in September 1964, but soon after the 74° thermostat became the standard fitting, to increase oil pressure and decrease oil temperature under normal working conditions; cars for cold countries were then fitted with the 82° thermostat. A revised design of thermostat with conical valve seating was introduced in January 1965, and Weston-Thomson latch-open thermostats were used from January 1967. All three types of thermostat were interchangeable. The 82° thermostat was re-introduced as the standard fitting in March 1969 and remained to the end of production, together with the 74° and 88° alternatives.

From the start of MGB Mark II production in 1967, there was a new radiator with the cap mounted centrally at the front of the header tank. At the same time, a six-blade metal fan was fitted on cars with the 18GF engines to the new North American specification, and this type of fan was also found on non-North American cars with the automatic gearbox. On all Mark II and subsequent engines, the original cylinder block drain tap was replaced by a simple plug. The drain tap at the bottom tank of the radiator was discontinued in June 1970.

Four different types of water pump were found on the early MGBs. The three main bearing engines had a unique type, while the three types found on five main bearing engines were interchangeable, assuming the correct pulleys are used. In October 1968, a new water pump with a pressure balance seal was introduced, and on the 18V engines from August 1971 the pump was commonised with that found on the BMC Austin/Morris 1800 models. The pump was changed again in 1974 and 1975.

On North American cars, the six-blade metal fan was replaced by a seven-blade plastic fan in December 1972. The new plastic fan was also fitted to non-North American cars with the automatic gearbox, but all other cars retained the original three-blade fan. Only in March 1974 was the type of fan commonised on all cars, when an alternative seven-blade plastic fan with metal inserts was introduced. Even so, the old three-blade fan returned on cars for Switzerland in October 1974 to meet local noise regulations.

A revised radiator with a new cap rated at 13lb/sq in was introduced on the 1976 models, but more important changes were in store for the 1977 cars.

To revert for the moment to 1967 and the MGC, this car had a rather different cooling system in that a sealed (or more correctly semi-sealed) system was used, with an expansion tank mounted at the front of the left-hand side of the engine compartment, below the level of the header tank, and connected by hose to the radiator filler cap inlet. The filler cap was mounted on a rearwards elbow extension of the thermostat housing and was of the plain type without a pressure relief valve. The expansion tank (which was of a different type on North American models) was fitted with a pressure cap rated at 10lb/sq in on standard cars but 14lb/sq in on North American cars. The radiator was mounted rather further forward on the MGC than on the MGB. The standard thermostat was rated at 82°C, with 74° and 88° alternatives being available. A six-blade yellow plastic fan was fitted to standard engines, but an eight-blade steel fan, also yellow, was used on North American engines.

The cooling system of the MGB GT V8 was more sophisticated, in line with 1970s practice. The radiator on this model was moved forward, and was of the new, more efficient cross-flow type. As on the MGC, the system was semi-sealed with a separate expansion tank, mounted in the same front left-hand corner of the engine bay. The system was pressurised at 15lb/sq in, and the thermostat setting was 82°C. In place of the mechanical fan of the MGB, the V8 employed two electric fans, mounted on brackets in front of the radiator, thus blowing cold air on to the radiator rather than sucking it through. The fans were thermostatically controlled with a trip setting of 90°C. The thermo-switch for the fans was mounted in the top of the inlet manifold.

On the MGC with its radiator mounted further forward it was a bit of a squeeze to get the oil cooler in as well – hence the awkward-looking pipe run on the bonnet locking platform.

The various radiator installations can be seen in the engine bay photos in the engine chapter, but this detail shot of a 1969 model shows the oil cooler installation particularly well, with the pipes passing through the radiator diaphragm panel on the right-hand side of the car.

On this 1980 model RHD car, the radiator is of the forward-mounted type with a separate expansion tank. The thermostatic switch for the electric fan is at the back of the top tank, between the top hose and the pipe connecting to the expansion tank. On this car the oil cooler pipes are attached to the bracket which holds the expansion tank in place. The bracket with the Leyland symbol at the back of the thermostat housing is for the air pump – the bracket was by now always there even on cars not equipped with an air pump.

This six-blade yellow plastic fan was found on standard MGC engines, but North American engines had an eight-blade steel fan. The remote radiator filler cap was another space-saving measure. The pipe from the filler is connected to the expansion tank, mounted low down in the left-hand front corner of the engine bay.

It was, broadly speaking, the V8 cooling system which was adopted on the four-cylinder cars for the 1977 model year, in that these cars were fitted with the forward-mounted radiator and semi-sealed system. The electric fan was also introduced, but only North American export models had the twin fans of the V8, other MGBs making do with a single fan. As on the V8, the fans of the four-cylinder models were in front of the radiator, with a mesh-type fan guard being fitted between radiator and bonnet locking platform to prevent fingers or tools accidentally coming into conflict with an operating fan. One difference compared with the V8 was that the 1976-80 four-cylinder models had the expansion tank in the right-hand front corner of the engine compartment. In this form the cooling system continued until the end of production with only minor changes, such as the introduction of a larger thermostatic switch for the fan, fitted with a retaining clip in a modified radiator header tank in January 1980.

An oil cooler, mounted in front of the radiator on all models with connecting pipes passing through the diaphragm panel to the right of the radiator, was fitted as standard on export MGBs from the start of production, but remained optional in the home market until the arrival of the five main bearing 18GB engine in 1964. The oil cooler was also fitted to all MGC and MGB GT V8 models. The original oil cooler (ARH 181) was replaced by one of intercalary construction (ARH 186) in January 1964. Home market cars used ARH 186 when they were fitted with the oil cooler as standard in October 1964, but export cars received an improved 13-tube oil cooler (ARO 9809). This latter version was then fitted on home market cars from August 1965. Subsequently the oil cooler was changed again at the start of Mark II production in 1967 and on the 'rubber-bumper' cars in 1974. On North American cars, the oil cooler was discontinued in December 1974 (1975 model year).

The MGC with manual gearbox used the ARO 9809 oil cooler but automatic MGCs had the ARH 186 type, fitted in conjunction with a smaller separate oil cooler for the gearbox. The MGB GT V8 also used the ARH 186 in 1973-74, but the ARH 185 found on 'rubber-bumper' V8s was the same as that used on the four-cylinder 'rubber-bumper' cars.

Most MGBs will have a heater, although this only became officially standard equipment on home market cars in October/November 1968. Until then, it was charged separately to UK customers but was normally supplied as standard on export models, except to certain countries with hot climates (notably Australia). The Smiths combined heater and fresh-air unit drew air through the grille mounted on the scuttle in front of the windscreen. The electric blower fan and the heater matrix were combined in a single casing fitted on the shelf at the rear of the engine compartment. Hot water was drawn from a valve situated towards the rear of the cylinder head on the right-hand side of the engine. Two rotary controls on the facia controlled air distribution and temperature, with a separate switch for the blower.

The type and principle of the heater barely changed over the years, and the heaters on the MGC and MGB GT V8 were little different from those on contemporary MGBs. In late 1968 the heater became standard equipment for all markets except Australia, Puerto Rico and Hawaii, and it was standardised on Australian CKD kits from April 1969. Only in April 1975 did a heater become standard also on cars for Puerto Rico and Hawaii.

Some improvements were made in August 1970 for the 1971 model year, notably to the heater air ducts, the demister hoses and the air outlets, and in August 1971 separate fresh-air vents were added, necessitating a partial redesign of the facia as they took the space originally intended for a radio. The heater controls were changed, and from August 1972 were illuminated on cars with the North American facia. New style heater control knobs were found on 'rubber-bumper' cars, both RHD and North American, but illuminated heater controls were only introduced on RHD cars for the 1977 model year with the new facia and console. At that point, a two-speed blower fan was also introduced.

A fresh-air unit could originally be fitted as an alternative to the heater. This was simply a heater without the heat exchange matrix, but still with the blower. Cars fitted with the fresh-air unit had only the air distribution control on the facia. The fresh-air unit was mainly fitted to cars for hot climates and was a regular option on Australian-assembled cars until April 1969; it was then discontinued for Australia, and a year later it was dropped altogether.

No MGB car ever had an air conditioning system fitted in the factory. However, proprietary air conditioning systems to fit the car were developed in the USA and were occasionally fitted to new cars prior to delivery to North American owners. This was particularly the case with the 1979-80 Limited Edition models, which are often seen fitted with air conditioning. By then, J.R.T. (the US importer) supplied special 'factory air' kits.

CARBURETTORS & FUEL SYSTEM

The majority of MGBs and their derivatives had two SU carburettors, the only exception being North American export models which used a single Zenith-Stromberg from December 1974. Most of the changes made to the carburettors coincided with the introduction of a revised engine specification. Each carburettor installation was covered by a part number or specification number which was sometimes stamped on a small tag attached to the float chamber lid of each carburettor.

The original carburettors were type HS4. The type designation indicates that these were horizontal semi-downdraught carburettors installed at a slight angle, and with 1½in diameter chokes. The jet size was .090in (2.2mm). The caps to the damper pistons at the top of the bellhousings were always in knurled black plastic. The carburettor installation used on the first 18G engine (1962-64) was specification number AUD 52 with standard needle MB (alternatively rich number 6, weak number 21). When the 18GA engine was introduced in 1964, the carburettor specification was changed to AUD 135, which was 99% interchangeable with the original set-up but the standard needle was now a number 5. The first 61 high compression 18GA engines, incidentally, still used the earlier AUD 52 specification but thereafter AUD 135 was used, and this was also used on 18GB engines through to the end of Mark I production. At some stage the standard needle was changed to an FX.

On Mark II models with 18GD engines the standard needle for the AUD 278 carburettors was definitely FX, with alternatives of GZ (weak) or number 5 (rich). Mark II cars for North America with 18GF engines had the slightly different AUD 265 carburettors for which only the standard FX needle was quoted. On 1969 models, carburettor specifications became AUD 325, still with the FX needle, on 18GG engines (not for North America), or AUD 326 with a spring-loaded AAE needle on the North American 18GH engines. In October 1969, from engine number 18GH/20290, new float chamber lids and levers were fitted, and the carburettor specification became AUD 405, still with the AAE needle. The same carburettors were used on the special evaporative loss control 18GJ engine. North American cars with 18GK engines for the 1971 model year still used the HS4 carburettors, now of specification AUD 465 with AAL needles.

With the introduction of the first 18V engines in 1971, more drastic changes occurred to export models. Home market cars continued with the HS4 carburettors, now specification AUD 492 fitted with spring-loaded AAU needles. These carburettors are found on engines of types 18V-581, 582 or 583 with a letter F after these code numbers in the prefix. All export cars were fitted with the new SU HIF4 carburettors with Horizontal Integrated Float chambers. Engines of types 18V-581, 582 or 583 with these car-

burettors had a letter Y after the code number in the prefix, and on these non-North American export cars carburettor specification was AUD 434, also with AAU needles. North American export models with HIF4 carburettors had engines of types 18V584 or 585, followed by the letter Z in the prefix. On these cars, carburettor specification was AUD 493, again with AAU needles. For the 1973 model year, North American cars with engine types 18V-672 or 673 adopted carburettor specification AUD 550 with ABD needles, but changes were minimal.

HIF4 carburettors were introduced on home market cars in November 1973 with engine types 18V-779 or 780. These were also fitted with the AAU needles and carburettor specification was AUD 616. These carburettors were carried over on the 'rubber-bumper' models in late 1974 but needles were changed to ACD and the carburettor specification became FZX 1001. The final change to the carburettor specification on home market cars was the introduction of tamper-proof carburettors of specification FZX 1229. These can be recognised by having much shorter necks to the bellhousings of the suction chambers. It is not certain when these were introduced, but they possibly came at the start of the 1977 model year (car number 410001 in June 1976).

On North American models, the twin SUs were replaced in December 1974 on 1975 model year cars with engine types 18V-797 or 798. These cars had a single Zenith-Stromberg type 175CD5T with an automatic choke, and have the letters AE for alternative single carburettor in their engine prefixes. The design and operating principles of the Stromberg-type carburettor are not dissimilar to the SU. There were several different variations of this carburettor, with different types being found on cars with or without catalysts, and changes being made on the 1977 and later models as well.

Essentially only two different types of inlet manifold were found on the MGB, for the twin SU carburettors or the single Zenith-Stromberg. The twin carburettor manifold consisted of two simple carburettor throats connected by a balance pipe. There were many variations, mostly because of changes to the number and position of adaptors fitted to the balance pipe. The single carburettor manifold for the late North American cars was combined with the exhaust manifold to a single unit. An electric induction heater was fitted between carburettor and manifold.

MGBs with two carburettors had two separate air cleaners, of a truncated cone shape, painted black, and of the dry paper element type. On all cars with 18G type engines up to 1971, the air cleaners were supplied by Coopers and carried labels with this name. Cars with 18V type engines from 1971 had a slightly different design of air cleaner carrying Unipart labels. Slight differences also occurred thereafter between air cleaners on UK, North American and other export cars, although the non-North American export type air cleaners were fitted also to UK cars with HIF4 carburettors from late 1973.

The air cleaner found on North American single carburettor cars was more complicated. It was shaped like a flat box combined with a horizontal drum extending forward to an air intake which incorporated an air temperature sensitive bi-metal valve, switching the air intake from heated air (drawn from a shroud surrounding the exhaust manifold) to ambient temperature fresh air as the engine warmed up.

On the MGC, two SU HS6 carburettors were fitted to all cars, similar in design to the MGB carburettors but with 1¾in choke diameter. There were, however, four different carburettor specifications. On 1967-68 cars with engine type 29G (and 29GB), carburettor specification was AUD 150, with standard needle type ST, weak C1W or rich SQ, while North American cars with engine type 29GA for the 1968 model year had specification AUD 287 with needle KM. On 1969 models, from engine numbers 29G/3201 or 29GA/1401, carburettor specification became AUD 341 (non-North American models) with the same needles as before, while North American cars were now fitted with specification AUD 342, incorporating spring-loaded needles of type BAD. There were two slightly different types of inlet manifold, one for the 29G and 29GB engines, the other for the North American 29GA engine. The air cleaners were different but appear identical, with an oval housing incorporating two paper elements, and an extended air intake at the front.

An interesting feature found only on North American MGCs with 29GA engines was a carburettor cooling system which consisted of a small electric fan, blowing cold air drawn from the air cleaner on to the carburettor float chambers. The system was controlled by a thermostat set at 70°C.

On the MGB GT V8, two SU carburettors of type HIF6 were used, with spring-loaded needles of type BBU. Like the contemporary MGB carburettors, these had horizontal integrated float chambers but the choke diameter was 1¾in. The jet size was .100in (2.54mm). The way in which the carburettors were installed was more interesting than the carburettors themselves. In order to avoid an MGC-like bonnet bulge, the MG engineers needed to position the carburettors at the back of the engine. While the V8 engine kept its standard Rover penthouse inlet manifold, a special V-shaped adaptor was bolted on top of this, with two throats reaching back to the carburettors. The carburettor chokes were thus more or less longitudinal in the car. At the back of the carburettors was a joint airbox, very shallow to fit in front of the heater, with the air filters jutting forward on either side of the carburettors. The teardrop-shaped air filters were of the dry paper element type, and each had an air intake extension at the front, incorporating a temperature sensitive device. The airbox and air filters were painted silver, and a Unipart label was fitted on each air filter.

All MGB, MGC and MGB GT V8 cars had an SU electric fuel pump, of the high pressure type, mounted behind the heelboard on the right-hand side of the car, inboard of the forward rear spring hanger. The first type of pump, specification number AUA 150, was fitted until August 1964 (with minor modifications this type of pump was later quoted as specification AUB 182 for replacement purposes). It was then replaced by an AUF 301 pump (also quoted as AUF 303) with a redesigned body. In February 1968, an AUF 305 pump was fitted, incorporating an additional breather. The MGC was fitted with the AUF 303 pump and the MGB GT V8 with the AUF 305. From the start of 'rubber-bumper' models in 1974, the pump was mounted so that the electrics end protruded into the boot where it was protected by a black-painted metal cover. The final type of pump, only introduced in January 1977, was specification number AZX 1307, which could be identified as the end cover was no longer stepped as on previous pumps. The new pump had an improved contact life and was less liable to buzzing. It was fully interchangeable with the AUF 305 type.

The fuel tank itself was mounted under the boot floor of all models. The original tank, used until March 1965, was shaped like a wedge, with a flat top and curved bottom, rounded off front and rear, and was made with separate end plates. From a change point quoted by body number in March 1965, it was

Most of the twin SU carburettor installations are featured in previous illustrations, but here is a detail shot of the single Zenith-Stromberg carburettor fitted to North American cars from December 1974.

MANUAL GEARBOX

replaced by a larger tank (12.7 gallons or 58 litres, compared to 10 gallons or 45 litres) which resembled a basin fitted with a lid. Where the original tank had been held by two straps, the new tank was simply bolted to the boot floor. The second type of tank was used also on the MGC, and continued in use on MGB cars – including the V8 – to the end of 'chrome-bumper' production in 1974. The fuel tank used on 'rubber-bumper' cars to 1976 was in fact inter-changeable with the previous design, allowing for a small modification to the filter and hose connection. From January 1974, however, the drain plug in the fuel tank had been discontinued.

On cars for North America with the evaporative loss control system, fitted from October 1969 for California and from August 1970 on all North American cars, a different fuel tank was found. To prevent the escape of fuel vapours or the fuel spillage which might occur if the tank was filled to capacity or fuel was allowed to expand in the tank, the fuel tank incorporated a capacity limiter in the form of an internal expansion chamber. This brought usable capacity back down to 10 gallons. There was also a vapour separation tank mounted within the right-hand side of the boot, and connected to the under-bonnet charcoal adsorption canister and the fuel tank. Cars with the evaporative loss control system were fitted with a non-venting fuel filler cap. Catalyst-equipped cars for North America from 1975 had a special restricted filler neck and filler cap to ensure that owners could not inadvertently fill up with leaded fuel. A label at the petrol filler also served as a reminder to use unleaded fuel only.

In August 1976, both RHD and North American cars were fitted with the full fuel integrity system, including a new fuel tank where the fuel feed and gauge unit were combined. The new tank had a short vertical filler neck in contrast to the earlier tank with its longer, sloping filler neck. There was only one further change, in late 1977, when a new filler tube and connection were introduced to meet new Californian legislation, and this revision was soon after commonised on all cars.

The fuel filler cap on all models was a plain non-locking cap with a knurled edge for fingergrip. Originally in stainless steel, it was replaced during the Mark I's life by a chrome-plated cap which continued to the end of production, and was also used on MGC and MGB GT V8 models. The only variation was the non-venting type of cap found on North American cars from 1969/70, as mentioned earlier. The filler cap was made by either Wingard or Westwood until 1968, when Westwood became the sole supplier. A factory-fitted locking filler cap was never offered, but locking caps were originally offered by BMC Service Limited as an after-market accessory. Unipart later offered locking caps suitable for the MGB in bright metal or matt dark grey plastic-coated finishes.

Until 1967, the MGB was fitted with the standard BMC B-type four-speed gearbox, which was broadly similar to the gearbox found on the MGA, with synchromesh on second, third and top gears.

The combined gearbox casing and clutch housing was cast in aluminium and normally left unpainted. A dipstick on the right-hand side was accessible from inside the car. Gearboxes were individually numbered, the number being stamped on the top of the casing adjacent to the dipstick. The gearbox numbers typically have a maximum of four figures, with a number/letter prefix. Where gearbox numbers are entered in the production records (1965-72 only), the serial number is recorded without prefix. It is therefore not possible to refer a gearbox number to a chassis number, or to date those gearbox changes which are recorded only by a gearbox number in the parts lists.

The gearbox had a detachable cover on the left-

There is plenty to see in this view from below the power unit, but in particular note the clutch slave cylinder, the gearbox drain plug, the speedometer drive and the black bolt-on crossmember at the rear of the gearbox which carries the rear power unit mounting point. Other points are the sump painted red engine colour, the twin exhaust downpipes, and the wiring and pipe runs.

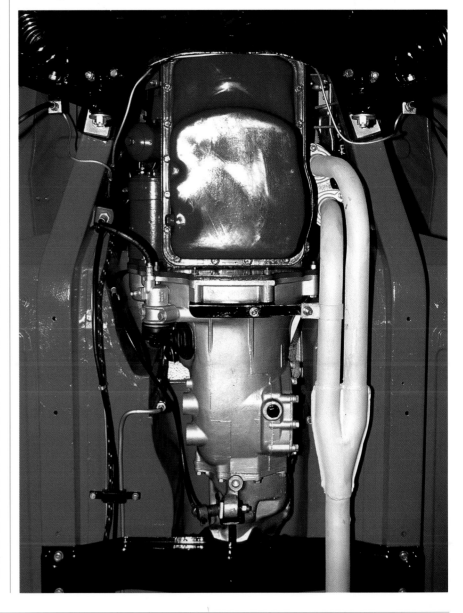

Cars fitted with overdrive had this 'shepherd's crook' switch from April 1965 to September 1974.

hand side and was fitted with a rear extension with a top cover giving access to the top-mounted selector levers, with the remote control gear lever at the rear of the extension. At the front underside of the extension was the gearbox mounting point which together with the front engine mountings completed the three-point power unit suspension. The gear lever was chrome-plated and had two bends so that the longer middle part of the lever was inclined to the rear, while the top part with the knob was vertical. The gear lever knob was pear-shaped and of black Bakelite with the engraved shift pattern highlighted in white. The shift was the normal H-pattern, with reverse on a dog-leg to the left and back.

From early 1963, a Laycock de Normanville D-type overdrive with a ratio of 0.802:1 could be fitted as an optional extra. This required a different rear extension where the remote control was a separate unit, bolted on to the top of the extension, and the actual overdrive housing took up the place of the rear half of the extension. The gear lever on overdrive cars was different as it had only a single bend at the bottom, so the top part and the knob were inclined to the rear. Engines that were originally fitted with an overdrive gearbox may be identified as they have an extra letter R in the engine number prefix (for instance, 18G-RU-H rather than 18G-U-H). The overdrive was electrically activated by a separate control originally mounted at the end of the facia on the driver's side, and operated on third and top gears.

The standard gear ratios for the three-synchro gearbox were as follows, quoted both as gearbox ratios and as overall ratios for the standard final drive ratio of 3.909:1 (11/43):

	Gearbox ratio	Overall ratio
First	3.6363:1	14.2142:1
Second	2.2143:1	8.6557:1
Third	1.3736:1	5.3694:1
Third o/d	1.101:1	4.3062:1
Fourth	1.00:1	3.909:1
Fourth o/d	0.802:1	3.1350:1
Reverse	4.7552:1	18.5881:1

Some major changes occurred to the three-synchro gearbox during the 1962-67 period. From the start of the 18GB engine series in October 1964, the first motion shaft input spigot was increased in diameter from 0.62in to 0.85in and the gearbox casing was modified. In December 1965 the second gear synchromesh was improved, and in September 1966 the reverse selector and detent were modified, while at the same time a reverse light switch was added to the gearbox. An improved larger diameter layshaft supported on four rather than three bearings was introduced in March 1967, together with caged needle roller bearings. These changes were quoted by engine numbers and the change points vary for standard and overdrive engines, and also for high and low compression (see page 140 onwards).

A special cluster of close-ratio gears was offered for the three-synchro gearbox as a competitions part, but as there is no evidence this was ever fitted to standard production cars, details will be found in the sections dealing with tuning and competition parts (see pages 116-118). It may be worth noting that the larger diameter layshaft introduced as standard in 1967 was in fact of the type that had already been fitted to the close-ratio gear cluster.

The all-synchromesh gearbox was introduced on the MGB in late 1967 from the start of production of the Mark II model, series GHN4/GHD4 with engines of the 18GD or 18GF types. The same basic gearbox was also found on the MGC and on the new Austin 3-litre saloon, and would continue to serve on the MGB until the end of production in 1980, including on the MGB GT V8 model. To indicate that a fully-synchronised gearbox was fitted, MGB engine number prefixes were modified and the letters 'We' for the all-synchro gearbox were substituted in place of the earlier letter 'U' (but MGC engine prefixes still contained the letter 'U', which simply meant centre-change gearbox).

The all-synchro gearbox had a totally new casing which was different on MGB and MGC models. Common to both, and also common whether or not overdrive was fitted, was a separate remote control unit which was bolted on to the rear extension. The gear lever was now completely vertical and had a ball-shaped knob. On cars not fitted with overdrive, the rear extension was of a simple tubular shape. On cars fitted with overdrive, the extension was terminated immediately after the point where the remote control unit was bolted on, and the overdrive housing substituted. The overdrive was now Laycock's LH type, with a reduction ratio of 0.82:1.

The ratios for the all-synchro gearbox were revised, and were now in effect a little closer. The original 1968 model MGC with standard (non-overdrive) gearbox shared the MGB gearbox ratios. However, on MGCs fitted with overdrive a special close-ratio gear cluster was found. On MGCs for the 1969 model year, the close-ratio set of gears was fitted also on non-overdrive cars from car number 4236 (coinciding with engine number 29G/3201, or 29GA/1401 for North America). The MGB continued with the same rear axle ratio as before, of 3.909:1 (11/43). The MGC was, naturally enough, fitted with higher rear axle ratios, originally of 3.071:1 (14/43) on non-overdrive cars and 3.307:1 (13/43) on overdrive cars. But from car number 4236, the 3.307:1 ratio was introduced on non-overdrive cars, while overdrive cars were fitted with a lower ratio of 3.7:1 (10/37), which was otherwise only found on later models of MGB with the automatic gearbox. Automatic MGCs retained the ratio of 3.307:1 throughout.

For the MGB between 1967–74, the following ratios are found (with the standard final drive ratio):

	Gearbox ratio	Overall ratio
First	3.440:1	13.446:1
Second	2.167:1	8.470:1
Third	1.382:1	5.402:1
Third o/d	1.133:1	4.429:1
Fourth	1.00:1	3.909:1
Fourth o/d	0.82:1	3.205:1
Reverse	3.095:1	12.098:1

Matters are more complicated on the MGC cars, as there were four different sets of ratios:

	1968 model, without overdrive		1968 model, with overdrive	
	Gearbox ratio	Overall ratio	Gearbox ratio	Overall ratio
First	3.440:1	10.56:1	2.98:1	9.85:1
Second	2.167:1	6.65:1	2.058:1	6.80:1
Third	1.382:1	4.24:1	1.307:1	4.32:1
Third o/d	-	-	1.0717:1	3.544:1
Fourth	1.00:1	3.071:1	1.00:1	3.307:1
Fourth o/d	-	-	0.82:1	2.71:1
Reverse	3.095:1	9.50:1	2.679:1	8.86:1

	1969 model, without overdrive		1969 model, with overdrive	
	Gearbox ratio	Overall ratio	Gearbox ratio	Overall ratio
First	2.98:1	9.85:1	2.98:1	11.026:1
Second	2.058:1	6.80:1	2.058:1	7.615:1
Third	1.307:1	4.32:1	1.307:1	4.836:1
Third o/d	-	-	1.0717:1	3.965:1
Fourth	1.00:1	3.307:1	1.00:1	3.7:1
Fourth o/d	-	-	0.82:1	3.034:1
Reverse	2.679:1	8.86:1	2.679:1	9.912:1

There were very few important changes to the all-synchro gearbox between 1967–80. North American cars for the 1972 model year included a seat belt inhibitor switch in the remote control unit. From August 1972, for the 1973 model year, the gear lever knob became pear-shaped but larger than the Mark I type. It was, in fact, a corporate British Leyland design, with the shift pattern under a clear plastic insert in the top of the knob which was otherwise covered in simulated leather. The overdrive switch had been moved from the facia to the steering column wiper/washer stalk on North American cars from the start of Mark II production in 1967. The first non-North American car to adopt this feature was the MGB GT V8, but from the start of 'rubber-bumper' production, in 1974, stalk operation was found on all four-cylinder models with overdrive.

The V8 used basically the same gearbox design as the four-cylinder cars but with a different casing to

As this Mark I gear lever has a visible bend towards the top, it is from a car without overdrive – with overdrive the top and centre parts of the lever were straight. The lower bend in the lever is hidden by the rubber gaiter. Note that the surround of the lever is elongated and that the transmission tunnel steps down behind the lever.

accommodate a larger clutch. It also had a unique set of internal gearbox ratios, more closely spaced than those on the four-cylinder models and with a higher first gear. While the V8 had overdrive as standard, on this model it operated only on top gear, although early production cars had the overdrive operating also on third. The final drive ratio on the V8 was 3.071:1 (14/43), the same as the early MGC without over-drive. The following are the ratios for the 1973–74 V8 model:

	Gearbox ratio	Overall ratio
First	3.138:1	9.637:1
Second	1.974:1	6.062:1
Third	1.259:1	3.866:1
Fourth	1.00:1	3.071:1
Fourth o/d	0.82:1	2.518:1
Reverse	2.819:1	8.657:1

Some small changes were made from the start of 'rubber-bumper' production in 1974. The gearbox casing on four-cylinder cars was revised, with a side-mounted filler plug instead of filler and dipstick at the

On Mark II and later models, the gear lever was straight, vertical and had a ball-shaped rather than a pear-shaped knob. It was mounted a little further back and the surround was circular.

This vinyl gaiter completely shrouding the gear lever was introduced on 1971 models.

top, and, there was a new speedometer drive, with a new gear and pinion. The overdrive unit on four-cylinder cars was modified and can be identified by its blue – instead of black – Laycock label. On 'rubber-bumper' cars, the first gear ratio was higher, at 3.036:1, on both four-cylinder and V8 models, giving an overall first gear ratio of 11.867:1 (four-cylinder cars) or 9.325:1 (V8). In June 1975, the overdrive became standard on home market four-cylinder cars.

In June 1976, from the start of the 1977 model year (car number 410001), further changes were made. The first gear ratio altered again, to 3.333:1 (overall ratio 13.03:1). A new gear lever was cranked rearwards and fitted with a larger mushroom-shaped knob which in the case of cars equipped with overdrive incorporated the overdrive switch. This gear knob was of the type used on Triumph cars for some years previously. Overdrive was fitted as standard on all right-hand drive cars from June 1976, but it remained an optional extra on North American cars until the end of production. While RHD cars continued to have the overdrive operating on third and top gears, on North American cars from February 1977 it operated only on top gear.

The type of clutch fitted to the MGB was a Borg & Beck single dry plate 8in diaphragm spring clutch, type DSG, with hydraulic actuation. The clutch pedal operated a Lockheed hydraulic master cylinder situated immediately above the pedal box, with an integral hydraulic fluid reservoir. The slave cylinder was located on the right-hand side below the clutch housing. The clutch pedal matched the brake pedal with its shield shape and rubber pad with vertical ribs.

There were only detail changes to the clutch system over the years, but it should be noted that a revised master cylinder was introduced from the start of the GHN4/GHD4 series with fully synchronised gearbox in 1967, with the mounting flange turned so that the reservoir leaned away from the brake master cylinder, to clear the bigger brake fluid reservoir found on North American cars with dual-circuit brakes. The master cylinder was changed again at an unknown point during production of the GHN5/GHD5 series, probably during 1973. The later type of master cylinder can be identified by the presence of two concentric rings around the cylinder barrel in front of the reservoir. This type is interchangeable with the previous type and is now recommended for fitting also to earlier cars with the all-synchro gearbox, as the original type of master cylinder for these cars is no longer available.

The MGC clutch was similar but was of 9in diameter, and the hydraulic actuation was provided by a Girling 0.625in master cylinder, with the integral reservoir at the very rear of the cylinder. On the MGB GT V8, the clutch was further increased in size, to 9½in, which incidentally meant that this car also had to have a different gearbox casing from the four-cylinder models. On the V8 model, the Lockheed clutch master cylinder was also bigger than on four-cylinder cars.

A new gear lever knob of a standard BL design (right) appeared on 1973 models, and was also fitted on the V8. The final design of gear lever knob (far right), fitted on 1977 and later models, had the overdrive switch built into the knob. The surround for the gaiter was changed from chrome to matt black.

AUTOMATIC GEARBOX

Offered as an optional extra on the MGB Mark II model from late 1967, as well as on the MGC, the automatic gearbox was the common Borg-Warner type 35 three-speed epicyclic unit, coupled to a hydraulic fluid torque converter. The auto 'box was basically the same, whether found on the MGB or the MGC, and had the same internal ratios. However, they can be identified, as the gearbox serial number had a prefix code of 23EA (MGB) or 17EA (MGC).

The most important change to the automatic gearbox affected only the MGC, which in February 1968 (car number 1300) changed from cable to rod control for the gear selector. The MGB always had a rod for the selector control. On the MGB, the automatic gearbox option was discontinued at the end of the 1973 model year, in August 1973.

Gear selection was controlled by a sliding lever moving in a quadrant which took the place of the normal gear lever on the transmission tunnel. The selector positions, from front to rear, were: P (Park), R (Reverse), N (Neutral), D (Drive), L2 (Low 2, intermediate gear hold), L1 (Low 1, low gear hold). The selector lever knob was shaped rather like an Edam cheese. A collar-shaped detent sleeve below the knob had to be lifted before R or P could be engaged.

The torque converter ratio varied between 1:1 and 2.2:1. The overall ratios on cars fitted with the automatic gearbox varied as three different rear axle ratios were fitted, respectively on the MGC, on the 1968 model MGB, and on the 1969 and later models of MGB. The ratios are as follows, assuming direct drive through the torque converter:

	Gearbox ratio	Overall ratios, MGC
First	2.39:1	7.903:1
Second	1.45:1	4.795:1
Top	1:1	3.307:1
Reverse	2.09:1	6.911:1

	Overall ratios, MGB (1968)	Overall ratios, MGB (1969–73)
First	9.34:1	8.843:1
Second	5.668:1	5.365:1
Top	3.909:1	3.7:1
Reverse	8.17:1	7.733:1

Cars with the automatic gearbox had a different brake pedal, with a wider rectangular pad and rubber. A special gear selector illumination lamp was also fitted originally, on the lower edge of the facia panel above the selector. This lamp came on together with the instrument lights but could be independently controlled by a switch next to it. It was discontinued at the end of the 1971 model year, as all 1972 and 1973 models were fitted with a courtesy lamp on the new centre console.

It has been speculated that the option of an automatic gearbox was introduced to cater for demand in the North American markets. While the MGC automatic was indeed sold in the USA and Canada, the MGB automatic was never offered regularly in either market. The great majority of MGBs with automatic 'boxes were sold in the home market. The only export market to take them in any quantity was Australia, which received a total of 228 MGB roadster CKD kits with auto 'boxes between August 1968 and July 1970. Otherwise, the GT was by far the most common model to be fitted with an automatic gearbox.

Engine number prefixes on automatic cars were different, and on the MGB these engines had their own number series. The following is a guide to the different types of engines found on cars with automatic gearboxes:

Although this automatic MGC GT has a non-original gear selector knob, the selector and the gate are of the correct style.

	Engine number prefix	Engine numbers
MGC, except North America and France	28G-Rc-H	101–4936[1]
MGC, North America	29GA-Rc-H	101–4397[1]
MGC, France (2850cc engine)	29GB-Rc-H	113 (one only)
MGB, 1968 model	18GD-Rc-H	101–240
MGB, 1969–71 models	18GG-Rc-H	101–955
MGB, 1972–73 models, home market	18V-583-F-H	101–870
MGB, 1972–73 models, export	18V-583-Y-H	101–870[2]

[1] Shared with non-automatic engine numbers
[2] Shared with home market engine numbers

The parts list also mentions 1968 model year US specification MGB engines with automatic, prefix 18GF-Rc-H with numbers from 101 to 110, but no such engines were ever fitted to production cars. Please note that, as usual, low compression versions of all MGB engines would have a final letter L rather than H in the prefixes quoted above.

Production figures for the automatic models have been the subject of speculation over the years, as these cars were never counted separately at Abingdon. For the MGBs, the engine number series give a reasonably good guide, but do not in themselves permit the oft-desired split between roadster and GT models. Definitive figures for the automatic models, checked very carefully against the production records, are published for the first time:

MGC

Roadster 92 home market, 2 RHD export, 9 LHD export, 453 North American export; total **556** cars. **GT** 258 home market, 11 RHD export, 11 LHD export, 484

REAR AXLE

North American export; total **764** cars. Grand total of **1320** MGC cars.

MGB

1968 models with 18GD series engines. **Roadster** 12 home market, 2 RHD export, 2 LHD export, 36 CKD for Australia. **GT** 74 home market, 10 RHD export, 2 LHD export (including 1 for Canada).
1969-71 models with 18GG series engines. **Roadster** 90 home market, 10 RHD export, 7 LHD export, 192 CKD for Australia. **GT** 475 home market, 40 RHD export, 30 LHD export.
1972-73 models with 18V-583 series engines. **Roadster** 92 home market, 3 RHD export, 6 LHD export. **GT** 603 home market, 29 RHD export, 22 LHD export. Total of all MGB models: **452** roadsters, **1285** GTs. Grand total of **1737** MGB cars.

It will be seen that the actual MGB production figures fall slightly short of the figures that might have been expected from the engine number series. Inevitably, a few engines were not fitted in cars.

A few oddities regarding automatic MGBs may be worth noting. Although the availability of the automatic gearbox was announced from the start of the Mark II model in late 1967, in fact the first cars were only delivered in early 1968, and regular production only occurred by May or June of that year. It will be noted that one 1968 car was shipped to Canada. The 1968 model year cars for Canada, of course, still had the UK-specification 18GD engine, not the emissions control US-specification 18GF engine. In addition to the cars counted above, there were also eventually two automatic MGBs built for the USA with the later 18GK series engine. These were a GT in October 1970 (car number G-HD5-UB/222653-G, engine number 18GK-Rc-H/101) and a roadster in February 1971 (car number G-HN5-UB/238235-G, engine number 18GK-Rc-H/106). These two cars appear to have been purely one-off experiments and one can only speculate what happened to engines with numbers between 101 and 106.

If you are the owner of an automatic MGB or MGC, you have quite a rare vehicle. At the last count, the MG Car Club's special register for automatic MGBs numbered little more than 120 cars. But it is a matter of opinion whether these cars are actually desirable. The automatic MGB seemed to lose out little on performance or even fuel consumption compared to the manual model, according to a road test – possibly the only full test ever carried out of the model – in *Autocar* magazine (16 April 1970). Incidentally, at that time the automatic gearbox added £104 to the MGB roadster's home market price of £1164. With the Borg-Warner type 35 being so common on other cars of the period, neither spare parts nor rebuilds should present too much of a problem to the restorer.

The original rear axle was of the banjo type with a one-piece case assembly including the differential housing and axle tubes, and a bolted-on nosepiece or differential carrier. It was of the three-quarter floating type and had final drive with hypoid bevel gears. From the start of GT production in 1965, this model was equipped with a new Salisbury tube type axle, characterised by its central differential housing with only a removeable rear cover, and separate axle tubes. This axle was of the semi-floating type, again with hypoid final gears. The tubed axle was later also introduced on roadster models, at widely varying car numbers depending on whether disc wheels or wire wheels were fitted, although research has shown that the change-over had taken place on all roadsters by July 1967.

Rear axles were individually numbered, the number being typically stamped on the front of the left-hand axle tube, and rear axle numbers were entered in the production records between approximately 1965 and 1972. It seems that the tubed axles had a different number series from the banjo axles, but otherwise there is little information about the number sequences.

The rear hubs were different on wire wheel and disc wheel cars. As the hubs were part of the rear axle assembly, different part numbers were quoted throughout the production period for disc wheel and wire wheel cars. The axle casing on wire wheel cars

The banjo rear axle was used on roadster models until 1967, but never on the GT. The fuel tank also seen here is the original bolster-type tank with strap fittings used until March 1965.

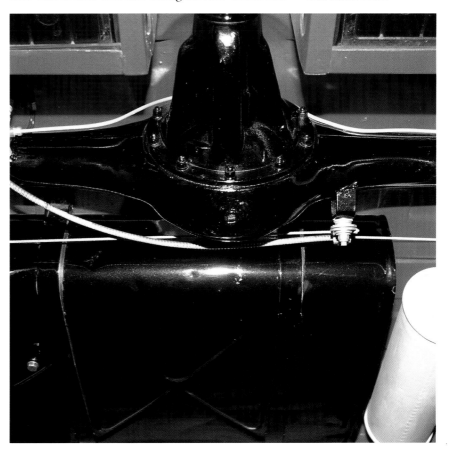

STEERING

was in any case almost 2in narrower than on disc or Rostyle wheel cars. Wire wheel hubs were changed early in 1964 when the original hubs with 12 threads per inch for the wheel nuts were replaced by hubs with 8 threads per inch. There were slight changes to the rear axle at the start of the Mark II model in 1967, but by and large the basic axle design continued in use until 1980. The MGC and MGB GT V8 rear axles were very similar, but final drive ratios differed.

The standard ratio for the MGB models was 3.909:1 (11/43) throughout production, while the automatic version had a ratio of 3.7:1 (10/37). Alternative ratios listed as part of the competitions equipment were 4.555:1 (9/41), 4.3:1 (10/43) and 4.1:1 (10/41), all quoted for the early banjo axle. For the tubed axle, only two alternative ratios were originally quoted, of 4.555:1 (9/41) and 4.22:1 (9/38), to which were later added the MGC ratios. A limited slip ZF differential was also quoted as part of the competitions equipment, for both axle types.

The MGC was at first introduced with a rear axle ratio of 3.071:1 (14/43) on standard cars without overdrive or 3.307:1 (13/43) on overdrive and automatic cars. However, on 1969 models (from car number 4236) the 3.307:1 ratio was introduced on non-overdrive cars, and overdrive cars were given the ratio of 3.7:1 (10/37). A limited slip differential was also quoted as a competitions part for the MGC. The MGB GT V8 was fitted with the final drive ratio of 3.071:1 (14/43), the same as the early standard MGC. Calculations of the overall gear ratios for the different standard final drive ratios will be found in the sections on the manual and automatic gearboxes.

The prop shaft on all cars was a Hardy Spicer tubular shaft of the telescopic type with a splined section towards the front end, and universal joints with needle roller bearings front and rear. Of 2in diameter, the prop shaft was originally 30in (762mm) long on cars with the standard gearbox, and 31⅛in (791mm) long on cars with the overdrive gearbox.

In April to June 1965, the so-called lip sealed type was introduced, with improved seals in the universal joints. When the tube type rear axle was introduced on the GT in 1965 and subsequently also on the roadster, the prop shaft had to be lengthened, so cars with the standard gearbox received the 31⅛in long shaft while overdrive cars were given a new shaft of 32in (813mm). However, modifications on the Mark II model with the fully-synchronised gearbox allowed the 31⅛in prop shaft to be used on all cars, including automatics, and this remained the specification to the end of production.

The MGC prop shaft was similar and also of 2in diameter, but was made of heavier 0.095in gauge material instead of the MGB's 0.064in gauge. The same prop shaft was fitted on all MGC cars regardless of type of gearbox, and was also found on the V8. On these models, larger universal joints were fitted.

Conventional rack and pinion steering was fitted on all cars. Until 1967, the only noteworthy change was that early roadsters had a grease nipple fitted on the pinion shaft, but this was deleted in 1965. From the introduction of the Mark II model in late 1967, cars for the USA (and for Canada from August 1968) were fitted with a collapsible, energy-absorbing steering column. Similarly, the MGC for the USA and later Canada was fitted with the collapsible steering column. On non-North American cars an energy-absorbing column was fitted on 1972 models (from car number 258001) in August 1971, but only from the start of 'rubber-bumper' production in 1974 was the same steering column fitted to all cars, including the V8 model, regardless of market. A steering rack with a lower ratio was introduced on 1977 models, from car number 410001 in June 1976. There were four types of steering column splines over the years – 1962-67 (Mark I), 1967-69 (Mark II), 1969-76 (GHN/D5 series) and 1976-80 (1977 model year and later) – which means that steering wheels are not interchangeable.

From 1962, MGBs for certain markets – at first Germany and Sweden, later also Finland (October 1967), Austria (January 1968) and France (September 1969) – were fitted with a combined steering and ignition lock, which necessitated a different steering column. Several different steering locks were fitted to the 1962-67 models, the parts list giving details of four, of which the final type was carried forward on the Mark II and MGC models. All of these locks had the key entering from the front, below and slightly to the right of the steering column. Early locks were sometimes made by the German firm of Neiman and were often marked on the lock face with the words 'Halt', 'Garage', 'Fahrt' and 'Start', other later locks being marked 'O', 'I', 'II' and 'III'. Some pre-1967 locks only found on export models had five-figure key numbers with a prefix and a suffix letter. In 1968 a new stronger Trico lock became a universal fitting on export cars with a steering lock.

From the start of Mark II production in 1967, most North American cars were fitted with a steering lock. This lock used a standard FS-series key and was rather weak, being easily defeated. These cars were the first MGBs to have a steering lock with the key entering on the right-hand side of the steering column. North American cars not fitted with a steering lock had their ignition lock in the same position. For the 1970 model year, steering locks were fitted on all North American cars, and the same type of side-entry lock was now used for Swedish/German specification.

In the home market steering locks became a legal requirement from 1 January 1971, so to simplify matters it was decided to fit them on all cars from 14 December 1970 (from car numbers roadster 230617 and GT 231339). The front-entry lock below the column persisted on non-North American cars until

The steering lock mounted on the side of the column was introduced on American cars from the start of Mark II production in 1967, but was only fitted across the range in 1974 – earlier non-North American cars had a front-entry lock below the column. The car pictured is a 1973 US model.

the end of 'chrome-bumper' production in 1974, with the exception of the V8 which had a side-entry lock from the start.

Several different types of locks were fitted to both North American and non-North American cars. Suppliers of steering locks included Neiman, Trico, Magnatex, Wilmot Breeden and Lowe & Fletcher. Some steering lock keys of the early 1970s had five-figure key numbers with the series letter A. Later locks, including the side-entry types, typically had four-figure numbers, often with the prefix BL. It is quite possible that steering locks of different makes were fitted at the same time.

The MGB GT V8, with its redesigned steering column, steering column cowl and column-mounted stalks, had a side-entry lock from the start of production. Similar to the locks used by this time on North American four-cylinder cars, the V8 lock had a small press button which needed to be operated before the key could be turned back to the locking

Many of the different steering wheels are illustrated in the 'facia & instruments' section of this book (starting on page 43), but here are a few of the more unusual variations, such as this wheel used only on 1970 models with stalk-operated horns. It features pierced spokes and a unique silver and red MG badge in the centre.

The solid-spoke wheel was used from 1973 to 1976, but this all-black version was very rare and possibly confined to the 1975 GT 'Jubilee' limited edition model as seen here.

position (marked 'O') and withdrawn. When the V8 steering column arrangements were introduced also on non-North American four-cylinder cars in 1974, these too adopted the side-entry lock with press button key release. This persisted until October 1977, when the final type of steering lock without press button key release was introduced, still with a slightly different type of lock for the North American specification cars.

The original type of steering wheel featured wire spokes in T-formation. The spokes forming the cross-bar of the T each had three wires and dropped slightly from the steering wheel centre to the rim, while the vertical spoke pointing downwards from the centre had two wires. The steering wheel hub and the plastic-covered rim, with finger grips on the reverse, were always black. The centre motif contained the horn push and carried an MG badge with silver letters and octagon on a background of red wavy lines. The steering wheel was 16½in (419mm) in diameter and required a little less than three turns from lock to lock.

The MGC steering wheel was of the same design and size but was distinguished by a sewn-on black leather cover for the rim – the product, apparently, of a small saddler local to Abingdon! The MGC had lower-geared steering so 3.5 turns were required lock to lock. On MGB Mark II and MGC models to North American specification with the energy-absorbing column, the horn was activated by a stalk switch and the centre motif was a simple push-fit. In 1969, the moulded material of the rim was changed from acetate to polypropylene, to remedy any tendency for the rim to crack.

A new design of steering wheel, of 15½in (394mm) in diameter, was introduced on the 1970 models. This had three spokes in natural colour alloy, each containing five potentially finger-trapping holes, with the spokes forming the crossbar of the T now horizontal. The rim and the surround of the centre were covered in simulated leather. Initially all cars with this type of steering wheel – including non-North American models – had the horn on a stalk switch and the MG badge on the centre motif was red and silver, but from the start of the 1971 model year the horn push was moved back to the centre of the steering wheel and the MG logo became all black. On 1972 models a touch of colour was re-introduced as the background of the MG logo became red, the letters and octagon staying black.

The next new design of steering wheel appeared for the 1973 model year, with the separate holes in the spokes replaced by slightly less finger-trapping slots. These did not last long as four-cylinder models had the slots filled in from June 1973, with only a slight depression in the centre part of each spoke. This solid-spoke wheel was used on the V8 model effectively from the start of production. The home market 'Jubilee' GTs with this design of steering wheel had black rather than alloy-coloured spokes. The solid-spoke wheel was carried over on the 'rubber-bumper' models. From January 1975 to January 1976, including 'Jubilee' GTs, the background colour for the MG octagon on the horn push was changed from red to gold – which was actually more like yellow – in the same way that exterior badges were changed to gold to mark MG's 'jubilee year'. This gesture supposedly applied to all cars built during the 1975 calendar year – but one wonders.

As part of the general update for the 1977 model year, an all-new 15in (381mm) steering wheel was fitted. This had a thicker padded rim and four spokes arranged in a slightly bent horizontal H. The spokes and the centre were in the same plane, while the wheel, including the embossed MG logo in the centre, was dark grey in colour, although on 1978 models the logo was changed to hot-foiled silver. The horn push was moved back on a steering column stalk switch on the 1977 models, and the same steering wheel was used on North American as well as non-North American cars. On home market Limited Edition models in 1980, the MG logo on the steering wheel acquired a red background, with silver letters and octagon.

The final type of steering wheel found on MGB cars was fitted only to the North American Limited Edition model of 1979-80. This was a Motolita-style wheel with three pierced alloy spokes, somewhat similar to the 1970-72 style except that the leather rim covering extended to the outermost part of the spokes, and each spoke had only three holes. The MG badge in the centre of the wheel was silver and black. This steering wheel was apparently the product of a French manufacturer.

A wood-rimmed light-alloy steering wheel (part number AHH 7208) was originally quoted as part of the competition equipment, but does not appear ever to have been fitted on the production line. It was deleted from the Special Tuning booklet in 1965. Curiously enough, a similar steering wheel – maybe even the same one – was fitted to 1000 MGB GTs sold in the USA in 1967, promoted as a limited edition to mark the first anniversary of the MGB GT being introduced in this market. This particular type of steering wheel was fitted by dealers at point of sale in the USA. It was a 16in (406mm) diameter wheel with three pierced alloy spokes and a wood rim, and came together with – would you believe? – a 'matching Australian coach wood shift knob'. Wooden steering wheels and gear lever knobs were popular after-market accessories in the USA before 1968, one leading supplier of such items trading under the name of 'MG Mitten' as it had started out making car covers for MGs.

Another unusual option theoretically available as a factory-fitted item was a steering column 1⅜in longer than normal. The availability of this may have been

More commonly used during the 1975 calendar year was this version where the background colour for the MG badge in the centre was gold but the spokes were natural metal finish.

Home market LE cars of 1980 basically had the standard post-1976 steering wheel, but the background colour of the MG badge was red.

The American market Limited Edition model of 1979-80 had this special steering wheel, looking very much like a Motolita design (but in fact made by another company, apparently in France) and having an all-black MG badge in the hub.

inspired by the fact that the MGB was never offered with an adjustable steering column. The longer steering column was quoted in publicity material until 1966, including the original GT brochure. I have never come across a car fitted with the longer steering column, nor seen one listed in the production records with this option…

SUSPENSION

The front suspension on all MGB models, including the V8, was the classic MG design with wishbones and coil springs. A hefty front suspension crossmember was attached to the bodyshell with two bolts on either side. The lower wishbones were pivoted from the crossmember, with spring pans between the front and rear wishbone arms to locate the coil springs. At the top, the coil springs were seated in inverted cups formed by the extremities of the crossmember. On top of these cups, hydraulic lever arm shock absorbers were located, the lever arms forming an upper wishbone. The upper and lower wishbones held the vertical swivel arm assemblies with stub axles for the wheel hubs.

A towing eye plate was added to the crossmember in July 1962 from car number 368, and soon after, from car number 619 in August 1962, a new pattern Armstrong front shock absorber with a built-in reservoir was fitted to eliminate damper fade. An extra greasepoint was added at the bottom of the swivel pin assemblies in November 1963. Wheel hubs were naturally different on disc wheel and wire wheel cars, and in February 1964 new hubs were fitted on wire wheel cars, with a coarser thread for the wheel nuts.

A front anti-roll bar was available as an optional extra from the start of production. It was a standard fitting on the GT model when this was introduced in 1965, the GT having a stiffer anti-roll bar than roadster models. From car number 108039 in November 1966, the anti-roll bar was standardised also on the roadster. Cars fitted with the anti-roll bar had the front lower wishbone arms modified to accept it. Also in November 1966, the towing eye was deleted from the front suspension crossmember.

Prior to the introduction of 'rubber-bumper' cars, the GT model had longer front coil springs with slightly different spring rates from the roadster. From August 1972, the coil springs on both roadster and GT models were changed to increase the height at the front of the car by 0.5in – this was done in order to overcome the problem of the springs settling too low, which sometimes occurred when export cars had been tightly lashed down on board ship. A further change seems to have been made to the roadster springs in November 1972, but this may simply have been a part number change as the modified springs were interchangeable with the previous type.

The GT springs with extra length were also used on all V8 models. On the other hand, the front anti-roll bar originally intended for the V8 was commonised on the four-cylinder GT in March 1973. The V8 had a modified front crossmember which raised the car by 0.5in, necessary in order to maintain reasonable ground clearance, which was otherwise somewhat compromised on this model.

From the start of 'rubber-bumper' production, the V8 front crossmember was fitted also on four-cylinder cars, helping to ensure that the cars met the new US requirement for bumper height. The crossmember was now different on LHD and RHD cars. In conjunction with other modifications also introduced on 'rubber-bumper' cars, the total increase in ride height on these models was in the order of 1½in. The roadster type coil springs were now commonised on the four-cylinder GT. A new anti-roll bar was fitted, common to GT and V8 models, but initially on 'rubber-bumper' roadsters no front anti-roll bar was fitted at all. It was only re-introduced on the roadster in June 1976 from the start of the 1977 model year, and stiffer anti-roll bars were then fitted on both roadster and GT models. Also at that point, V8 front hubs were introduced on the four-cylinder models with Rostyle wheels. A later modification to the Rostyle wheel hubs in March 1979 permitted use of the cast alloy wheels which were then being introduced on North American Limited Edition models.

Because of the much deeper and longer engine fitted to the MGC, there was no room for the traditional crossmember and coil spring suspension of the MGB. Instead a deep U-shaped welded-in crossmember was fitted, incorporating engine and suspension mounting points. A new suspension was designed, with the swivel pin assembly being located between a triangular top arm and a back-to-back lower arm. The lower arm acted directly on a torsion bar which had its rear end located in the crossmember under the floor at the rear of the gearbox. Shock absorbers were of the telescopic type, anchored to the lower suspension arms. On the early cars the shock absorbers were different on roadster and GT models,

Taken from the rear and looking towards the front of the car, this photo shows the black bolted-in cross member which carries the front suspension, together with the lower wishbones enclosing the spring pans and the bottom of the coil springs.

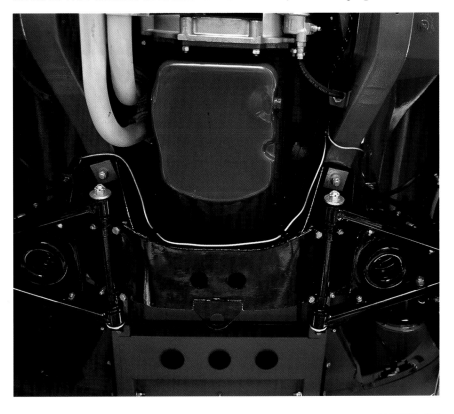

Although this front hub (left) is from a 1973 car fitted with Rostyle wheels, it is typical of all MGB front hubs for cars without wire wheels.

The front hub and brake disc of a 1964 wire-wheeled car (above). As this photo is taken from the front we can see the anti-roll bar and the track rod end coming out of the rubber boot enclosing the end of the steering rack. Above the brake disc is the V-shaped lever arm of the shock absorber which forms the upper wishbone, and the shock absorber housing in natural metal finish.

As this photo (left) of the MGC front suspension is taken from the rear it shows a different aspect compared to the MGB view. The shock absorber (painted blue) is telescopic and therefore independent of the upper triangular suspension arm. The lower back-to-back arm works on the torsion bar, a section of which can just be seen behind the flexible brake hose.

Brake drums and rear hubs from a 1964 wire-wheeled roadster (far left) and an MGC (left). The MGC has five studs for the hub, and the 9in Girling brake drum is also rather different from the 10in Lockheed drums found on MGBs. To the left of the MGC view is a corner of the fuel tank, to the right a corner of the battery box, and above the brake drum are (from left) the rebound strap, rubber bump stop and lever arm for the shock absorber.

but from car number 570 the GT shock absorbers were introduced also on the roadster. Otherwise there were no important changes to the specification of the MGC front suspension.

Semi-elliptic leaf springs were used at the rear on all models, with hydraulic lever arm Armstrong shock absorbers. The original roadster springs had six leaves without any interleaving, but from car number 11313 in May 1963 interleaving was added, and at the same time the springs were made slightly softer to lower the rear end of the car. The GT model in 1965 was given seven-leaf springs to offset this car's increased weight at the rear. On the MGC, seven-leaf springs were fitted to both roadster and GT models but with an increased free camber and higher load rating for the GT springs. MGC springs were modified in January 1968. On the MGB GT V8, the only difference to the rear springs compared with a four-cylin-

der GT was that the load rating was slightly higher.

Important modifications to the rear suspension only occurred in September 1974 from the start of 'rubber-bumper' production. As it became necessary to increase the ride height of the four-cylinder cars to meet US bumper height legislation, the rear spring hangers were slightly lowered and the rear springs were stiffened up, while the rear shock absorbers were also revised and given longer links. The ride height of the V8 was not altered. From the start of 'rubber-bumper' production, the roadster was equipped with the GT-type seven-leaf springs, although this model reverted to six-leaf springs in September 1975. The adverse comments incurred by the inferior handling of the early 'rubber-bumper' cars undoubtedly influenced the decision to fit – belatedly – a rear anti-sway or anti-roll bar, which was introduced from the start of the 1977 model year, in June 1976.

BRAKES

A Lockheed hydraulic braking system was fitted to all MGB models, with 10.75in diameter discs at the front and 10in x 1.75in drums at the rear. All cars had a conventional handbrake, operating mechanically in the rear drums, with cable actuation from the handbrake lever mounted on the right-hand side of the transmission tunnel. The handbrake lever was the ordinary ratchet type with thumb-button release. A fly-off handbrake conversion kit was quoted as a competitions part in the early days but was probably discontinued in the early 1970s.

The brake and clutch pedals were pivoted under the front of the cover of the master cylinder box, with small shield-shaped pads and vertical ribs to the rubber pedal covers. The brake pedal operated directly on the pushrod of the brake master cylinder. Originally all cars had a combined master cylinder and brake fluid reservoir, but from car number 119500 in 1967, cars destined for France and the Benelux countries had a separate transparent brake fluid reservoir. Mark II cars for the USA, and cars for Canada from August 1968, had a dual-circuit braking system with a new tandem master cylinder incorporating an angled brake fluid reservoir.

Pipe runs were similar on all the early cars, with slight differences at the rear depending on whether a banjo or tubed axle was fitted. A much revised pipe layout was employed on North American cars with dual-circuit braking systems from 1967. Dual-circuit brakes were found on cars for Sweden and Germany for the 1970 model year, and were also introduced for Norway from early 1971, for Switzerland from August 1971 and for the Benelux countries from September 1974.

One piece of standardisation was that US-type brake pads and linings were fitted to all MGBs from May 1968. On the other hand, when a Lockheed type 6 brake servo became available as an optional extra in February 1970, it was only fitted on cars with single-line braking systems and was therefore not available at all in North America. An improved servo unit with a bigger bore was fitted from May 1970. The V8 model had the servo fitted as standard from the start of production, and it became standard on four-cylinder cars for the home market in August 1973, although a few export cars may have continued without one until 1976. On North American cars, a standard-fit servo finally appeared in December 1974, at the start of the 1975 model year. This was the direct-acting type of servo which was combined with the master cylinder and the supply tank. UK cars continued with the non-direct-acting servo mounted on the opposite side of the car to the master cylinder until May 1977, when the dual-circuit brakes and direct-acting servo were introduced for the home market at car numbers 436465 (GT) and 437181 (roadster). Meanwhile, the braking system on North American models had been extensively revised from the start of the 1976 model year, with an improved master cylinder and servo being fitted.

The brake pipes on all cars had been given a corrosion-resistant coating in April 1969, and in early 1970 protection improved again when the pipes were coated in passivated zinc. Otherwise there were no important changes to the brake pipes and their runs. Cars with dual-circuit brakes were fitted with a brake pressure failure warning switch and a corresponding warning light, which was also employed as a handbrake warning light on 1976 and later models.

The Girling brake system on the MGC was in principle similar and again showed regional variations, such as the remote transparent brake fluid reservoir for France and Benelux, and dual-circuit brakes on all cars for the USA, as well as Canadian cars from August 1968. Early US models with dual-circuit brakes had a remote transparent brake fluid reservoir shaped like a drum, but from car number 3018 this was replaced by a box-shaped reservoir sitting on top of the master cylinder body.

All MGC cars had servo-assisted brakes, using Girling Mark 2B servo units which were commonised on US and non-US cars from car number 1154.

Two types of pedal cluster. On the MGC (below), in common with other cars from 1967 to 1976, the accelerator pedal is shield-shaped and lacks a rubber pad – the Mark I cars had a smaller square pedal with a pad. Brake and clutch pedals stayed the same shape and size. There was a foot-operated dipswitch. On the 1980 car (bottom), the brake and accelerator pedals have moved closer to each other for easier 'heel-and-toeing'; the larger, re-shaped accelerator pedal seen here had been introduced in 1976.

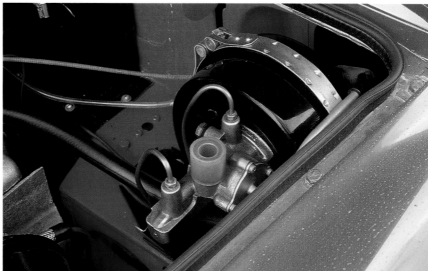

These two views (above) show the two types of Girling servo that may be found on the MGC: the green car is a very early one, while the red car has the type of servo found on all US models and also on other cars from around February 1968.

This Lockheed servo is from a 1973 model MGB but is typical of the unit found on all servo-equipped cars with single-line brakes from 1970 to 1977, when it was replaced by the direct-acting type.

However, on North American cars with dual-circuit brakes there were two servo units, for the front and rear brakes respectively. The rear servo at the right-hand rear of the engine compartment functioned on the rear brakes, while the front servo on a bracket on the right-hand side of the engine compartment adjacent to the oil filter functioned on the front brakes. The single servo on cars with a single-line braking system was mounted at the rear of the engine compartment, on the side opposite to the master cylinder box. The bracket for mounting the front servo to the side of the engine bay is found also on most cars with a single-line braking system, except on very early models. On North American cars with two servos, the pipes from both servos run through a joint pressure failure switch.

Apart from minor improvements to the thumb-button release, the handbrake assembly remained unchanged until 1971, and even thereafter the mod-ifications were minimal. On 1972 and later cars, the handbrake lever was cranked over to the right to clear the new centre console. The same handbrake grip was used throughout the production period. In the early years, different handbrake cables were found, depending on whether the car had a banjo or tubed rear axle, and differences also persisted depending on whether the car had disc wheels or wire wheels. In 1977, from car number 412301 (GT) or 415001 (roadster), the handbrake activating mechanism was re-designed and now featured the so-called rod-type plastic-coated cables with greaseless inner cables and no compensating lever. The purpose of this change was to improve clearance to the fuel tank. The MGC handbrake assembly was the same as found on contemporary MGBs, with only a difference in the cables to suit the Girling brake drums. The MGB GT V8 handbrake was identical to that of the four-cylinder cars of the period.

WHEELS & TYRES

Until 1969, the standard MGB wheel was a simple four-stud steel disc wheel with 12 oval ventilation holes. The roadster had 4J×14 wheels, the GT 5J×14 wheels. The alternative wheels were exactly the same in appearance, and were always painted in a silver-grey colour called Aluminium (paint code AL.1 in the BMC paint code system). These disc wheels had a very plain bright hubcap with no logo or embossing. Alternatively, Ace Mercury full-width louvred aluminium wheel discs were offered as factory-fitted optional equipment from 1963 to 1965, when they became a dealer-fitted accessory. They featured an octagonal centre piece with an embossed MG logo picked out in red. They were only offered until 1967 or possibly 1969.

Alternatively, centre-lock 60-spoke wire wheels were available as an optional extra, size 4½J×14 on both roadster and GT models. These wheels were normally also painted Aluminium, but chrome-plated wire wheels were fitted to the first 200 or so MGB roadsters for the USA in 1962 and became generally available in October 1965, continuing to be offered until June 1971. It is questionable whether they were always offered in the home market and, generally speaking, seem to have been most commonly found on cars exported to North America, but also on some cars bound for Europe. Wire wheels, incidentally, were standard on export GTs until 1969. Stronger 70-spoke wire wheels were quoted as competitions equipment for the MGB.

Wire wheels were retained by two-eared knock-ons, except when replaced by a simple octagonal hub nut in those markets where wing nuts were illegal (Germany and Switzerland from the start of production, some US states from 1965–66 and all of the USA from February 1967). From the start of Mark II production in late 1967 all export cars had octagonal nuts, and they were introduced on home market cars in August 1968 or possibly a little earlier. Both knock-ons and octagonal nuts had an altered section for increased strength from car number 28951 in January 1964, but were interchangeable with the earlier versions. Only a month later, from car number 30851 in February 1964, the hub threads were altered from 12 threads per inch to the coarser 8 threads per inch.

Knock-ons and octagonal nuts of all types were made of chrome-plated aluminium bronze and carried the words 'Right Side' or 'Left Side', and 'Undo' with arrows in the appropriate direction – but they never had the MG logo. An alternative type of octagonal nut was introduced in June 1972 but this was interchangeable with the previous type. Wire wheels were withdrawn from the German market in March 1972 as the wheel nuts protruded beyond the body line, contravening local regulations. In later years wire wheels became increasingly uncommon in all markets except for North America. However, they remained available in the home market until the end of production. In September 1976 the wire wheels were modified for improved tyre clearance to the wheelarches. Wire wheels were fitted to 208 of the 421 LE home market roadsters in 1980.

The MGC was fitted with 15in wheels, size 5J×15 for both disc and wire wheels on roadster and GT models. The disc wheels were quite different to the MGB style, with ten rectangular ventilation holes, hubcaps with characteristic bevelled edges and five-stud fixings. The MGC wire wheels, which were far more common than disc wheels, had 72 spokes. Both types of wheel were normally painted Aluminium, with optional chrome-plating for the wire wheels. The knock-ons and octagonal nuts for the wire wheels were the same as on the MGB.

Let us now dispose of a long-lived red herring: the MGC parts list claims that 1969 models were available with five-stud 15in Rostyle wheels. It can be

Fitted as standard equipment on MGB cars from 1962 to 1969, the pierced disc wheel was painted in a silver colour – probably the BMC colour 'Aluminium' – and fitted with this simple hubcap design. The narrow-band whitewall tyres seen on this car are probably not the correct type for a pre-1965 car.

Painted wire wheels were available throughout the production period, this one being from a 1980 LE roadster. Until 1968 some cars had knock-ons, but thereafter all wire-wheeled cars featured this octagonal nut.

stated quite categorically that there is not a single car listed in the production records with these wheels. They simply did not exist. The MGB parts list for Mark I/II models (AKD 3547) similarly claims that 1969 MGBs were available with Rostyle wheels, and chrome-plated ones at that. Again, no car so equipped has ever been found in the production records.

Rostyle wheels, however, replaced disc wheels on MGBs for the 1970 model year (GHN5/GHD5 series, from car number 187170). These wheels had a quartered design, with four prominent dividing spokes and two rectangular ventilation holes in each quarter circle. They were painted a combination of silver and black, and finished off with a small hubcap for the centre hole bearing a black and silver MG logo. From February 1970 or maybe a little earlier, chrome-plated Rostyle wheels were also available: the rim and spokes, normally painted silver, were chromed, with the central cloverleaf area still in black. They were at first offered only on export cars but became available in the home market on 1972 models. They were withdrawn from North America in August 1972, but at the same time became standard on non-North American export cars. They were discontinued in June 1976. The painted Rostyle wheel was standard wear until the end of production, with an altered paint finish on 1977 and later models.

The V8 had cast alloy wheels supplied by Dunlop, although actually only the wheel centres were cast, the rims being chrome-plated steel. These wheels featured ten square ventilation holes whose edges, like the circles around the wheel nuts, were a bright alloy finish, the wheel centres otherwise being painted black. Rim size was 5J×14, the wheels had four-stud fixing and special chrome-plated nuts fitted with captive washers, and the chrome-plated metal centre cap with a black and silver MG logo was similar in design to the Rostyle wheel cap. This cast alloy wheel was found also on the 1975 GT 'Jubilee' model, but on these cars the wheels were painted black and gold, while the hubcap was matt black with a dark green and gold MG badge. Similar wheels were fitted to the one-off 1975 North American roadster which was the millionth car built at Abingdon, and which was generally kitted out like the GT 'Jubilee' cars.

The final type of MGB wheel, in cast alloy with five spokes in a pentastar design, was found on the North American Limited Edition roadsters of 1979-80, on all the GT LE models, and on 213 of the roadster LE models. It was also optional equipment on non-LE home market cars in 1979 and 1980. The design of this wheel was based on that of the Triumph Stag. The rim size was 5J×14 and the wheels had the normal MGB four-stud fixing. These wheels were given an epoxy finish to overcome corrosion. The inset areas of the spokes and the recessed wheel centre were painted dark metallic grey, with rims, raised spoke edges and the raised circle around the centre

The 15in disc wheels fitted to the MGC were quite different from those on the MGB, with elongated instead of circular holes, and the characteristic bevelled edge to the hubcap.

Alternatively the MGC could be fitted with 72-spoke wire wheels, either painted or chrome-plated as seen here. The knock-ons were fitted only during the first year of MGC production.

in a lighter alloy colour. The small centre hubcaps carried the MG logo, which was silver and black on North American and non-LE home market models, but silver and red on the home market LE cars.

When the MGB was introduced, radial tyres were rare on British cars. The 1962 standard tyre on the MGB was a Dunlop Gold Seal nylon tubed crossply, size 5.60-14, available in either normal or whitewall versions. Alternatively, the keener motorist could specify Dunlop Road Speed RS5 tyres from January 1963, again with normal and whitewall versions, and again always fitted with inner tubes. The Road Speed tyres may have been standard equipment on early cars supplied to Germany. The whitewall versions of both the early types of crossply tyres had wide white bands beginning at the wheel rim.

In 1965, the standard crossply tyre was changed to Dunlop C41, of which the whitewall version had a

Rostyle wheels were introduced in 1969 and lasted with minor modifications until 1980. This 1973 car has the standard painted Rostyle wheel, but there was also a chrome version.

The V8 model had this style of composite wheel, with a cast alloy centre and a chrome-plated steel rim. This wheel was also found on the 1975 GT 'Jubilee' model, on which the bright parts were painted gold.

This cast alloy wheel is from a 1980 North American Limited Edition model, but the same wheel was also available as optional equipment on other cars in the 1979-80 period, and was found on most of the home market LE models built in 1980.

narrow white band with a black inner circle next to the wheel rim. In February 1971 the crossply tyres were changed to Dunlop D75, which remained the standard tyre for home market cars until March 1972 on GTs and August 1972 on roadsters. They may have been fitted to a few non-North American export cars later on, but were deleted in August 1973. The whitewall option was not available in the home market after the end of the 1969 model year.

Also in 1965, the optional Road Speed tyres were deleted and the MGB instead became available with radial tyres for the first time. The first type of radial tyre was Dunlop SP41, size 155-14 on roadsters and 165-14 on GTs. From March 1968, the SP41 was gradually replaced by the new SP68, which became the universal fitting by April 1969. The MGB was now specified with SR-rated tyres. Whitewall radial ply tyres were offered from December 1969, or possibly earlier, with narrow white bands which did not extend inwards to the wheel rim.

The MGC always had radial tyres, 165-15 Dunlop SP41 at first but 165HR-15 SP68 on 1969 models – note that HR-rated tyres were now specified on the MGC. Around the time MGC production stopped in August 1969, Michelin ZX and Pirelli Cinturato were also approved for fitting. From the start of the 1970 model year, radials became standard on North American MGBs.

The V8 in 1973 became the first MGB to be fitted with tubeless tyres. The tyre size was 175HR-14 and three different makes were specified – Goodyear G800 Grand Prix, Michelin XAS and Pirelli CN36. The 175HR-14 tyres were also fitted on the GT 'Jubilee' model. Home market four-cylinder cars with Rostyle wheels were only fitted with tubeless tyres from the start of 'rubber-bumper' production in 1974; by now the recommended Dunlop tyres were SP68 tubeless or SP73 Sport tubed. On 'rubber-bumper' cars, tyre size became 165SR-14 on roadsters and GTs. North American cars with Rostyle wheels continued with tubed tyres until 1976.

Steel-braced radial tyres were introduced instead of the textile-reinforced type in January/February 1978, and approval was at first given to Dunlop SP4, Pirelli P3 and Michelin XZX tyres, in tubed as well as tubeless versions. This was soon extended to Goodyear G888+S (tubed or tubeless), Uniroyal Rallye 180 and Firestone S1 (both only in tubeless form). Cars with cast alloy wheels in 1979-80 had low-profile tubeless tyres, of size 185/70SR-14, either Dunlop SP4 or Uniroyal Rallye.

MGB cars assembled abroad would typically have had locally-manufactured tyres. For instance Australian MGB cars originally often had Dunlop B7 crossply tyres made in Australia, and were later fitted with Olympic GT radials. These tyres always had inner tubes as wire wheels were standard equipment on the Australian cars.

ELECTRICS & LAMPS

The 12-volt electrical system was originally of the positive earth return type, but from the start of MGB Mark II production in 1967 a negative earth system was introduced and remained on all subsequent models, including the MGC and the MGB GT V8. Electrical components were originally all supplied by Lucas but some components on later models were sourced elsewhere.

With extreme variations in specifications and equipment over the years, the main wiring harness was changed time and time again. The harness was split into the so-called main harness for the front end of the car, and the body and boot harness, the two harnesses joining up in the scuttle area. Individual wires were typically PVC-covered with the normal Lucas colour code system, with a braided cloth cover for the main harness. There were additional sub-harnesses for some equipment which was not necessarily fitted as standard on all cars, such as the overdrive. The electrical system was protected by two main fuses rated at 35 amps until 1969, when a new fusebox with four fuses was fitted. In addition there were a number of line fuses for individual items.

Until 1974, two six-volt batteries were used, located in battery boxes under the tonneau floor behind the seats. The standard battery type was Lucas SG9E (or STGZ9E in dry-charged form on some export cars) until June 1966, when BT9E batteries without external bus-bars were introduced (BTZ9E dry-charged). Some export cars, including some for Canada, were supplied without batteries, and CKD cars would also typically have batteries supplied locally. Early MGB Police cars could be supplied with higher-capacity batteries, originally type SFLY17E-6 or SFF17E-6, which were bulkier and therefore required modified battery boxes. The MGC, later MGB Mark I Police cars and some cars supplied to cold countries had FG11E batteries (FGZ11E dry-charged); as the number indicates, these had 11 plates rather than the normal nine.

In June 1969, single-fill batteries were introduced, of type CA9E on MGB or CA11E on MGC (as well as MGB to special order). The 11-plate batteries were also fitted on the MGB GT V8. From the start of 'rubber-bumper' production, a single 12-volt battery was fitted in a new battery box under the right-hand side of the tonneau floor. This was typically also a Lucas battery with a single vent cover for all six cells. In February 1976 the original screw-fixing helmet-type battery terminals were replaced by battery cables with clamp fixings.

On most cars prior to 1967, current was supplied by a Lucas C40/1 dynamo, normally painted in the red engine colour. A Lucas RB340 control box was fitted to the right-hand side of the engine bay, together with the fusebox. The exception concerns MGB Mark I Police cars, for which originally a higher-output C42 dynamo was quoted, with a mod-

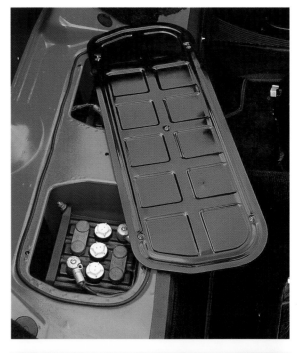

From 1962 to 1974, all cars had two six-volt batteries connected in series and fitted in battery boxes below the floor of the tonneau area, accessible through this joint cover panel.

The 'rubber-bumper' cars from 1974 to 1980 had a single 12-volt battery mounted in a box on the right-hand side of the tonneau floor, with this smaller cover.

ified control box, wider ½in fan belt and the larger batteries. In 1964, however, MGB Police cars became available with a Lucas 11AC alternator fitted in conjunction with a 2TR control unit.

On the Mark II models from 1967, together with the MGC, an alternator became standard on all cars. The 1967-68 cars used a 16AC alternator with a remote-mounted 4TR electronic control unit, but 1969 models had a 16ACR alternator with a built-in regulator. In March 1972, the 16ACR alternator was fitted with a modified regulator and a surge-protection device, and in February 1973 it was replaced by a 17ACR type. The final change was to an 18ACR alternator: although an exact change point is not available, it is thought that this occurred on all cars from June 1976. The V8 used an AC Delco alternator, number 7982707.

A Lucas M418G starter motor was fitted from the start of production, with a new armature shaft and drive assembly being introduced in January 1967. From the start of Mark II production, the original Bendix drive starter was replaced by a pre-engaged type under the same Lucas type number. A starter solenoid switch was fitted on the right-hand side of the engine compartment until 1967. It appears that a separate starter relay, type 6RA, was only fitted from the start of the 1970 model year.

A Lucas 2M100 starter motor was introduced together with the 18V engines for the 1972 model year, and continued until the end of production. In January 1976, a starter relay type 26RA was introduced instead of the 6RA type. While the MGC had used the same M418G starter motor as the MGB, the V8 was fitted with a 3M100 type starter motor. Starter motors were typically painted engine colour, red on all 18G engines until 1971, black afterwards, and silver-green on MGCs. All cars had key starting, either with a conventional ignition lock or from a combined ignition and steering lock.

Headlamps were originally Lucas F700 on all cars, of either the Mark VI or the Mark X type – the difference lies mainly in the design of the lamp unit retaining plate. The Mark X headlamps were introduced at different times depending on market specifications, but certainly by 1965 all cars had these later headlamps. Sealed beam units were fitted to RHD cars for home and export, and on cars for North America. Some early cars for the USA may have used sealed beam units of American manufacture but it seems that Lucas units were standardised in 1963. On RHD cars, the headlamps dipped to the left, on North American cars and non-European LHD cars they dipped to the right, while European cars had double vertical dip headlamps. Except for North America, LHD cars had ordinary light units with replaceable bulbs rather than sealed beam units, with special yellow bulbs being required for France, and a

An alternator became standard equipment from the start of Mark II production in 1967. Several different types were used over the years: on this 1969 model it is the 16ACR type with a built-in regulator. Only the alternator fan has received a dash of red paint, while the traces seen on the brackets for the alternator are typically overspray.

few cars for Germany in 1965 had the sidelamps built into the headlamps.

Improved sealed beam headlamps were introduced on RHD cars for the 1970 model year, and on 'rubber-bumper' cars the sealed beam headlamps were replaced by ordinary headlamps with built-in sidelamps, except on North American cars. While cars for the North American market continued with sealed beam headlamps with ordinary tungsten bulbs to the end of production in 1980, RHD cars were fitted with H4 halogen headlamps with built-in sidelamps from June 1976.

A headlamp flasher was optional at the start of production, and was operated by the indicator stalk switch on the steering column. It became standard on the GT from launch, and also became standard on the roadster (except for North America) from October 1965. From the start of Mark II production, if not earlier, the headlamp flasher was also fitted on North American cars. All cars had a foot dipswitch until 1967, but North American Mark II models had the main and dipped beam controlled by the combined indicator and headlamp flasher stalk switch. This arrangement was adopted on all other cars from the start of the 1970 model year.

'Chrome-bumper' cars generally had combined side/indicator lamps below the headlamps. Normally the lens for this lamp was white and amber, with the more prominent amber part (for the indicators) positioned towards the radiator grille. All-white lenses, however, were found on cars for the USA, Canada and Italy, and some other export cars may have had the lamps fitted so that the amber indicator was on the outside. On a few German cars in 1965, it appears that this lamp acted only as an indicator, as the sidelamps were built into the headlamps. From April 1966, Canadian cars adopted the amber indicator lenses, and on later cars for North America, probably from the start of the Mark II model in 1967, all-amber lenses were fitted. The lamp units were moved slightly closer to the radiator grille on 1969 models. On 1968 and 1969 model year North American cars a two-piece lens was still fitted, on 1970-74 models a single-piece lens was used, and a single bulb with twin filaments.

On the 'rubber-bumper' cars, new front indicator lamps were fitted in the bumper. On North American cars these units also incorporated the sidelamps. Lenses were amber on all cars except those for Italy, which still required white front indicator lenses. There are no known instances of cars being fitted in the factory with side repeater lamps for the front indicators, but such lamps were often fitted by importers in those European markets where they were a legal requirement. From the start of the 1969 model year, MGBs and MGCs were equipped with side marker reflectors for North American markets, of a small rectangular design fitted just behind the wheelarches, with amber lenses for the front and red lenses for the rear. From the start of the 1970 model year until the end of production, MGBs for North America had proper side marker lamps to front and rear wings, of a bullet-shaped design with black plinths, at the front fitted in front of the wheelarch, at the back moved further rearwards. On 1970 models they came on together with the headlamps, on all later cars together with the sidelamps.

The rear lamp units combined the stop and tail lamps with flashing indicators and reflectors. The only major change to the rear lamps occurred from the start of the 1970 model year when the lenses became larger and more angular in section. For most markets, the lenses for the indicators were amber and the stop/tail lamp lenses red, but cars for Italy and originally North America had red indicator lenses. Special bulbs were introduced for the German market in 1965. From the 1970 model year, North American cars also adopted amber lenses for the rear indicators. The indicator lamp was normally at the top of the unit, but on North American cars for the 1970 model year and later, it was moved down to the centre part, with the stop/tail lamp at the top.

Reversing lamps were introduced as standard on all cars from March/April 1967, with the point of introduction being quoted by body number. The small rectangular reversing lamps were mounted on the lower rear panel by either bottom corner of the boot lid and required slight depressions with apertures pressed in the panel. Lenses were usually white, but France required amber inserts inside the standard lenses. So-called 'diakon' lenses were introduced (except for France) in January 1972, and reversing (and rear) lamp lenses were given SAE markings in January 1973 to comply with North American regulations. In May/June 1977, the fixing screws were changed to the self-tapping type.

A pair of Lucas red rear fog guard lamps was fitted below the rear bumper from June 1979 on all home market 1980 models, but not on North American cars. Rear fog guard lamps became a legal requirement in the UK from 1 April 1980. The parts list does not specify exactly when they were introduced, but the switch for them was added in June 1979!

Hazard flashers were found on North American cars from the start of the MGB Mark II and MGC models in 1967. They were fitted to home market cars probably from the start of the 1974 model year, although the evidence is a little conflicting. They were certainly standard on the V8 from the start, while 1973-74 GT brochures quote them as an optional extra on four-cylinder cars in a package together with twin exterior mirrors and servo brakes, available only in the home market. They are not mentioned at all in 1974 roadster brochures, but handbooks and workshop manuals seem to suggest they were fitted to all 1974 models, and they were certainly found on

Lucas sealed beam headlamps were fitted to all cars until 1974, and for most markets the combined sidelamps and indicators had white and amber lenses.

Mark I cars for North America (and the much rarer Italian specification cars) were fitted with all-white sidelamp lenses.

'rubber-bumper' cars. Until 1967, an FL5 flasher unit was fitted, replaced on Mark II and MGC cars by an 8FL unit – although German cars reverted in 1971 to the FL5 type. A separate flasher unit, typically a Lucas 9FL, was fitted for the hazard warning flashers.

A pair of number plate lamps, Lucas type L534, was fitted to all cars from the start of production, one each on the inside of the rear bumper overriders. From 1965, German cars were fitted with two L467 lamps on a special rear number plate bracket, and a similar arrangement (although with a different bracket) was adopted for Japan. For 1970 model year cars for North America, a pair of L749 number plate lamps was tucked inside the ends of the rear quarter bumpers. This arrangement lasted only one year, as all 1971 models – including those for North America, Japan and Germany – had their number plate lamps mounted on the overriders.

When in early 1974 North American cars acquired big rubber overriders, these cars were fitted with number plate lamps on the number plate bracket, of a unique design which thereafter stayed the same in principle on North American cars. However, from June 1976 these lamps were made by L.E.Pirie rather than Lucas, and in March 1977 their finish was changed from chrome to black.

Non-North American cars from January to September 1974 had two Lucas L780 number plate lamps mounted on the central part of the rear bumper bar between the overriders. With the coming of the 'rubber-bumper' model, non-North American cars were fitted with number plate lamps on the rear number plate bracket, but these cars used the classic L467 design, with the twin-bulb L467/2 type being used on German cars from March 1975. Originally finished in chrome-plate, these lamps later became black on all cars, probably from November 1976.

Originally, the only means of illuminating the interior had been the facia-mounted map light with its adjacent switch. For the GT, a roof lamp was added on the rear header rail from the start of Mark II production in 1967, and was activated either by courtesy switches in the doors or by a switch on the lamp. From August 1970, door-operated courtesy switches were added also on the roadster model. The door switches on both roadster and GT now operated a new facia-mounted lamp on North American cars, or the old-style map light on non-North American vehicles, but in August 1971 the North American courtesy lamp was specified for all cars and the map light was discontinued. GT models continued with the roof lamp, but from August 1970 this was activated by a courtesy switch at the top of the tailgate. At the same time, roadsters were fitted with a boot lamp, with a switch operated by the boot lid. A new round courtesy lamp was fitted to the facia of all RHD cars from June 1976, while North American cars had a rectangular lamp fitted on the lower edge of the facia, with a switch built into its rocking lens.

Lucas 9H horns were fitted from the start of production. A single high-note horn was standard on home market cars until the start of the 1970 model year, with an additional low-note horn quoted as optional equipment in the home market. All export cars and later home market cars had twin horns as standard, as did MGCs. It is likely that most pre-1970 home market MGBs were in fact fitted with twin horns. The horns were at first located on the bonnet locking platform, but they were moved in January 1963 to the wheelarch panel where they were mounted horizontally on new angled brackets. Despite slight changes, the 9H horns stayed in use until 1974, when the 'rubber-bumper' models were given Mixo horns, which remained in use until the end of production.

The wiper motor on early roadsters was a Lucas DR3A, giving 106° of wipe with 10in blades on 10¼in arms. The GT, with its higher windscreen, required longer blades and 12in arms, and the wiper motor was quoted as a type 12W, giving 115° of wipe. GT wiper blades were 11in until 1967, then 13in until August 1972, when 12in blades were introduced. From the start of Mark II and MGC production, roadster and GT models were fitted with the same 14W two-speed wiper motor. On North American roadsters for the 1969 model year, three wipers were fitted to comply with legal requirements governing the wiped area of the windscreen, and the triple wipers were also fitted to 1970 and later export cars for Sweden, Germany and Norway. The GT retained two wipers for all markets. At the end of 1968, the Lucas wiper blades and arms were replaced by Magnatex items. In August 1972, the chrome-plated wipers were replaced by matt black ones. Some later

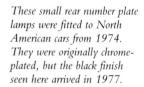

The lens for the combined rear lamp unit was of this type (far left, top) until 1969, with amber indicator at the top, red tail/stop lamp in the centre and reflector at the bottom. On North American and Italian cars of this period, however, the indicator lens was also red. This 1969 car also has reversing lamps and the number plate lamps are in the overriders. From 1969, larger and more angular lenses were adopted for the rear lamps (far left, below). The indicator lenses became amber on North American cars, but the indicator was then normally in the centre of the lamp unit, as can be seen on this 1977 model. This car also has the sidemarker lamp on the rear wing. By contrast, the more familiar home market rear lamps (near left) still had the amber indicator at the top. On this 1980 car, one of the two rear fog guard lamps below the bumper can be seen.

cars – at least GTs – used Trico windscreen wipers.

Of other electrical accessories, a heated rear window was made available as an optional extra on the GT in July 1966 and was subsequently also available in a tinted version. With the exception of some export cars, it became standard in August 1972. Triplex Hotline was the type most often seen, but some late cars had a Sicursiv rear window. A radio aerial mounted in the driver's front wing, together with a pair of door-mounted loudspeakers, became standard on North American cars from the start of the 1977 model year in June 1976, but only appeared on RHD cars on the 1979 models in May/June 1978. Radios, which were generally not factory-fitted, are discussed in the section about extras and accessories.

North American cars from the 1970 model year were fitted with an 'anti-theft warning buzzer' which sounded if the driver's door was opened with the steering lock key in the off or auxiliary positions. From December 1971, North American cars incorporated an audible seat belt warning system as well as a warning light, both of which would operate if the ignition was switched on or a gear selected without both the driver's and the passenger's seat belts being fastened. This originally had a mechanical buzzer, but this was replaced by an electronic type in July 1973.

From August 1973 to February 1975, North American cars had the delightful sequential seat belt warning system which rendered the starter motor inoperative unless both driver and passenger had put

on their seat belts. This must have gone down like the proverbial lead balloon in New Hampshire, where the state motto is 'Live free or die'! On later cars, this particular piece of big-brotherism was replaced by a time delay system where the warning light and buzzer came on for 8sec if the ignition and starter were operated before the seat belts were fastened. Owners of RHD cars were spared such indignities, although 1977 and later RHD cars were fitted with a seat belt warning lamp which would flash if the ignition/starter was operated without the driver having buckled up.

These small rear number plate lamps were fitted to North American cars from 1974. They were originally chrome-plated, but the black finish seen here arrived in 1977.

LIMITED EDITIONS

The first limited edition of the MGB will be virtually unknown to most UK readers as it was marketed only in the USA. This was 'the first anniversary MGB GT Special', an edition of 1000 cars which appeared in 1967 a year after the American introduction of the GT. The special equipment fitted to these cars was added by the US dealers at point of sale. A plaque was mounted on each front wing just in front of the door bearing an octagonal Union Jack and the words 'MGB/GT Special'. There was a 16in wood-rimmed steering wheel, a matching Australian coach wood gear lever knob, and a vibration-free non-glare racing wing mirror on the driver's side. Wire wheels were standard, and so probably were whitewall tyres. The advertising did not mention whether the overdrive was available. Efforts at identifying these cars in the Abingdon production records have proved fruitless.

Some words must be said about the University Motors Specials, although these MGC cars were not factory products. The subject was covered in detail in Graham Robson's book *The Mighty MGs* (David and Charles, 1982). When MGC production was coming to an end in 1969, University Motors, the long-standing MG main distributor for London, bought on a bulk basis some cars, mostly GTs, remaining in factory stock. The number of cars has been estimated between 141 and 176. Some, but by no means all, of these cars were transformed with Downton-tuned engines, in ultimate stage 3 form

with three SU carburettors, special exhausts and a Downton-modified cylinder head carrying their stamp and number. Power output was claimed to be 174bhp at 5500rpm.

A distinguishing feature of the University Motors Specials was a new grille with bold horizontal black alloy slats in the original chrome-plated frame. Many cars had special paint jobs, such as a contrast-colour roof or black paint on the part of the bonnet bulge in front of the chrome trim. Other features were an under-bumper air dam, Koni shock absorbers, a Motolita steering wheel and J.A.Pearce centre-lock cast alloy wheels. Some cars were partially re-trimmed and a few GTs had rear seats modified to give more room, while some may have been fitted with a fabric sunroof. A 'U.M.S.' badge was fitted at the front of the bonnet. Not all cars had all of the features listed here and it is probable that no two of them were alike.

John Hall's 1975 'Jubilee' GT was one of 751 cars of this type, with a gold tape stripe for its Racing Green paintwork and V8-style wheels partly painted gold.

A rare sight: the original 'limited edition' plaque (below left) bearing the 'car number' and the name of the original owner, who in this case still has the car. The gold tape stripe (below) incorporates this logo on each front wing. Uniquely on this model, the body trim strips (visible below the gold stripe) were painted body colour.

All are thought to have been sold when new in the UK. Again, the Abingdon production records are of no help in identifying them.

It was decided that 1975 would be the right year to celebrate MG's 50th anniversary, although strictly speaking this was a year or two late. But it was the 50th anniversary of 'Old Number One', the first real MG sports car. A special limited edition of the MGB GT was brought out, called the 'Jubilee' (or sometimes 'Anniversary') model. The intention was to make 750 of these cars, but when one was destroyed in a TV advertising stunt a replacement was built, bringing the total to 751. The cars were built between April and June 1975 and carried car numbers from G-HD5/374858-G to G-HD5/379588-G.

The 'Jubilee' model was painted Racing Green (BLVC 25), a standard MGB colour during the 1971 model year and also known as New Racing Green, and had a gold tape decoration scheme on each flank, incorporating the MG badge surrounded by a laurel wreath and the legend '1925-1975'. Special equipment included V8-style cast alloy wheels painted gold and black, and overdrive, headrests and tinted glass were all standard. A black-spoked steering wheel and matt black door mirrors were unique to the model. The trim colour was black and these cars had full carpeting, which was not yet offered on ordinary MGBs or V8 models. The front and rear badges, and the steering wheel badge, were all of the 'gold' type commonly found on 1975 calendar year MG cars.

Each of the 'Jubilee' cars was shipped from the factory with a numbered plaque. The idea was that the selling dealer should arrange to have the name of the first owner engraved on the plaque, which could then be fitted on the facia. But most plaques were probably never fitted to the cars at all, and often became separated from the cars when they changed hands. Unfortunately the 'limited edition' numbers were found only on the plaques and were not recorded by the factory. Replica plaques are now available but the correct number is most often not known.

In addition, three other MG cars were decorated in a scheme similar to the 'Jubilee' models. One was a Midget which was raffled among the workforce and still exists with a minimum mileage (see *Original Sprite & Midget* by Terry Horler, Bay View Books, 1993); one was an MGB GT V8 (G-D2D1/2605-G in June 1975) which was sold to the British School of Motoring as a high-speed instruction vehicle; and one MGB Roadster to North American specification was billed as the millionth car built at Abingdon. This landmark MG, car number G-HN5-UG/388950-G (October 1975), was raffled in the bi-centennial year of 1976 among members of The New England MG T Register and was won by Bryan Wladis and George Cookson. The car, affectionately known as 'Millie', was last reported in the care of Don Bridger, who runs an MG parts business in Arkansas. It was, incidentally, painted Brooklands Green, but had the gold tape stripe and cast alloy wheels of the UK-market 'Jubilee' GTs.

To increase interest in the ageing MGB in the North American markets, the 'Limited Edition' roadster (also known as the 'Special') was launched in 1979, continuing into 1980. This model was originally sold throughout North America, but at the end of

This plaque was fitted on the glovebox lid of the 1979-80 American Limited Edition model.

The 1979-80 American Limited Edition model in black, dressed up with its special cast alloy wheels, tape stripe and front spoiler – as well as an appropriate front number plate.

On the home market LE cars of 1980, the front spoiler was of the same type that had been fitted on the American Limited Edition cars.

'And now the end is near'. This 1980 LE roadster from the BMIHT collection at Gaydon was the last but one of all MGBs. Finished in Bronze Metallic, it has the wire wheels found on some of these LE roadsters.

1979 it was withdrawn from California (as were all MGBs) and so 1980 models were sold only in the 49 states and Canada. As no fewer than 6682 cars were built, one questions the description 'limited'! The cars were produced from March 1979 (car number 492071), the last Californian car was 500344 (December 1979) and the last Federal car of all was 523000 (August 1980), which was presented by Graham Whitehead of Jaguar Rover Triumph Inc to Henry Ford II for the Ford Museum, which has since sold it. What may be the factory development car for the 'Limited Edition', registered AJO 788V, was photographed for my book *The MG Story* (Haynes, 1982) when it was owned by the Beer family. It featured non-North American silver and grey nylon seats.

The 'Limited Edition' cars were all black, and came with either black or beige trim. They had a silver striped tape scheme just above the sill, between the wheelarches and behind the rear wheelarch, with a Union Jack motif incorporating the letters MGB on the front wing. The wheels were five-spoke cast alloys, similar in design to Triumph Stag wheels and partly painted dark metallic grey. The cars had an under-bumper air dam in black hard rubber at the front. In the interior was a special three-spoke light alloy steering wheel with a leather-covered rim, and on the glovebox lid a plaque with the MG badge and the words 'Limited Edition' in gothic script.

The 'Limited Edition' model was available with or without overdrive. A tonneau cover was standard. Equipment added by the North American distributors typically included a luggage rack, floor mats and a stereo radio, all American-sourced, and sometimes air conditioning, which was never available from the factory. The 'Limited Edition' cars had their spoilers added in the USA or Canada, and both spoilers and tape stripes were of American manufacture.

Finally, there were the UK-market 'LE' models. These were not quite the last 1000 cars built – not by VIN numbers anyway. The first LE roadster was car number 518492 (but most cars were from 518988) and the first LE GT was car number 519867 (most from 519999). These cars were built between August and October 1980, but they were stockpiled and only released for sale in January 1981. The last roadster, 523001, and the last GT, 523002, were both completed on 22 October 1980 and went straight into BL's Heritage collection. Both have been photographed for this book at The Heritage Motor Centre at Gaydon, where they can normally be seen. There were 580 GTs, all with cast alloy wheels, and 421 roadsters, of which 208 had wire wheels and 213 had cast alloy wheels.

The sister car to the LE roadster, also from the BMIHT collection, was this LE GT in Pewter Metallic with cast alloy wheels: car number 523002 was the last of all MGBs and came off the assembly line at Abingdon on 22 October 1980.

The wheels were the main item of special equipment on these cars. The cast alloy wheels were the same type as found on the American 'Limited Edition' models, while the wire wheels were the standard 60-spoke versions. The tape scheme was also the same as found on American models – but was gold on roadsters – and exterior mirrors were fitted on both doors. The front bumper and steering wheel badges were red, as were the hubcap badges on the cast alloy wheels. The front spoiler was the same as found on the North American 'Limited Edition' model. Both this and the tape stripes were imported from the USA. The paint colours, taken from the Princess saloon range, were Pewter Metallic (with silver and grey trim) on GTs or Bronze Metallic (with orange and brown trim) on roadsters. The paint colour codes stamped on the VIN plates were MMD (Pewter) or BMC (Bronze). Otherwise there was no special equipment on the cars, which nevertheless sold quickly and at rather higher than normal list prices. Some were kept in dealer showrooms for quite some time and registered late, a few may not have been registered at all, and it is not only the Heritage cars which have been preserved in mint condition with low mileage. The 'LE' cars were neither individually numbered nor fitted with commemorative plaques.

One must draw the line somewhere and I do not intend in this section to discuss vehicles which could not be called production cars, whether experimental cars (such as the O-series engined MGBs), or the 1972 experimental safety MGB GT (SSV1), or the works competition cars (which are overdue for a book of their own). But it is worth mentioning finally three

The cast alloy LE wheels were the same as those on the American Limited Edition cars, except for the red background colour of the hubcap. The silver version of the tape stripe was also the same, although the Bronze Metallic home market LE roadsters had a gold-coloured version of the tape scheme.

cars which were not all that special but each of which has a bit of history attached.

The 250,000th MGB was a Blaze MGB GT built on 27 May 1971 to North American specification. Although originally scheduled to have car number 252280, with a bit of sleight-of-hand it was instead given the special number G-HD5-UB/250000-G (in the middle of a batch of roadster car numbers). It was awarded by British Leyland Motors Inc in a sweepstake which attracted 80,000 entries, the lucky winner being one Bill Newton of Alabama. The half-millionth MGB, car number 509313 built on 17 January 1980, was a North American specification 'Limited Edition' roadster. Now owned by Moss Motors in California, it has covered only around 100 miles. Finally, G-HD5/431669-G, a Tahiti Blue GT built in April 1977 and labelled as the 'Silver Jubilee' car, was unusually equipped with a factory-fitted radio, and became a raffle prize for the Vale of the White Horse District Council.

COUNE BERLINETTE

The MGB Coune Berlinette is by any standards a very unusual variation. Mike Akers' car is one of possibly eight survivors and the only car of this type to have been in Britain since new.

Jacques Coune was a gifted Belgian coachbuilder whose workshop in Brussels turned out, among other projects, Mercedes-Benz based estate cars and a convertible based on the Volvo 'Amazon' 121/122. At the Brussels Motor Show in January 1964, he exhibited the first example of his interpretation of a GT car based on the MGB – the Berlinette. By June of that year, he was reported to be turning out 12 to 15 cars a month, and to be looking for a British company which might be prepared to assemble four cars a month.

Over a period of approximately two years, Coune created some 56 of these coachbuilt cars, each costing about two-thirds more than an MGB roadster. Apart from Belgium, they were sold in The Netherlands, Germany and France. When MG's own much cheaper MGB GT was introduced in October 1965, the Berlinette became a lost cause. The final attempt was a one-off 'Spider' shown at Turin in 1966, resembling the Berlinette but with a targa-style roof, notch-

back tail and fixed rear window *cum* roll bar. There are eight known surviving Berlinettes including the only RHD car, which is owned by Mike Akers and illustrated here. At least one more Berlinette resides in the UK, having been recently imported from The Netherlands.

The Akers car has a particularly interesting history. It was ordered by Walter Oldfield, managing director of Nuffield Press (BMC's printing and publishing subsidiary at Cowley), and came off the Abingdon production line in April 1964 as a standard Tartan Red roadster, supplied without hood and fittings. It was immediately shipped to Brussels and converted by Coune on Oldfield's orders. It seems to have been finished by June 1964, when it returned to the UK and was registered in Oxfordshire as CBW 55B. The car was considered as a production possibility by Alec Issigonis and George Harriman of BMC, but was eventually rejected as 'too Italian looking'. BMC instead went ahead with Syd Enever's GT design, as

refined by Pininfarina. Oldfield kept the car until 1978, when it was acquired by the present owner with 24,000 miles on the clock. By 1994, the mileage had advanced to 31,000.

Some of the Coune Berlinettes were based on new cars which were obtained – at dealer discount – from the Belgian MG importer. Others were based on cars brought to the company by customers. One possibility that remains unproven is that some Berlinettes were based on CKD cars exported to Belgium from May 1964. This would certainly have made life easier for Monsieur Coune and his Italian panelbeaters!

The modifications were quite extensive. All of the sheet metal behind the doors was cut away, leaving just the wheelarches and the floorpan. To provide extra rigidity, a three-sided box section was welded between the wheelarches. Further metal strengthening was carried out at the rear of the car. The first few cars had the roof and new rear body made in metal, but a one-piece fibreglass assembly was soon substituted. The shape was a graceful fastback with a fixed rear window and a small boot lid between this and the Kamm-style recessed vertical tail panel. All of the glass was unique, including quarterlights and drop glasses in the doors.

Other body modifications included headlamps set further back than normal and covered with perspex cowls (this conversion was also offered by Coune for MGB roadsters). The chrome trim strip along the side of the car was deleted and the holes filled. All four

wings were teased out in small wheelarch lips. The rear bumper was unique, and most cars had vertical overriders above the rear bumper. There was also a slim front bumper with similar overriders on the 1964 show car, but production cars used the standard MGB front bumper. Round rear lamp units were fitted, probably standard units from some European car – possibly the Simca 1000. Most cars had little badges

The rear end of the Coune Berlinette shows a distinctly Italian influence, with a Kamm-type tail design similar to some Ferraris of the time. The cowled headlamps are actually set further back in the wings.

The interior is at first glance like that of a nice original 1964 MGB, but the wood-rim steering wheel is non-standard and the rear view mirror is mounted on the scuttle, just out of sight. The scuttle panel itself has additional padding. Behind the seats it is a different story, with a large luggage platform with this quilted cover.

Monsieur Coune's plate appeared on both rear pillars.

on the rear quarter pillars and the bonnet locking platform marked 'Jacques Coune – Carrossier'. The original show car was red (shade unknown), but the Akers car is metallic silver-blue and has a strip of Dynotape on the bonnet locking platform stamped 'Peinture Acrilique Lucite'. The cars could be painted in any colour desired by the original customer.

The interior specification could also be adjusted according to customer preference. The Akers car has standard front seats but some cars are said to have been specially trimmed – but trim colours are not known. Many cars had wood-rimmed light-alloy steering wheels of various patterns. The rear-view mirror was mounted on a stem above the facia. The scuttle panel behind the windscreen was given extra padding and sometimes fluted. A typical Coune feature was that

The rear end was all new. While the rear bumper is unique, this car seems to have the standard overriders with number plate lamps that appear to have no function – this car has an additional number plate lamp fitted below the centre section of the bumper.

While the luggage area was accessible from within the car, the other way of reaching it was through this small external boot lid below the rear screen.

the headlining was quilted. A quilted cover was also provided for the generous luggage platform behind the seats. Some cars had a folding rear seat for children, and this may have become standard on the later Berlinettes. The boot lid was opened by a remote control behind the driver's seat. Fibreglass matting was used extensively for sound-deadening between the external skin and the inner structure.

The completed car was stated to be 126lb (57kg) lighter than a standard roadster. As the aerodynamics were also improved, the claimed top speed of 180kph (112mph) seems quite realistic – less so the 195kph (121mph) which has also been claimed. The only mechanical alteration was a dual Abarth exhaust system, an Italian product for which Coune held the Belgian agency.

The Coune Berlinette was a splendid effort and remains a fascinating car. But in commercial terms, it was a lost cause from the start.

The only mechanical alteration on the Coune Berlinette was this Abarth dual exhaust system (far left). The wheelarch lips (left) were unique to the Berlinette and also meant additional work for the panelbeaters.

OPTIONAL EQUIPMENT

The items listed in this section are those that could be fitted in the factory when a car was manufactured, as opposed to dealer-fitted accessories or competition parts (see later sections). Because there was some overlap between these categories, the same item may be listed in more than one section. Optional equipment discussed here will be listed roughly in the order that it was introduced.

Oil cooler Always standard on export cars, except North American cars of the 1975-80 model years. Optional in home market until 1964, when it became standard. See section on cooling system (page 78).

Car radio Usually a Smiths HMV Radiomobile in the UK, available in manual tuning or push-button versions, medium wave only, long/medium wave, or medium/shortwave. Supplied with loudspeaker and aerial. Soon discontinued except for some export cars and company vehicles, and became dealer-fit instead. Factory-fitted loudspeakers were found on North American cars from June 1976, on UK cars from May 1978, together with a wing-mounted aerial. In the USA, many locally-supplied dealer-fit radios were marked with the legend 'British Motor Corporation' or 'British Leyland'.

Heater and demister Standard on export models except for some hot climates (Australia). Standard for home market from October/November 1968, and for all export cars from April 1975. Alternatively a fresh-air unit could be fitted for export, discontinued for Australia in April 1969 and a year later for all markets. See section on cooling system (page 78).

Road Speed tyres Possibly offered only from early 1963 (but may have been standard on early cars to Germany), discontinued in 1965 and replaced by radial tyres. See section on wheels and tyres (page 95).

Whitewall tyres Popular mostly in American markets, but quoted in the home market until October 1969. Whitewall radial tyres also available, 1969 and later. Continued for North American market until 1980.

Wire wheels, painted Available in 60-spoke form throughout production, but rarely seen in the home market after 1974. See section on wheels and tyres (page 95).

Wire wheels, chrome-plated Fitted to the first 200 cars built for North American markets in 1962 but only quoted as a regular option on the GT at introduction in 1965 and shortly afterwards on the roadster. Discontinued in June 1971.

Twin horns Standard on export cars from the start of production, and on home market cars from October 1969.

Wing mirror Usually Desmo Boomerang Continental in the UK, quoted as factory-fit until 1965, then dealer-fit. Other mirrors were also available for dealer-fit, see section on accessories (page 114). Exterior mirrors standard on 1968 model year and later North American cars. Two door-mounted mirrors standard on V8 from 1973, and offered as extra on four-cylinder GT; standard on all home models from October 1974 to 1977, subsequently mirror on driver's door only, except 1980 LE models which had two mirrors. In the first years of production, a wing mirror was always added if the luggage carrier was factory-fitted.

Fog lamp (one or two) or fog lamp and long-range driving lamp Factory-fit only to 1963 (home market) or 1965 (export), afterwards dealer-fit except on Personal Export Delivery cars.

Tonneau cover Standard on home market cars from August 1972 and on North American export models from December 1977 (although it appears some later North American cars still lacked a factory-supplied tonneau cover).

Anti-roll bar Standard on GT model from start of production in 1965 and on roadster from November 1966. Other stiffer front anti-roll bars were listed as competition parts (page 117). Omitted on 'rubber-bumper' roadster from September 1974 to June 1976. A rear anti-roll bar was never optional but became standard equipment in June 1976.

This was the only style of hard top offered by the factory from 1963 to the end of production. Originally available in a variety of colours, from 1966 it came only in black. A white hard top, therefore, is not strictly correct on this Pale Primrose Yellow car, as this colour was only introduced in 1967! But it looks pretty...

Headlamp flasher and switch Standard on GT model from start of production and on roadster from October 1965 – except where not permitted by local regulations. Standard in North America only from start of Mark II production in late 1967.

Folding hood In original form, optional until August 1970, when both this and the standard pack-away hood were replaced by an improved folding hood design. See the section on weather equipment (page 53).

Luggage carrier Fitted on the boot lid, chrome-plated with tubular frame, cross bars and rear guard, supported on two skis which bolted to the boot lid with rubber interleaving strips. If factory-fitted, a driver's side wing mirror was also supplied. After 1965 available only as an accessory, except on some export cars. A different style carrier was available for North American cars.

Ashtray Fitted on the transmission tunnel in front of the gear lever. Standard on export cars from August 1968, on home market cars from December 1969.

Front bumper overriders Standard on export cars from start of production, on all GTs, and on home market roadsters from 1966. In practice, early home market cars almost invariably also had front bumper overriders – only one or two cars are known not to have had them.

Rear compartment cushion Available in main trim and piping colour combinations to suit all trim schemes. Discontinued in 1969. Also available as an accessory.

Cigar lighter Also offered as an accessory. Standard on GT during 1972 model year, and on roadster from start of 1973 model year. On North American cars, standard on Mark II models (1968 model year) and all cars thereafter.

Steering column 1½in longer than normal Quoted until approximately 1966, but one wonders if it was ever actually fitted to a production car.

Map pocket This was fitted to the scuttle side liner in the passenger footwell, in various colours to match the trim. Fitted as standard on the GT in 1965 and on North American roadsters from 1967, as well as on all MGCs. Not available on home market road-sters after 1971; 1974 GTs may have had two map pockets, but later GTs had only one.

Passenger footrest The same item was also quoted as a competition part. The following quote is taken from British Leyland Special Tuning data sheets: 'These enable the passenger to comfortably brace themselves against the seat when the car is being driven in a spirited manner.'

Ace Mercury wheel discs Offered from 1962 (or maybe 1963) to 1965, then a dealer-fitted accessory, possibly discontinued in 1967 (and certainly by 1969 as they were not suitable for Rostyle wheels).

The items listed above were those which were quoted at the time the new model was introduced in 1962. The second part of the list concerns items which became available later on:

Overdrive Available from January 1963. Standard on V8 model 1973-76, and on RHD four-cylinder cars in 1976. Remained an option on North American cars to the end of production, and always compara-tively rare in these markets. See the section on the manual gearbox (page 82).

Hard top Available from June 1963. Officially listed in the home market until 1976, and still fitted to a few export cars through to 1979-80. See section on weather equipment (page 53). In the USA in 1978 and later, dealers would sometimes give a free hard top away with the car as an incentive to buy.

Radial-ply tyres Introduced instead of Road Speed tyres in 1965, and standard on all cars from 1973. See

Inside a car with a hard top (below left). The top fits in the hood mounting sockets and to the hood brackets on the rear tonneau panel, as well as with clamps to the windscreen frame. This car also has the early type of static seat belts. The map pocket on the side of the passenger footwell (below) was always standard on GTs. The rubber mat seen here is not original.

This is quite an unusual radio, found in a 1964 roadster, and more likely to be of American manufacture – no known British radios were ever marked 'British Motor Corporation'.

This is the most common type of door mirror fitted to MGBs. Although it only appeared as standard fit on the V8 model in 1973 and afterwards also on four-cylinder cars, it has been retro-fitted on many earlier cars as well. A matt black version was found only on the 1975 GT 'Jubilee'.

section on wheels and tyres (page 95).

Heated rear window Available on GT model from 1966, but always standard on home market GTs from August 1972.

Reversing lamps May have been factory-fitted as optional equipment on some cars before becoming standard equipment in March-April 1967.

Locking petrol cap, badge bar Usually both were quoted only as accessories but were factory-fitted on some cars (mainly export models) in the 1960s.

With the introduction of the MGB Mark II and MGC models in 1967, there were some alterations to the list of optional equipment, the most notable being the addition of:

Automatic gearbox Available from 1967-68 to 1973. Not offered on MGB in North America.

Hazard warning lights Standard on North American cars from 1967, and on V8 from 1973. Available on home market four-cylinder GTs 1973-74 together with brake servo and twin door mirrors. Standard on all 'rubber-bumper' cars.

Metallic paint finish Choice of Metallic Golden Beige or Riviera Silver Blue. Standard on MGC GT, optional on MGC roadster and MGB GT, not available on MGB roadster. Discontinued late 1968.

The following is a list of those items which were specifically quoted for the MGC models and which will also, broadly speaking, summarise those options which could be fitted to the MGB in the period 1967-69. Availability differed depending on market, some items being standard for certain markets, others only being available on export cars.

Wire wheels Painted or chrome-plated
Wheel discs For disc wheels
Cigar lighter
Heater Alternatively, fresh-air unit
Fog lamp, long range driving lamp
Wing mirror
Radio
Passenger footrest
Overdrive
Automatic gearbox

Folding hood Roadster only
Luggage carrier, with wing mirror Roadster only
Tonneau cover Roadster only
Hard top Roadster only
Rear compartment cushion Roadster only
Heated rear window GT only

On the MGB Mark II models, the only variations compared to the MGC were that radial tyres were an option (standard on MGC), and the ashtray, second low-note horn and map pocket (roadster) were also options on the MGB but standard on the MGC.

Seat belts Factory-fitted static seat belts were supplied on North American Mark II and MGC vehicles from late 1967 but remained dealer-fit in the UK until January 1971, when they became standard factory-fit. Later static seat belts were gradually replaced by inertia reel belts.

Headrests Standard on North American cars for 1969 model year. Optional in the home market from April 1970, standard from June 1976.

Brake servo Optional on cars with single-line braking system from February 1970. Standard on V8 model, and on all home market cars from August 1973. Not offered in North America until standardised on North American 'rubber-bumper' models from December 1974 onwards (1975 model year). Also standard on all MGCs.

Chrome-plated Rostyle wheels Offered between February 1970 and June 1976, with some variation depending on market.

Tinted glass Available only on GT. Standard on North American cars from start of 1971 model year, optional on home market cars from start of 1972 model year. Standard on V8 and on 1975 'Jubilee' GT. Standard on all GTs from June 1976.

The V8 model was particularly well equipped, with the following items all being standard: overdrive, cast alloy wheels, tinted glass, headrests, brake servo, two door mirrors, hazard warning lights and inertia-reel front seat belts. The only item listed as an option in the brochure was a radio, and that was available only for export. Since no V8s were officially exported, they must have been joking...

When the 1977 models were introduced, the only quoted home market option was painted wire wheels. Everything else was now either standard or had been discontinued. Factory-fitted options still quoted for 1977 North American models included overdrive, tonneau cover and whitewall tyres, apart from the wire wheels.

Only one addition to the list of options was introduced later. This was cast alloy wheels, introduced around March 1979 and fitted to small numbers of home market cars, apart from the North American 'Limited Edition' models and most of the home

This luggage rack is another American-made item, of the type commonly seen on the 1979-80 Limited Edition models as well as other late US-specification cars.

market LE cars of late 1980. The only other option at the end of production was wire wheels, and overdrive and whitewall tyres on North American cars.

It is not my intention to list within this section items which were peculiar only to specific export markets, but which were part of the standard specification for these markets, nor items which were found initially only on export cars but later became standard also on home market cars (such as octagonal wheel nuts, steering lock). It would be worthwhile, however, to quote details of the rather special 'option pack' which was fitted on UK Police cars, most notably for the Lancashire Constabulary. This equipment included larger-capacity batteries (if necessary in larger battery boxes), special wiring prepared for a variety of extras, a Lucas ammeter, an 11AC alternator (on Mark I models until 1967), a specially calibrated speedometer and heavy-duty rear springs (Police roadsters were often fitted with GT springs). Police cars were normally painted a special colour called Police White and inevitably took black trim and hood (or, if black was not available, the darkest trim colour available). One well-known early V8 was prepared by British Leyland as a Police demonstrator and the Thames Valley force used six V8s as 'unmarked pursuit cars'. A few MGCs were also supplied as Police cars.

Finally, a word on some items which, despite persistent rumours, were *not* available. There was never a factory-fitted sunroof for the GT model. However, the fact that a particular GT in North America is known to have been supplied with a British sunroof when new has led me to conclude that, in the case of Personal Export Delivery and similar cars, MG would farm out the finished car to a company like Webasto or Goldie to have a sunroof installed. The other is air conditioning, never fitted in the factory, but often installed in North American cars when they were new. The air conditioning units and installation were of American design and manufacture, and seem to be particularly common on the 1979-80 Limited Edition models in North America.

ACCESSORIES

The items listed in this section were – with a few exceptions – not available as factory-fitted optional equipment but were purchased by customers at the point of delivery or later. However, they were BMC-approved accessories and were listed in special leaflets produced from time to time, the first appearing in September 1962. Many such items – for instance, car care products – were not specific to the MGB and can be ruthlessly disregarded. Those which were specific to the model or which were at any rate attached to the car were as follows:

Anti-roll bar Also available as factory-fit, but later standard.
Extra Lucas Windtone low note horn Also available as factory-fit, later standard.
Headlamp flasher switch Also available as factory-fit, later standard.
Lucas fog and driving lamps 5WFT and 5WLR, or WFT 576 and WLR 576.
Reversing lamp Desmo, Lucas or Lucas flush-fitting.
Parking lights 'All rubber'.
Locking petrol cap
Wing mirrors Desmo Boomerang Continental (trapezoidal head), Desmo Boomerang Continental (short arm), Desmo Boomerang round head, Magnatex Viewmaster round head (curved or straight arm). All available with convex or flat glass, except the Boomerang short-arm type, and with Boomerang or Viewmaster escutcheon plates to suit.
Seat belts Britax, later Kangol (later became standard factory-fit).
Switch panels Two types.
Chrome luggage carrier Also available as factory-fitted optional equipment.
Badge bar 17in by ⅜in.
Ashtray Also available as factory-fit, later standard.
Casco Tex cigarette lighter With fixing bracket if required.
Seat covers Available in Ocelot/Leopard, Wool Tartan, Moquette, Rayon, Bedford Cord, Duracour/Leathercloth, plastic. Offered for both seats or driver's seat only.
Rubber mats Red, black, grey, blue or green.
Rear compartment cushion Matching front seats (also available as factory-fit).
Touch-up paint All standard colours in ¼-pint tins.

Subsequent additions listed in 1963 and 1964 included the following:

Wingard Turina wing mirror With convex glass.
Exhaust deflector With MG badge.
27in badge bar For the really keen clubman!
Chrome-on-brass tailpipe extension
Tonneau cover Also available as factory-fit, later becoming standard.

Heater kit Also available as factory-fit, later becoming standard.

Lockheed brake servo kit

Hard top Supplied in primer (and also available as factory-fit, in colour).

Raydyot reversing lamp

Non-specific badge bars

Plastic licence holder With BMC rosette.

Ace Mercury wheel trim discs Also available as factory-fit.

Wheel trim rings So-called 'rimbellishers'.

Tudor mud flaps

In 1965 or later, a roof rack was offered for the GT, this being simply the same type and size as was recommended for the Mini. Also for the GT, a heated rear window conversion kit was listed.

As policy and emphasis changed over the years, many accessories were discontinued or replaced by non-specific items. On the other hand, some items which originally had been available as factory-fit options became dealer-fit accessories, for instance the luggage carrier, fog lamps or radios. Some items were listed as being available as factory-fit only on export models, which in practice probably meant Personal

Export Delivery cars. Certain types of radio remained 'recommended', most notably the Smiths HMV Radiomobile range but also Ekco Escort, at least on export cars. But in later years of production, factory-fit radios were largely confined either to PED cars, or to cars supplied to company staff, as direct sales or as company vehicles. After 1968, when Unipart took over from BMC Service Limited, the list of accessories was drastically pruned and very few items specific to the MGB were available in later years.

Only in the USA (and presumably Canada) did the market for accessories continue to flourish, and this was exploited by British Leyland Motors Inc. The following are some of the items listed in US market MGB sales brochures, but this list is not necessarily exhaustive (many items were made by Amco):

Radios Typically of US manufacture, with accessories; later stereo radios, also with eight-track or cassette tape decks.

Racing equipment Approved by SCCA (Sports Car Club of America).

Grille guard For Mark II and later models to 1974 model year.

Leather armrest With cubby hole (Mark II, 1968 model year).

Hardwood gearshift knob Mark II through to 1976 model year.

Wood-rim steering wheel 1969-70 model years.

Centre console With armrest, ashtray and electric clock (1969-71 model years).

Luggage carrier With ski adapters if required (1971 model year on). This item was very different from the UK luggage carrier.

Striping kits From 1973 model year, but a variety of designs were offered over the years.

Trim rings for Rostyle wheels 1970 model year onwards.

Electric clock 1972-76 model years.

Rubber floor mats

Door edge guards

'Coco' floor mats 1977-80 model years.

Driving lamps 1980 model year.

The most intriguing items are undoubtedly the unspecified SCCA racing equipment. Were these simply British Leyland special tuning parts or US-developed tuning kits? Some tuning parts were made in the USA in the 1960s and were supplied by Huffaker Engineering, of San Rafael, California, under part numbers prefixed HAE. An item not listed above is air conditioning, which is known to have been fitted to some US cars when new, including 'Limited Edition' models of 1979-80. Finally, the existence of some GTs in the USA with sunroofs prompts the thought that these were undoubtedly at times installed in the USA when the cars were new, as they were in the UK.

This picture is the joker in the pack, showing a 1980 American car with air conditioning installed. The pump for this appears to have displaced the normal air pump altogether and the alternator sits uneasily on brackets above the air conditioning pump. Lots of extra plumbing, and what looks like a heat exchanger in front of the radiator top tank. This car has only one electric fan but there may be a mechanical fan below the shield behind the radiator. Barely visible behind the washer container are the dual carbon canisters, but the 1980-style blue Austin Morris logo on the rocker cover shows up well.

SPECIAL TUNING

As had been the case for earlier MG models, MG published a Special Tuning booklet (AKD 4034) for the MGB. This was periodically revised and updated. In the booklet, six (later seven) different stages of tune were described in detail for the owner who wished either to improve road performance or to embark on competition. Any present-day enthusiast with a strong interest in these matters should obtain a copy of the booklet because the details quoted here can only be a brief summary.

Stage 1 simply advised carrying out routine polishing of the cylinder head and ports, but otherwise leaving all parts as standard, including the distributor and the camshaft. This was intended for road work and would yield a power increase of some 3bhp. Later on, a polished cylinder head complete with valves and stronger valve springs became available under part number C-AHT 100, the initial letter 'C' indicating that this was a Competition part. The 1971 edition of the booklet defines Stage 1 as fitting two 1¾in SU carburettors, with KP needles.

Stage 2 was intended to improve mid-range performance and acceleration, still for road use. It involved fitting a special camshaft, 1H 603, with the following valve timing: inlet opening 5° BTDC, inlet closing 45° ABDC, exhaust opening 40° BBDC, exhaust closing 10° ATDC. This was later replaced by camshaft 48G 184 with the following timing: inlet opening TDC, inlet closing 50° ABDC, exhaust opening 35° BBDC, exhaust closing 15° ATDC. Both of these camshafts had a valve lift of .322in (8.2mm). With a standard distributor this should result in 2-3bhp extra at the lower rev range, with slightly impaired performance above 5000rpm. Stage 2 could be combined with Stage 1 if desired. By 1971, stage 2 instead called for polishing head and ports together with fitting the 1¾in carburettors. Alternatively cylinder head C-AHT 100 could be fitted, or .027in (.656mm) could be skimmed off the standard head for a compression ratio of 9.2:1.

Stage 3 was described as competition tuning. A special camshaft (AEH 714) was fitted, with valve timing of 24°/64°/59°/29°, valve lift of .250in (6.35mm) and tappets set at .017in (.43mm) hot; ¹⁄₁₆in (1.59mm) was machined off the face of the cylinder head, to a finished head thickness of 3⁵⁄₆₄in (79mm), for a compression ratio of 9.7:1. Two SU carburettors of 1¾in size were fitted, with .100in jets and SY needles, together with a new inlet manifold and no air cleaners. The standard distributor was re-set at static ignition timing 10° BTDC. With a few other tweaks, the result should be 105/108bhp at 6000rpm. The revised 1971 booklet suggested fitting the C-AHT 100 head with .035in (.89mm) machined from the head face.

Stage 3A was similar but instead of machining the cylinder head, flat-top pistons were fitted, with a similarly increased compression ratio.

Stage 3B required both the machining of the head and the fitting of flat-top pistons, for a compression ratio of 10.5:1 and some 112-115bhp at 6000rpm.

Stage 4 took the competitions tuning a step further. First, the head was polished, as with Stage 1. Then special valves were fitted, with special valve guides if desired, and stronger double or triple valve springs. Next came special rocker shaft brackets and tubular steel distance pieces between the rockers. Then there were special tappet adjusting screws. A special high-lift wide-overlap camshaft (AEH 770) was fitted, with valve timing of 50°/70°/75°/45°, valve lift of .452in (11.5mm) and tappet clearance of .018in (.457mm). Larger tappets and shorter pushrods could be fitted if desired, as well as steel timing chain sprockets. The flat-top pistons were fitted, with special con rods in the case of three-bearing (18G, 18GA series) engines but standard con rods on the five-bearing (18GB, etc) engines. The 1¾in carburettors from stage 3 were used, as well as a special distributor with static ignition set at 6° BTDC. The result should be 121bhp at 6000rpm. In addition, the 1971 instructions suggested machining the cylinder head as per Stage 3.

Stage 5 was the same as Stage 4 but with a twin-choke Weber 45 DCOE 13 carburettor instead of two SUs. This would give 122bhp at 6000rpm.

Stage 6 was as Stage 4 or Stage 5, but with the cylinder head machined as described under Stage 3. With SU carburettors this should result in 129bhp at 6500rpm, or 130-131bhp at 6000rpm with the Weber carburettor.

Stage 7 was first quoted in the 1969 edition of the Special Tuning booklet. It resembled Stages 4 to 6, but in addition required the cylinder head to be machined to take larger valves, and prescribed the fitting of 2in SU carburettors and a wide-overlap camshaft, with the engine bored out to +.080in (2.00mm) so that oversize lightweight forged pistons could be fitted. This would give a size of 1892cc.

A complete Special Tuning booklet was never issued for the MGC, but a Stage 1 cylinder head was approved for the model. This was sold as a complete kit on an exchange basis and included a fully polished and assembled cylinder head with new valves, springs, cotters, etc; a matched inlet manifold; two three-branch exhaust manifolds; a new exhaust system; sparking plugs; and all necessary gaskets (part number C-AJJ 3392 for the complete kit).

A power output figure for the MGC was not quoted but the car's maximum speed was claimed to exceed 130mph when the kit was fitted. British Leyland did not quote a supplier for this conversion kit, but it may have been related to the Downton tuning carried out on some of the University Motors Special MGCs (see page 103).

No tuning instructions were given for the MGB GT V8 model.

Most tuning levels prescribed improved carburation, but stage 7 included the use of larger 2in SU carburettors together with larger valves and a wide-overlap camshaft.

COMPETITION EQUIPMENT

Inevitably there was a degree of overlap between out-and-out competition equipment, normal optional equipment, standard equipment and mere accessories – more than one item figures under several of these headings. The equipment listed in this section was generally listed in the Special Tuning booklet and later in an appendix to the parts list.

While these parts were originally sold by BMC Service through distributors or dealers, many parts subsequently had to be ordered direct from British Leyland Special Tuning, based in the MG factory at Abingdon. Sometimes competition parts were identified with the letter C in front of the normal part number, but later parts sold directly from Abingdon were identified in the parts list with the code C–MG. The list of competition parts was longest in the early years, and was gradually reduced. There was no reference at all to these items in the parts list for 1977 and later models.

Many parts have already been referred to in the previous section about Special Tuning. Starting with the engine, the following were available: induction-hardened crankshaft, for either three- or five-bearing engines; nitrided competition crankshaft, three-bearing engine only; special main and big end bearings; special Hidural bronze valve guides; nimonic valves, standard size or larger size; stronger valve springs, double or triple, with associated parts; special rocker shaft brackets, distance pieces for rockers; tappet adjusting screws; larger tappets and shorter pushrods; competition cylinder head gasket; steel timing gears; a choice of four special camshafts, described as half race, full race, sprint and super sprint; lightened steel flywheel; flat-top pistons; special con rods to be used if fitting flat-top pistons to 18G or 18GA three-bearing engines; lightweight forged pistons (.080in oversize only); special exhaust manifold; special low-speed dynamo pulley and fan belt; competition distributor, for use with full race camshaft; deeper oil sump, with baffle (available for three-bearing and five-main bearing engines); and larger capacity oil pump. In 1969, a polished cylinder head became available.

On the induction side, the choice was between a pair of 1¾in SU carburettors (HS6) or a Weber twin-choke carburettor, both offered with all the associated parts necessary for installation, including special inlet manifolds. From approximately 1969, 2in SU HS8 carburettors were also available.

The transmission system could be upgraded with a competition clutch and associated parts. A close-ratio gear cluster was offered but only for the early three-synchro gearbox, with ratios as follows: first 2.45:1, second 1.62:1, third 1.268:1 and fourth 1.00:1. There is a modification note (number 6480, March 1968) which suggests that a close-ratio gear cluster with spur gears rather than helical gears was then becoming available for both the MGB and the MGC, which

must mean it was suitable for the all-synchro gearbox, with ratios quoted as follows: first 2.45:1, second 1.815:1, third 1.306:1, fourth 1.00:1 and reverse 2.46:1. A year later, modification note number 6943 in March 1969 stated that strengthened material was introduced for the spur gears and ratios were now quoted as follows: first 2.449:1, second 1.748:1, third 1.306:1 and fourth 1.00:1. Originally the close-ratio cluster was supplied with a larger-diameter layshaft, but this became a standard fitting in March 1967 (see engine change point list on page 140).

For early cars with the banjo rear axle (roadsters until July 1967), alternative crown wheel and pinion sets were available for the following final drive ratios: 4.1:1 (10/41), 4.3:1 (10/43) and 4.555:1 (9/41). For cars with the tubed axle (all GTs, and roadsters from July 1967, including all MGC models), the following final drive ratios were available: 3.071:1 (14/43), 3.307:1 (13/43), 3.7:1 (10/37), all used as standard on MGC cars; 3.909:1 (11/43), the standard MGB ratio; and 4.1:1 (10/41), 4.22:1 (9/38) and 4.555:1 (9/41). Also, for MGC only: 3.58:1 (12/43) and 4.875:1 (8/39). ZF limited-slip differential units were available for both banjo and tubed axles. Speedometers to suit the various non-standard ratios were available in both mph and kph forms.

Chassis parts could be upgraded with competition brake pads for the front discs, competition rear brake shoes or brake linings, a brake servo kit (quoted before the introduction of the optional equipment servo in February 1970), a fly-off handbrake conversion kit, competition shock absorbers, stiffer front and rear springs, a choice of front anti-roll bars, including the ⁹⁄₁₆in (14.3mm) diameter bar which later became standard, and anti-roll bars of either ⅝in (15.8mm) or ¾in (19.1mm) diameter. A wood-rim light-alloy steering wheel was quoted until 1965. GT-size disc wheels with 5in rims were available for the MGB roadster. There were also Dunlop wire wheels with 5.5in wide rims. In May 1967 these were upgraded from 60 spokes (Dunlop 2257, BMC part number AHH 8334) to 70 spokes (Dunlop T2399, BMC part number AHH 8530). I confess to being puzzled by 70-spoke wire wheels – did they possibly have 72 spokes? The Special Tuning booklet also mentions a centre-lock magnesium alloy wheel, 5.5×14, available only in the USA, but it is not clear whether this was simply a wire wheel with a magnesium alloy rim or a complete cast alloy wheel. The RAC homologation form lists Minilite-style centre-lock magnesium electron wheels, 5.5×14, part number C-ART69, from July 1967.

Among other assorted parts was a supplementary fuel tank of 10 gallons which was available until 1967. It was fitted inside the boot and the spare wheel then had to be strapped to the top of the tank. It had an Enots quick-release filler cap, coming through a hole in the boot lid on the right-hand side. The 1967

Among the competition equipment was a supplementary fuel tank, which was mounted in the boot and filled through an Enots quick-release filler cap in the boot lid.

IDENTIFICATION

homologation form quotes a 21 gallon tank. Then there was a higher capacity fuel pump, various Champion competition sparking plugs (N3, N63R, N62R, N58R, N57R), a thermostat by-pass blanking sleeve, leather bonnet straps, Sebring-type perspex headlamp cowls, the oil cooler which later became standard equipment, a higher-efficiency competition oil cooler, an oil cooler cover, and a passenger footrest in the various trim colours, for either RHD or LHD cars. Tuning parts supplied by Huffaker in the USA were, as far as engine and chassis modifications are concerned, mostly similar to parts offered in the UK, but included a racing windscreen and a bucket seat.

Fewer competition parts were quoted for the MGC. Most important was the cylinder head Stage 1 conversion kit, C-AJJ 3392, supplied on an exchange basis and discussed in the previous section on Special Tuning. Obviously many MGB competition parts could be used on the MGC. The following were specifically listed for the model: bonnet securing strap kit; Sebring headlamp cowl kit; footrest for passenger (LHD); rod and pawl for conversion to fly-off handbrake; limited slip differential, which could only be used with MGB final drive gears; a large-capacity oil cooler; and an oil cooler cover.

It does not appear that any special competition equipment was quoted for the MGB GT V8. One part added late, and which could be used on both V8 and four-cylinder models, was a Leyland Special Tuning front air dam which completely replaced the standard front fairing.

Each MGB was given a 'car number', which in common parlance is still often referred to as the 'chassis number' or, in North America, the 'serial number'. It would now be more correct to call it the 'Vehicle Identification Number' (VIN).

The car numbers were issued in one series for all MGB models – except the V8 – starting with 101 in 1962 and continuing up to 523002 in 1980. From 1965 onwards, batches of numbers were allocated alternately to roadster and GT models. For each of the two types, a batch of numbers – typically 350 or a multiple thereof – would be issued in advance, and the cars built side by side. When MGB production was at its height, no fewer than four final assembly tracks at Abingdon were devoted to the model. For this, and other reasons, the car number sequence is never exactly identical with the actual build sequence. Starting in 1970, there was usually a gap in the car number series between each model year, with the car numbers for a new model year starting at a convenient higher number.

The MGC had its own series of car numbers which also started from 101. They finished at 9102, with all numbers being used. Batches of roadsters and GTs within this number series were much smaller, and MGC cars were built on a complicated batch system which means that the car number series is even less of a guide to the build sequence. The third series of car numbers was that used for the MGB GT V8, which ran from 101 to 2903, with gaps between model years. It is always the car number which should

Since all MGB production records survive at the Heritage Motor Centre, Gaydon, any car can be precisely identified. This Tartan Red roadster's car number, GHN3/47459, pinpoints its date of manufacture to 24 September 1964.

be quoted on the registration document (the title document in the US) for identification purposes.

The prefix letters found in front of each car number give some information about the type and specification of the car. The MGB codes start with the letters GHN for roadsters or GHD for GTs. **G** indicates that the car is an MG, **H** that it has an engine within the bracket 1400cc to 2000cc. The third letter is for the body style – **N** for 'two-seater tourer' or **D** for coupé. Next comes a number, either 3, 4 or 5, where **3** indicates the Mark I models of 1962-67, **4** the Mark II models of 1967-69, and **5** all cars from late 1969-79. Until 1967 these codes were followed by an **L** on all cars with left-hand drive. Then a distinction was introduced so that cars to the new North American specification were given a letter **U**, and L was reserved for other left-hand drive cars, although the practice of using L was discontinued altogether in 1969. The final code letter which may be found in the prefix applies only to North American export vehicles, which from 1969 were given an extra letter to indicate the model year, starting with **A** on the 1970 models. The following letters were subsequently allocated: 1971, **B**; 1972, **C**; 1973, **D**; 1974 and '1974½' **E**; 1975, **F**; 1976, **G**; 1977, **H**; 1978, **J**; 1979, **L**. Note that these code letters stand for *model* year, not calendar year (the 1976 model year, for instance, ran from August 1975 to June 1976), and that this extra letter is found *only* on North American cars.

From 1967, each car number was given a suffix letter **G**, which indicates that the cars were built in the MG factory at Abingdon. A typical example of a complete car number would be G-HN5-UA/200000-G, indicating a roadster built to North American specification in the 1970 model year. A home market GT of the same period would have a number of G-HD5/201000-G. The suffix letter G is the cause of many problems for the British vehicle registration authorities as the DVLA computer frequently renders it as an extra '6' or '9' on the registration document.

The MGC car number prefixes follow exactly the same system, except that the letter H is replaced by the letter **C** (it should really have been a 'B' under the BMC system) and the number following the letter code is always **1**, for first series. Typical MGC numbers are G-CN1/1234-G for a right-hand drive roadster, or G-CD1-L/5678-G for a left-hand drive GT which is not to North American specification.

The MGB GT V8 car numbers have the prefix of G-D2D1, where the first **D** is again for the size class of the engine, the body code is now **2D** for two-door coupé, and the final **1** is for the first series. All series production MGB GT V8 cars were right-hand drive models destined for the home market, so there were no further variations. All MGB GT V8 car numbers are also suffixed with the letter **G**.

For the last model year of MGB production, BL

SCHEDULE OF CAR NUMBERS – MGB, 1962-80

Date	Roadster	GT	Notes
May 62	101	-	Start of roadster production
Jan 63	4619	-	First car built in 1963
Jan 64	27927	-	First car built in 1964
Jan 65	54469	-	First car built in 1965
Sep 65	-	71933	Start of GT production
Jan 66	79362	77774	First cars built in 1966
Jan 67	111418	113658	First cars built in 1967
Oct 67	138360	137795	Last GHN3/GHD3 models (approx date)
Nov 67	138401	139471	First GHN4/GHD4 Mark II models
Jan 68	138961	139800	First cars built in 1968
Sep 68	158371	-	First 1969 model roadster
Nov 68	-	158231	First 1969 model GT
Jan 69	165721	165382	First cars built in 1969
Sep 69	-	187841	Start of 1970 model, GHN5/GHD5 series
Oct 69	187170	-	Start of 1970 model, GHN5/GHD5 series
Jan 70	196222	195915	First cars built in 1970
Aug 70	218651	217910	Last 1970 models
Aug 70	219001	219002	First 1971 models
Jan 71	232725	233466	First cars built in 1971
Aug 71	254942	256646	Last 1971 models
Aug 71	258001	258004	First 1972 models
Jan 72	268645	269271	First cars built in 1972
Aug 72	293525	294250[1]	Last 1972 models
Aug 72	294251	296001	First 1973 models
Jan 73	307716	310578	First cars built in 1973
Aug 73	327741	327990	Last 1973 models
Aug 73	328101	328801	First 1974 models
Jan 74	338744	338535	First cars built in 1974
Sep 74	359169	360069	Last 1974 models (last 'chrome-bumper' cars)
Sep 74	360301	361001	First '1974½' models (first 'rubber-bumper' cars)
Dec 74	367647	367818	Last '1974½' models
Dec 74	367901	368601	First 1975 models
Jan 75	368082	369069	First cars built in 1975
Aug 75	386267	380574	Last 1975 models
Aug 75	386601	-	First 1976 model roadster
Nov 75	-	391501	First 1976 model GT
Jan 76	393834	394663	First cars built in 1976
Jun 76	409401	406357	Last 1976 models
Jun 76	410001	410351	First 1977 models
Jan 77	424714	422728	First cars built in 1977
Sep 77	444499	445979	Last 1977 models
Sep 77	447001	447036	First 1978 models
Jan 78	455670	455283	First cars built in 1978
Jun 78	468880	469149	Last 1978 models
May 78	471001	-	First 1979 model roadster
Jun 78	-	471036	First 1979 model GT
Jan 79	485110	483820	First cars built in 1979
Jun 79	-	497613	Last 1979 model GT
Dec 79	500904	-	Last 1979 model roadster
Jun 79	501001	501036	First 1980 models
Jan 80	507309[2]	508070	First cars built in 1980
Oct 80	523001	523002	End of production

[1] GHD5/294951 to GHD5/294987 were also 1972 models.
[2] First North American LE model built in 1980 was 508885

introduced the new VIN prefix coding which applies to all MGB cars with numbers from 501001 upwards, built between June 1979 and October 1980. These prefix codes are composed of eight characters which may be read as follows:

1 Marque: **G** = MG.
2 Model range: **V** = MGB.
3 Specification class: **A** = Base line roadster (ie, all RHD cars); **G** = GT (only available in RHD form); **J** = Japanese specification roadster; **L** = Canadian specification roadster; **V** = North American Federal (49-state) roadster; **Z** = Californian specification roadster.
4 Body type: **D** = Roadster; **E** = GT coupé.
5 Engine type and size: **J** = 1800cc B-series.
6 Steering, transmission: **1** = RHD, four-speed manual; **2** = LHD, four-speed manual.
7 Model year: **A** = 1980
8 Assembly plant: **G** = MG, Abingdon.

Typical examples of complete numbers with prefixes are GVVDJ2AG/501234 for a roadster to US Federal specification, or GVGEJ1AG/523002 for a GT. It may be mentioned, incidentally, that the VIN codes on the much later MG RV8 follow the same principles but with the addition of three more prefix letters, SAX, which form the world manufacturer code for Rover Group. The SAX world manufacturer code was only introduced in 1981, so is never found on an MGB.

Different identification plates were used on MGB cars over the years. Until January 1967, a small rectangular plate with the MG octagon logo was used. It bore the words 'Made in England' and 'When ordering replacements quote', followed by 'Car No.' and the stamped-in number. There was also a space for the engine number, which was pre-printed with the words 'see engine'. This plate was screwed to the inner wing valance in front of the radiator, on the left-hand side (when looking from the front).

In January 1967 a new type of plate, rectangular and with rounded ends, was headed 'The MG Car Company Ltd, Abingdon-on-Thames, England'. Below the space for the car number was a statement that the front seat belt anchorages comply with specification BS.AU.48.1965. There was no space for the engine number. This type of plate was used also on the MGC, on which it was normally attached to the inner wing behind the radiator, on the right-hand side when looking from the front. In February 1970, the fixings for the plate were changed from self-tapping screws to pop rivets.

In the autumn of 1972, and certainly on all cars from January 1973, the name of the manufacturer was changed to 'Austin Morris Group, British Leyland UK Ltd', and this style was used until 1979. The shape, size and location of the plate was the same.

SCHEDULE OF CAR NUMBERS – MGC, 1966-69

Date	Roadster	GT	Notes
Nov 66	101	110	Pre-production, only 13 cars built in 1966
Oct 67	115	116	Pilot production
Nov 67	138	-	Start of roadster series production
Dec 67	-	638	Start of GT series production
Dec 67	580	754	Highest numbers issued in 1967[1]
Jan 68	146	640	Lowest numbers issued in 1968[1]
Oct 68	4266	-	Start of 1969 model roadster
Nov 68	-	4236	Start of 1969 model GT
Dec 68	6032	5884	Highest numbers issued in 1968[1]
Jan 69	4793	4467	Lowest numbers issued in 1969[1]
Aug 69	9099	9102	End of production

[1] Please note the considerable overlap in car numbers between years. In practice this means that cars with numbers between 146 and 754 might have been built in either 1967 or 1968, while cars with numbers between 4467 and 6032 might have been built in either 1968 or 1969.

SCHEDULE OF CAR NUMBERS – MGB GT V8, 1972-76

Date	Car number	Notes
Dec 72	101	Pre-production, only three cars built in 1972
Jan 73	103	First pre-production car built in 1973
Apr 73	124	Start of series production
Aug 73	604	Start of 1974 model year
Jan 74	1173	First car built in 1974
Sep 74	1956	Last 1974 model, last 'chrome-bumper' car
Sep 74	2101	First 1975 model, first 'rubber-bumper' car
Jan 75	2167	First car built in 1975
Aug 75	2632	Last 1975 model
Oct 75	2701	First 1976 model
Jan 76	2721	First car built in 1976
Jun 76	2901	End of series production
Jul 76	2903	End of production[1]

[1] The last two cars built, 2902 and 2903, could be described as '1977' models and were built in July 1976 after the end of series production

The British Leyland plate was used also on the MGB GT V8 where it was mounted behind and below the oil filter. On four-cylinder cars from June 1976, the plate was fitted on the bonnet lock platform, on the left-hand side when looking from the front.

A special North American identification plate was introduced in September 1969. This was a much larger rectangular plate which confirmed compliance with FMVSS (Federal Motor Vehicle Safety Standards) and EPA (Environmental Protection Agency) standards in force at the time of manufacture. The plate also had a stamping indicating month of manufacture, for instance 10/69 for October 1969. The manufacturer's name was originally quoted as 'The British Motor Corporation Ltd', but changed in 1970 to 'British Leyland (Austin-Morris) Ltd', and in 1972 to 'British Leyland UK Limited'. The North American plate was riveted to the shut pillar of the left-

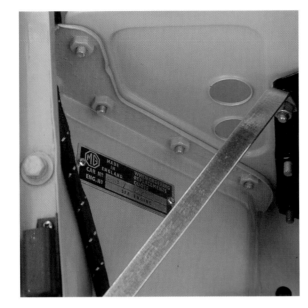

This type of car number (chassis number) plate was used from 1962 to early 1967, and located on the right-hand inner wing valance in front of the radiator diaphragm panel. This 1962 car, with the low number of 576, is believed to be the earliest surviving right-hand drive MGB.

This battered plate is of a similar type, but is interesting because the car number quoted, G-CN1/100, is the first prototype MGC. The riveted aluminium plate to the left covers a hole that was cut to reduce under-bonnet temperatures during development.

The plates found on an MGC – on the left the body number above the commission number plate, on the right the car (chassis) number plate of the type commonly in use from early 1967 to late 1972. All are located on the left-hand inner wing valance behind the radiator.

hand door. North American vehicles also had an additional plate used from 1 January 1969, fixed to the top of the dashboard so that the car number could be read from the outside through the windscreen.

The identification plate found on the final year's production of non-North American vehicles was of the new 'BL Cars Ltd' type. This was a larger rectangular plate which carried the EEC approved number, the vehicle weights (including permitted gross weight and axle weights) and three-letter code stampings for the paint and trim colours. This was also mounted on the bonnet lock platform.

Identification plates differed for certain export markets apart from North America. German cars had special plates quoting vehicle weights from the start of production in 1962, and CKD cars assembled in Australia had plates where the name of the manufacturer was given as 'BMC Australia' and the name of the paint colour was printed on the plate. Australian cars were also identified by their Australia assembly or chassis numbers with prefixes of YGHN, these numbers having no relationship at all with the car numbers issued to the CKD kits at Abingdon.

There remains the vexed question of whether the car number was actually stamped into the body structure. This was not a legal requirement in the UK until almost at the end of MGB production. MGB cars for the USA (and Canada?) had the car number stamped inside the front right-hand side member in the engine compartment just behind the front engine mount, adjacent to the starter motor. The stamped-in number is not found on the very first US export cars but seems to have been introduced quite early in the production run. The number is stamped in a similar location on North American MGCs.

At least some cars had the car number stamped in the floor pan in front of the right-hand seat, although this may only have been introduced in 1967. While it seems likely that the stamping was always made on cars destined for those export markets where it was a specific legal requirement, quite possibly it was omitted on many home market cars. There is a note in the factory records that cars for Sweden had to have the car number stamped into the floor of the boot (1970-73). Only from October 1979 did all cars, including home market models, have the number, complete with VIN prefix, stamped into the right-hand side member of the boot floor.

Of the other numbers found on the car, commission numbers were only issued from the start of Mark II and MGC production in 1967. The plate bearing the commission number had a red border and was riveted to the bonnet lock platform on MGB and MGB GT V8 cars, or to the inner wing near the car number plate on the MGC. The commission number prefixes start with **G** for MG, followed by a number representing BMC's ADO project code number for each model – **23** on MGB, **52** on MGC and **75** on

MGB GT V8. The last letter in the prefix is for body type, **N** on a roadster or **D** on a GT.

Commission numbers were suffixed with a letter indicating where the body had been 'commissioned', as commission numbers were issued and the plates attached in the body finishing plant, rather than at Abingdon. On MGBs, the following commission number letter suffixes may be found:

F Bodies Branch, Coventry (MGB roadsters 1962-69, early MGC roadsters)

P Pressed Steel, Swindon (MGB roadsters 1969-70, later MGC roadsters, MGB and MGC GTs 1965-70)

Z Pressed Steel, Cowley (all cars from 1970-76)

The change from suffix letter P to Z in 1970 is curious as it does not actually appear that earlier bodies were any more 'commissioned' at Swindon than later bodies were.

The commission number series each started from 101, and, in the case of the MGB and MGC models, different series were used for roadster and GT models respectively. A new series of numbers was started for both MGB and MGC roadsters when production of these bodies was moved from Coventry to Swindon/Cowley, but the new series of roadster commission numbers, and the GT number series, continued through the change from suffix letter P to suffix letter Z. Abingdon stopped recording the commission numbers in April 1971, but they were still issued to cars well into the 'rubber-bumper' era, certainly to June 1976.

Since engine numbers have been discussed in the engine sections of this book, this leaves just the body numbers. As Abingdon ceased to record the body numbers in 1972, information is scant on the later cars. The body number question is further complicated by the fact that each MGB roadster with a Coventry-built body had *two* body numbers, only one of which was written into the production records at Abingdon. And the number in the records is *not* the number which is described as the body number in most of the parts lists (except very early issues of the MGB parts list).

Of the two numbers on early MGB roadsters, one number is prefixed 'MGB' and is stamped on an alloy tag screwed to the inner wing valance behind the radiator diaphragm in the engine compartment, on the right-hand side when looking from the front. This number is *not* listed in the records. The other number has no prefix and is stamped on a tag which is spot-welded in a similar position to the wing valance on the left-hand side when looking from the front, and this is the body number which is quoted in the production records. The 'MGB' prefixed numbers start their number series from 101, while the un-prefixed numbers start from 1, and both ran up to over 110000

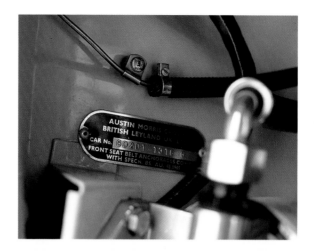

On the V8 model, the plate is on the right-hand wing valance but behind the radiator, below the oil filter. The plate headed 'Austin Morris Group – British Leyland UK Ltd' was used from 1972/73 through to 1979, except on North American specification cars.

The final year's production had the new-style VIN numbers and a prominent plate fitted on the bonnet locking platform, again with the exception of North American cars.

A special American identification plate was introduced in 1969 and was typically mounted on the left-hand rear door pillar. For the first year the manufacturer's name was given as 'The British Motor Corporation Ltd', but then it changed to 'British Leyland (Austin-Morris) Ltd' as seen on this car, which according to the date stamp was built in August 1970 (as an early 1971 model).

The commission number system was introduced from the start of Mark II production. The style of plate did not change but locations varied. Here it is on a 1969 model MGB roadster with a Coventry-built body, on the bonnet locking platform next to the safety catch.

Later American plates gave information about vehicle weights and listed the manufacturer simply as 'British Leyland UK Ltd'; the red MG sticker disappeared. On this 1977 model the plate is also further down than it was earlier, to clear the anti-burst unit next to the catalyst label.

The extra car number plate fixed to the top of the scuttle was found on all American cars from 1 January 1969 – a 1973 model is shown. It was designed to be read from the outside of the car through the windscreen, as demonstrated here.

for the Mark I models. On Mark II roadsters, the 'MGB' number tag moved in front of the radiator diaphragm panel.

On roadsters from 1969, with Swindon/Cowley-built bodies, it appears that there is only the one body number with the MGB prefix, and that this is now listed in the production records. However, from the start of Mark II production the special North American roadsters had their own body number series, with a prefix of MGBU. Similarly, the Swedish/German export model of 1969-74 had its own series of body numbers, with a prefix of GBSN.

The MGB GT is simpler to deal with. The GT always had only one body number, originally with the prefix GBD and the suffix letter P. GT body numbers started from 101 in 1965. Mark II and later North American export models had their own body number series, prefix GBUD, and on Swedish/German export cars from 1969 the body number prefix was GBSD, again with a special series of numbers. With some variation in the number series, the prefixes stayed the same until the end of 'chrome-bumper' production in 1974.

MGCs had four different series of body numbers, roadsters and GTs each being split into North American and non-North American models. The roadster prefixes were MGC or MGCU, the GT prefixes GCD or GCUD, the extra U in each case indicating the North American types. Non-North American MGC GTs had body numbers from 101, North American roadsters from 601 and North American GTs mostly from 500601. There were two series for non-North American roadsters: early cars with Coventry-built bodies had body numbers from 1 to 1123, later cars with Swindon/Cowley-built bodies had numbers from 501001 to 502166. It is likely, in fact, that MGC roadsters with Coventry-built bodies had two body numbers, of which only one was written into the records. The number series quoted here refer in all cases to the body numbers that can be found in the production records.

MGB GT V8 body numbers were prefixed with the code GB75D – in other words very similar to the commission number prefix code for this model. Similar body number prefixes were used on the four-cylinder MGB cars from the start of 'rubber-bumper' production in 1974, the following being found:

GB23T Right-hand drive roadster
GU23T North American roadster
GB23D Right-hand drive GT
GU23D North American GT ('1974½' model year)

All of these numbers were suffixed with the letter P, indicating that the 'body-in-white' was produced at Swindon. Because the body numbers were by then no longer entered in the production records, there is little information about the series of numbers issued.

On the V8, and also on 'rubber-bumper' cars in general, the commission number plate moved to the left of the bonnet lock platform (the right in the picture) and a new larger body number tag was fitted adjacent to it.

The bonnet lock platform of a 1977 American roadster, with a typical emissions control label and an electrical warning label, while the body number tag is next to the safety catch. But there is no commission plate as it appears that the practice of issuing commission numbers ceased with the end of the 1976 model year.

One of the two body number tags commonly found on early roadsters. This is the MGB-prefixed number on the riveted tag. On Mark I cars this was found on the left-hand inner wing valance in the engine bay behind the radiator, just about on a level with the carburettors, but on this 1969 Mark II model the tag has moved just forward of the radiator diaphragm panel.

In later years the body number tag or strip became larger, and on the V8, as well as on four-cylinder cars from 1976 with the forward-mounted radiator, the body number is on the bonnet lock platform.

The accompanying tables give the schedule of car numbers for the MGB, MGC and MGB GT V8 models over the years, with indications of the first and last numbers for each model or model year, and the first numbers issued in each calendar year. Because of the way in which the cars were produced, the first numbers in calendar years must be treated with care because they are only approximate: there were always cars with higher numbers built in the previous year

and cars with lower numbers built in the following year. This factor was particularly apparent in the case of the MGC, for which the car numbers fluctuated quite wildly, but the MGB was similarly affected until 1969. Only in the later years of production is it possible to specify fairly accurately which was the first number to be used in any given calendar year.

One final note on the MGB numbering systems. While CKD kits were issued with car numbers and engine numbers, as far as is known they had neither body nor commission numbers, for the simple reason that their bodies were not assembled prior to being shipped abroad.

PRODUCTION FIGURES

It might have been thought that sufficiently detailed and accurate production figures for the MGB and other models were already available from other publications, but this has turned out not to be so. Certainly, previously published figures did not match those standards which I feel obliged to set in such a prestigious series as the *Original* books!

My initial misgivings about other figures have been proved correct only after a great deal of hard work which, for instance, included counting every single 'rubber-bumper' car in the production records. While the figures published here are far more complete and accurate than those found elsewhere, at the time of publication of the first edition of this book some research still remained to be done, notably in the period 1971-74.

MGB ROADSTER PRODUCTION

		RHD Home	RHD Export	LHD North America	LHD Other export	LHD Sweden/ Germany	LHD Japan	RHD CKD	LHD CKD	Total	Total, calendar year	Total, model year
1962		540	111	2946	841	-	-	80	0	4518	4518	
1963		3020	531	15054	4179	-	-	524	0	23308	23308	
1964		4321	629	16753	3783	-	-	960	96	26542	26542	
1965		4742	524	13815	3642	-	-	1048	408	24179	24179	
1966		4050	341	14543	2289	-	-	1200	252	22675	22675	
1967	Mark I	2747	253	8611	1597	-	-	1240	120	14568	}15128	
	Mark II	2	14	520	24	-	-	0	0	560		
												}12540 (1968 models)
1968	Mark I	0	0	0	0	-	-	108	0	108		
	Mark II	1020	109	9169	438	-	-	1220	24	11980	}17355	
	1969 models	589	139	3953	374	-	-	212	0	5267		
												}19227 (1969 models)
1969	1969 models	1710	160	10527	635	-	-	928	0	13960	}18887	
	1970 models	565	69	4157	52	46	-	38	0	4927		
												}20072 (1970 models)
1970	1970 models	1845	220	11841	575	90	-	574	0	15145	}23662	
	1971 models	958	317	6995	*	15	-	232	0	8517		
												}24031 (1971 models)
1971	1971 models	2374	506	11999	*	105	-	530	0	15514	}22511	
	1972 models	684	179	5988	*	56	-	90	0	6997		
												}23960 (1972 models)
1972	1972 models	3737	504	12263	*	165	-	294	0	16963	}26222	
	1973 models	1161	319	7648	*	131	-	0	0	9259		
												}21801 (1973 models)
1973	1973 models	2017	501	9755	*	269	-	0	0	12542	}19546	
	1974 models	1017	184	5766	*	37	-	0	0	7004		
												}20779 (1974 models)
1974	1974 models	1138	356	12242	*	39	-	0	0	13775		
	1974½ models	439	15	5274	51	28	-	0	0	5807	}19757	5807 (1974½ models)
	1975 models	145	3	5	20	2	-	0	0	175		
												}13467 (1975 models)
1975	1975 models	895	21	11987	208	181	-	0	0	13292	}20171	
	1976 models	220	23	6411	141	84	-	0	0	6879		
												}19997 (1976 models)
1976	1976 models	783	26	11260	368	681	-	0	0	13118	}25527	
	1977 models	1110	5	11294	0	0	-	0	0	12409		
												}29955 (1977 models)
1977	1977 models	1620	31	15825	0	0	70	0	0	17546	}24483	
	1978 models	691	1	6205	0	0	40	0	0	6937		
												}17365 (1978 models)
1978	1978 models	1436	17	8795	0	0	180	0	0	10428	}21702	
	1979 models	1391	85	9464	0	0	334	0	0	11274		
												}25144 (1979 models)[5]
1979	1979 models	530	27	13289[1]	0	0	16	0	0	13862	}19897	
	1980 models	392	65	5578[2]	0	0	0	0	0	6035		
												}16918 (1980 models)
1980	1979 models	0	0	8	0	0	0	0	0	8	}10891	
	1980 models	1810[4]	222	8112[3]	0	0	739	0	0	10883		

Notes

[1] including 2321 Limited Edition models; [2] including 1856 Limited Edition models; [3] including 2505 Limited Edition models; [4] including 421 LE models; [5] including 8 cars built in 1980

* Separate figures for LHD export are not available for the model years 1971 to 1974, but are included with RHD export figures. Cars for Sweden and Germany are included in general LHD export figures to the end of the 1969 model year. Cars for Japan are included in general LHD export figures prior to 1977 calendar year.

MGB GT PRODUCTION

		RHD Home	RHD Export	LHD North America	LHD Other export	LHD Sweden/ Germany	RHD CKD	LHD CKD	Total	Total, calendar year	Total, model year
1965		350	3	164	7	-	0	0	524	524	
1966		2415	362	5851	1477	-	72	64	10241	10241	
1967	Mark I	5269	571	4142	1013	-	32	40	11067	}11396	
	Mark II	7	25	272	25	-	0	0	329		
											} 7242 (1968 models)
1968	Mark I	0	0	3	0	-	0	0	3		
	Mark II	2200	383	3792	490	-	48	0	6913	} 8352	
	1969 models	550	47	775	60	-	4	0	1436		
											} 9701 (1969 models)
1969	1969 models	2261	189	5245	546	-	24	0	8265	}12135	
	1970 models	983	71	2711	66	31	8	0	3870		
											}11380 (1970 models)
1970	1970 models	2628	346	3890	531	99	16	0	7510	}12510	
	1971 models	1885	603	2506	*	6	0	0	5000		
											}13612 (1971 models)
1971	1971 models	3673	482	4384	*	61	12	0	8612	}12169	
	1972 models	1656	340	1542	*	19	0	0	3557		
											}11952 (1972 models)
1972	1972 models	5434	749	2067	*	145	0	0	8395	}13171	
	1973 models	2449	364	1898	*	65	0	0	4776		
											}11550 (1973 models)
1973	1973 models	4114	613	1949	*	98	0	0	6774	}10208	
	1974 models	1646	453	1294	*	41	0	0	3434		
											}10965 (1974 models)
1974	1974 models	3324	691	3456	*	60	0	0	7531		
	1974½ models	289	20	1247	67	14	0	0	1637	} 9626	1637 (1974½ models)
	1975 models	428	7	0	20	3	0	0	458		
											} 4274 (1975 models)
1975	1975 models	3409[1]	51	0	253	103	0	0	3816	} 4517	
	1976 models	609	32	0	40	20	0	0	701		
											} 2607 (1976 models)
1976	1976 models	1348	113	0	294	151	0	0	1906	} 3656	
	1977 models	1735	15	0	0	0	0	0	1750		
											} 4352 (1977 models)
1977	1977 models	2529	73	0	0	0	0	0	2602	} 4198	
	1978 models	1594	2	0	0	0	0	0	1596		
											} 4614 (1978 models)
1978	1978 models	2979	39	0	0	0	0	0	3018	} 5652	
	1979 models	2539	95	0	0	0	0	0	2634		
											} 4703 (1979 models)
1979	1979 models	2015	54	0	0	0	0	0	2069	} 3503	
	1980 models	1328	106	0	0	0	0	0	1434		
											} 4858 (1980 models)
1980	1980 models	3334[2]	90	0	0	0	0	0	3424	3424	

Notes

[1] including 751 'Jubilee' models; [2] including 580 LE models; *Separate figures for LHD export are not available for the model years 1971 to 1974, but are included with RHD export figures. Cars for Sweden and Germany are included in general LHD export figures to the end of the 1969 model year.

At the root of the problem lie the figures originally compiled by MG's Production Control Department at Abingdon. In many cases these are simply not believable as the production figures exceed the maximum possible numbers of cars built, according to the car number ranges. There are also other discrepancies. While the Abingdon figures are beautifully detailed and split in all the appropriate production groups for the period up to approximately 1969, in later years some export versions are uncritically lumped together. The mistake – if mistake it can be called – of some other historians, including some very eminent ones, is to have simply repeated the Abingdon figures given to them without attempting any critical analysis – but I can't really blame them!

In the tables which follow, the figures are split by calendar year, and for 1968 and later, also in model years. They are split in the following production groups: home market; RHD export; LHD North American export; LHD export; CKD cars, with

RHD or LHD; and, where appropriate, separate figures have also been listed for the Swedish/German sub-species (1969-76), and for the Japanese roadster (1977-80). North American cars have *not* been split into US Federal, US Californian and Canadian cars – there is a limit to what even I will do! Some impression, however, of the relative numbers of these types in the later years of production may be gleaned from studying the engine number tables on pages 60 and 64. The exact numbers of Limited Edition models are quoted in the section on these cars on page 103. Some cars were never counted by Production Control even if given production type car numbers. This would apply to certain experimental vehicles as well as to the works competition cars.

The MGC and MGB GT V8 models are simpler to deal with, although in the case of the MGCs I always wondered why the published production figures were a few cars 'short' compared to the car number series. So I counted them in the records and

MGC ROADSTER PRODUCTION

Year	RHD Home	RHD Export	LHD North America	LHD Other Export	Total	Total by calendar year
1966	6	0	3	0	9	9
1967	176	0	0	6	182	182
1968 (1968 models)	1009	33	668	225	1935	} 2596
1968 (1969 models)	45	8	510	98	661	
1969	169	23	1302	263	1757	1757
Total	1405	64	2483	592	4544	4544

MGC GT PRODUCTION

Year	RHD Home	RHD Export	LHD North America	LHD Other Export	Total	Total by calendar year
1966	2	0	2	0	4	4
1967	30	0	0	8	38	38
1968 (1968 models)	1112	57	534	257	1960	} 2491
1968 (1969 models)	303	10	173	45	531	
1969	583	32	1064	246	1925	1925
Total	2030	99	1773	556	4458	4458

MGB GT V8 PRODUCTION

Year	RHD Home	LHD North America	Total	Total by calendar year
1972	0	3	3	3
1973 (1973 models)	496	4	500	} 1070
1973 (1974 models)	570	0	570	
1974 (1974 models)	783	0	783	} 853
1974 (1975 models)	70	0	70	
1975 (1975 models)	462	0	462	} 482
1975 (1976 models)	20	0	20	
1976 (1976 models)	181	0	181	} 183
1976 (1977 models)	2	0	2	
Total	2584	7	2591	2591

Note: Total chrome-bumper cars, 1856; total rubber-bumper cars, 735.

MGB PRODUCTION SUMMARY, BY CALENDAR YEAR

Year	Roadster	GT	Total
1962	4518	0	4518
1963	23308	0	23308
1964	26542	0	26542
1965	24179	524	24703
1966	22675	10241	32916
1967	15128	11396	26524
1968	17355	8352	25707
1969	18887	12135	31022
1970	23662	12510	36172
1971	22511	12169	34680
1972	26222	13171	39393
1973	19546	10208	29754
1974	19757	9626	29383
1975	20171	4517	24688
1976	25527	3656	29183
1977	24483	4198	28681
1978	21702	5652	27354
1979	19897	3503	23400
1980	10891	3424	14315
Total	386961	125282	512243

MGB PRODUCTION SUMMARY, BY MODEL

	Roadster	GT	Total
Mark I (1962-68)	115898	21835	137733
Mark II (1967-69)	31767	16943	48710
GHN/D 5 (1969-74)	110643	59459	170102
Rubber-bumper (1974-80)	128653	27045	155698
Total	386961	125282	512243

came up with slightly different figures, in this case including pre-production cars. The V8 figures have also been checked fully in the production records.

Further references to the numbers of cars with automatic gearboxes and the numbers of CKD cars will be found in the appropriate sections, respectively on pages 86 and 128. While I can appreciate that there are enthusiasts who would dearly like to know how many cars were built in certain colours, with respect I find requests for such information a little frivolous, although those who really want to know the number of cars in Mirage or Black Tulip are welcome to spend a holiday in the archive of the Heritage Motor Centre at Gaydon and count for themselves.

Country-by-country export figures are sadly not available, although I would find them fascinating. There is little doubt, however, that apart from the USA and the UK, some of the biggest markets were Australia, Canada and Germany – but MGBs did end up in some very obscure places. Sales to Libya, Iceland or Okinawa, even Greenland, can be explained by the presence of US bases, which also accounts for the large number of cars shipped to Germany, but the same explanation can hardly account for sales to what was then Yugoslavia.

The first table covers all MGB roadsters and the second all MGB GTs, while the third table is a simple summary of MGBs by calendar year. The final tables are for the MGCs and the MGB GT V8 respectively. The bottom line is that the discrepancy between my overall total and those published by others is exactly 637 cars, or about 0.1 per cent of MGB production. If you think that's a disappointment after my considerable build-up, who am I to disagree?

CKD PRODUCTION

From 1962 to 1972, a total of 10,498 MGB cars were not assembled at Abingdon but were shipped abroad in the form of CKD (Completely Knocked Down) kits to be assembled locally, in Australia, Belgium and Eire. The reasons why this was done were mostly to do with the desire to circumvent tariff barriers, but conceivably also to save some shipping costs.

As all of the CKD cars were allocated a car number by Abingdon and were entered in the production records with special codes, they are fairly easy to track. The CKD kits were put together in batches of varying size, typically of four, six or 12 cars, and certain ranges of numbers were normally pre-allocated to CKD cars, which may therefore have car numbers that do not follow the normal build sequencing. It should also be born in mind that there was typically quite a delay between the dates at which a CKD kit was packed for shipment and recorded by Abingdon's production control department, and the date of assembly in the receiving market. Finally, at the time of the change-over from Mark I to Mark II in 1967-68, production of Mark I CKD kits continued for much longer than of Abingdon-assembled cars – perhaps to use up stocks of Mark I parts.

The first and most important market to receive MGB cars in CKD form was Australia. The first batch of cars was shipped around November 1962, starting with car number 1734. These first cars came off the assembly line of BMC Australia on 4 April 1963. The last Mark I type cars were shipped out in January 1968, the total of Mark I roadsters being 5064 cars. The first Mark II CKD kits were shipped to Australia in March 1968. The first face-lifted 1970 models followed in October 1969, and the last kit was car number 271843 shipped in June 1972. The last Australian-assembled car came off the line on 6 November 1972, by which time a total of 9090 MGB roadsters had been shipped to Australia in CKD form. This figure contrasts with Australian sources which claim a total of 9993 cars, but the discrepancy may be accounted for if the higher Australian figure includes the small number of MGB GTs sent out from England in fully assembled form.

When an MGB was assembled in Australia it was given its own locally-devised identification number, prefixed by YGHN. The initial Y was used to distinguish Australian-assembled vehicles, while the rest of the prefix was the same as used on Abingdon-built cars. The 1962-68 Mark I models had this prefix followed by the number 3, the 1968-69 Mark II models by 4 and the 1969-72 facelift models by 5 – again just as for UK production. The number series issued in Australia started from 501 and reverted to 501 for each of the subsequent models. Thus, the Australian Mark I models should have car numbers from YGHN3/501 to YGHN3/5564, the Mark IIs from YGHN4/501 to YGHN4/2792, and the 1970-72 models from YGHN5/501 to YGHN5/2234.

In terms of specification, CKD cars to Australia were not painted, trimmed or supplied with hoods. When they were painted in Australia, they were typically given colours never offered on UK-built cars. Interior trim and hoods were probably mostly black. It is believed that all Australian cars had wire wheels, an ashtray and the front anti-roll bar even before this became standard on UK roadsters. Originally they came with or without the overdrive, but overdrive was standardised on Australian cars in 1971. Rather more interesting is the fact that between 1968-70 a total of 228 MGB roadsters for Australia were supplied with the automatic gearbox. Until April 1969 they did not have a heater but could be supplied with the fresh-air unit as an option, while from then on the heater became standard equipment and the fresh-air unit was deleted from the specification.

Apart from paint, trim and hood, parts sourced in Australia typically included glass, some electrical parts, and tubes and tyres. Australian-made tyres used on MGBs included Dunlop B7 crossplies and Olympic GT radials. Although it appears that B-series 1800 engines were made in Australia for the local versions of the Austin/Morris 1800, it seems that all MGBs had engines supplied as part of the UK-sourced kits. The MGB was finally discontinued in Australia because it became impossible to achieve the local content required by new tariff legislation.

Mark II models assembled in Australia had a small 'MkII' badge fitted on the rear panel, just above the left-hand overrider, and an 'Overdrive' script on the boot lid between the MG badge and the boot lock – if equipped with overdrive. Cars with the automatic gearbox may have had a similar 'Automatic' script. Australian 1969 models may have continued with the original style seats, possibly with black rather than contrast-colour piping, although reclining seats were introduced later. Also seen on an Australian 1969 model were unique door trims with vertical flutes to the centre panel of the door trim, and a steering wheel similar to the wheel found on British cars only for the 1970 model year, with three pierced alloy spokes.

The second market to receive CKD MGBs was Belgium. The reason for this was the convenience of having a manufacturing base in an EEC country in the days before Britain became a member. Most Belgian-assembled MGBs, in fact, do seem to have been sold in Belgium or The Netherlands, whereas Germany, France and Italy took fully-assembled cars direct from Abingdon. Belgian CKD production started with car number 35083, a roadster shipped in May 1964, and from October 1966 GTs were shipped as well. To the end of Mark I production, the total number shipped was 876 roadsters and 104 GTs. Only 24 Mark II roadsters were shipped, the last car being 141813 in April 1968 when CKD shipments to Belgium ceased. The total number of cars was 1004.

COLOURS

The Belgian cars were, of course, left-hand drive and came with a kilometres speedometer. They were not painted but it is probable that they ended up in the same colours found on UK cars. The kits were supplied with interior trim – mostly black but a few early cars had red trim – and in the case of roadsters with a hood which was always of the folding type. They had wire wheels, a heater, headlamp flasher switch, ashtray, cigar lighter and the anti-roll bar. They were available with or without overdrive. Although I have yet to prove it, I suspect that some of the Belgian CKD kits ended up as raw material for Jacques Coune's coupés.

Finally, there was Eire. Like Belgium, Eire took both roadsters and GTs. The first car was number 53409 in December 1964, while GTs followed in March 1966. Shipments of both continued until February 1971, the highest car numbers being 225064 for roadsters and 232312 for GTs. The production figures were 188 roadsters and 216 GTs, for a total of 404 cars of which 200 were Mark I models.

The Irish CKD kits were not painted, but it is again probable that they ended up in the colours which were available in the UK. They came complete with trim, mostly black except for a few early cars with red trim. The roadsters had a black hood of the pack-away type until the 1970-71 models received the new folding hood. They were fitted with wire wheels until the 1970-71 models, which had chrome Rostyle wheels. Equipment always included a heater, headlamp flasher switch and (on roadsters) a tonneau cover, and the Irish cars were always available with or without overdrive.

Neither the MGC nor the MGB GT V8 was ever supplied in CKD form.

The MGB roadster was available in five paint colours when it was introduced in 1962 – Black, Iris Blue, Chelsea Grey, Tartan Red and Old English White. With the exception of Chelsea Grey, which was offered only with red trim, all were available with either black or coloured trim (red on cars in Black, Tartan Red, or Old English White; blue on cars in Iris Blue). Hoods were originally only coloured, grey on cars in Black, Grey or White, and red or blue to match the paintwork on cars in these colours. This gave rise to the now famous – or infamous? – all-red or all-blue colour schemes. In December 1962, a sixth paint colour – British Racing Green with black trim and grey hood – was introduced, but replaced after only a few months, reputedly at the request of the export sales department, by a darker colour known as Dark British Racing Green, also with black trim and grey hood.

The relatively unpopular Chelsea Grey colour was discontinued in 1965, and later the same year the GT model made its appearance. The GT was offered in most of the roadster colours, but from introduction it was available in the darker Mineral Blue rather than Iris Blue, and had an additional two unique paint colours, Sandy Beige and Grampian Grey. Soon after, Iris Blue was discontinued on the roadster and replaced by Mineral Blue, although some roadsters may still have been finished in Iris Blue into early 1966. In February 1967, Pale Primrose Yellow was added for both roadster and GT models.

The MGB Mark II and the MGC models from late 1967 to 1969 were offered in the Mark I colours, except that from the start of MGC production, and soon after also on the MGB, Old English White was replaced by Snowberry White. Two additional metal-

Some of the cars in this book have been chosen to illustrate relatively unusual colours. This 1973 GT is in Black Tulip with Ochre trim.

This early GT, built in 1965, is painted Sandy Beige, a colour that was never available on roadsters. The auxiliary lights, wing mirrors and sunroof are period accessories.

COLOUR SCHEMES, MGB MARK I ROADSTER (1962-67)

Paint	Seats, liners	Piping for seats and liners[1]	Mats, carpets	Door seals	Hood[2]	Hood cover, tonneau cover	Hard top[3]	Remarks
Black	Black	White	Black	Black	Grey or Black	Black	Black/Red/Grey/White	
Black	Red	Black	Red	Red	Grey or Black	Red[4]	Black/Red/Grey/White	
Iris Blue	Black	Pale Blue	Black	Black	Blue or Black	Black	Black/Blue/White	To Oct 65
Iris Blue	Blue	Pale Blue	Blue	Blue	Blue or Black	Blue	Black/Blue/White	To Oct 65
Mineral Blue	Black	Pale Blue	Black	Black	Blue or Black	Black	Black/White	From Oct 65
Mineral Blue	Blue	Pale Blue	Blue	Blue	Blue or Black	Blue	Black/White	From Oct 65 to Dec 66
British Racing Green or Dark BRG	Black	White	Black	Black	Grey or Black	Black	Black/White	From Dec 62; Dark BRG from Aug 63
Chelsea Grey	Red	White	Red	Red	Grey or Black	Red	Black/Red/Grey/White	To Aug 65
Tartan Red	Black	Red	Black	Red[5]	Red or Black	Black	Black/Red/Grey/White	
Tartan Red	Red	Black	Red	Red	Red or Black	Red	Black/Red/Grey/White	To late 66
Old English White	Black	White	Black	Black	Grey or Black	Black	Black/Red/Grey/White	
Old English White	Red	White	Red	Red	Grey or Black	Red[4]	Black/Red/Grey/White	
Pale Primrose Yellow	Black	White	Black	Black	Black	Black	Black	From Feb 67

Notes

[1] Door waist rail piping in seat piping colour until 1966, then in black on all cars.

[2] Black hoods gradually introduced from 1964; coloured hoods discontinued in December 1966.

[3] Coloured hard tops to approximately December 1966, all hard tops black thereafter.

[4] Red hood cover and tonneau cover replaced by black in 1966.

[5] Red door seals replaced by black in 1966.

COLOUR SCHEMES, MGB MARK I GT (1965-67),
MGB MARK II GT AND MGC GT (1967-68)

Paint	Seats, liners	Piping for seats and liners	Mats, carpets	Door seals	Other trim[1]
Black	Black	White	Black	Black	Grey
Black	Red	Black	Red	Red	Grey
Sandy Beige	Black	White	Black	Black	Beige
Sandy Beige	Red	White	Red	Red	Beige
Mineral Blue	Black	Pale Blue	Black	Black	Grey
Mineral Blue	Blue	Pale Blue	Blue	Blue	Grey
Dark British Racing Green	Black	White	Black	Black	Grey
Dark British Racing Green[2]	Red	Black	Red	Red	Grey
Grampian Grey	Black	White	Black	Black	Grey
Grampian Grey	Red	Black	Red	Red	Grey
Tartan Red	Black	Red	Black	Red or Black[3]	Grey
Tartan Red	Red	Black	Red	Red	Grey
Old English White or Snowberry White[4]	Black	Red	Black	Red or Black[3]	Grey
Old English White or Snowberry White[4]	Red	Black	Red	Red	Grey
Pale Primrose Yellow[5]	Black	White	Black	Black	Grey
Metallic Golden Beige[6]	Black	White	Black	Black	Beige
Metallic Golden Beige[6]	Red	White	Red	Red	Beige
Metallic Riviera Silver Blue[6]	Black	Pale Blue	Black	Black	Grey
Metallic Riviera Silver Blue[6]	Blue	Pale Blue	Blue	Blue	Grey

Notes

[1] Comprises roof lining, sun visors, header and cant rail covers, rear quarter upper liner and quarterlight rear edge cover.

[2] Green with red trim was found on very few cars after the end of 1966, although at least five MGC GTs were finished in this scheme.

[3] Red door seals only on early cars, changed to black in late 1965.

[4] Snowberry White on MGC from start of production, on MGB from January 1968.

[5] Pale Primrose Yellow from February 1967.

[6] Metallic colours standard on MGC GT, optional extra on MGB GT 1968 model.

lic colours were introduced, Metallic Golden Beige and Metallic Riviera Silver Blue. These were listed as standard colours on the MGC GT, optional extra on the MGC roadster and the MGB GT, and were not available on the MGB roadster. Both were discontinued early in the 1969 model year, but otherwise the existing colour range continued for 1969.

Black hoods were introduced from 1964 as an alternative to the coloured hoods, which were discontinued altogether at the end of 1966. From then on, hoods were always black, as were hood covers (for the folding type hood) and tonneau covers. Similarly, the optional extra hard-top, which in the early years was available in a variety of colours, was offered only in black from 1966 to the end of production.

The original style of trim used from 1962 to 1968 featured contrast-colour piping for the seats, door liners, and rear quarter liners on each side behind the doors. The piping behind the waist rails at the top of

each door was in the seat piping colour until 1966, but black thereafter. The waist rails themselves were always black on all cars until 1970, as were the crash roll at the top of the facia (and its piping), the scuttle top or screen shroud panel behind the windscreen, and the moulding to the rear edge of the cockpit. The main trim colour extended to the seats, liners, rubber mats, carpets and usually the door seals – and this continued in principle until 1976.

Similarly, a number of trim parts were always black on the GT model until 1970, regardless of trim colour. These included the door waist rails and piping, the rear quarter waist rails and lower edge of the rear quarterlights, the A-post and centre pillar coverings, the scuttle top, and the facia crash roll with piping. The roof lining, header and cant rail covers, sun visors, rear quarter upper liners and quarterlight rear edge covers were typically grey on most GTs, but were beige on GTs in beige paint colours until late 1968.

COLOUR SCHEMES, MGB MARK II ROADSTER AND MGC ROADSTER (1967-68)

Paint	Seats, liners	Piping for seats and liners	Mats, carpets	Door seals	Hood[1]
Black	Black	White	Black	Black	Black
Black	Red	Black	Red	Red	Black
Mineral Blue	Black	Pale Blue	Black	Black	Black
Dark British Racing Green	Black	White	Black	Black	Black
Tartan Red	Black	Red	Black	Black	Black
Old English White or Snowberry White[2]	Black	White	Black	Black	Black
Old English White or Snowberry White[2]	Red	White	Red	Red	Black
Pale Primrose Yellow	Black	White	Black	Black	Black
Metallic Golden Beige[3]	Black	White	Black	Black	Black
Metallic Golden Beige[3]	Red	White	Red	Red	Black
Metallic Riviera Silver Blue[3]	Black	Pale Blue	Black	Black	Black
Metallic Riviera Silver Blue[3]	Blue	Pale Blue	Blue	Blue	Black

Notes
[1] Plus hood cover, tonneau cover and hard top.
[2] Snowberry White on MGC from start of production, on MGB from January 1968.
[3] Metallic colours only available on MGC as optional extra.

COLOUR SCHEMES, MGB MARK II ROADSTER AND GT AND MGC ROADSTER AND GT, 1968-69 (1969 MODEL YEAR)

Paint	Seats, liners[1]	Mats, carpets	Hood[2]	Other trim[3]
Black	Black	Black	Black	Grey
Sandy Beige[4]	Black	Black	n/a	Grey
Sandy Beige[4]	Mushroom	Brown[5]	n/a	Grey
Mineral Blue	Black	Black	Black	Grey
Dark British Racing Green	Black	Black	Black	Grey
Grampian Grey[4]	Black	Black	n/a	Grey
Tartan Red	Black	Black	Black	Grey
Snowberry White	Black	Black	Black	Grey
Pale Primrose Yellow	Black	Black	Black	Grey
Metallic Golden Beige[6]	Black	Black	n/a	Grey
Metallic Golden Beige[6]	Mushroom	Brown[7]	n/a	Grey
Metallic Riviera Silver Blue[6]	Black	Black	n/a	Grey

Notes
[1] Includes piping and door seals, plus headrests on North American cars only.
[2] Roadster models only: includes hood cover, tonneau cover and hard top.
[3] GT models only: comprises roof lining, sun visors, header and cant rail covers, rear quarter upper liner and quarterlight rear edge cover.
[4] GT models only.
[5] Toeboard trim pad and engine casing in Mushroom, map pocket in Brown.
[6] Metallic colours only on GT models, discontinued in late 1968.
[7] Toeboard trim pad, engine casing and map pocket in Brown.

COLOUR SCHEMES – MGB ROADSTER AND GT (1970 MODEL YEAR)

Paint	Trim, hood[1]
Black[2]	Black
Antelope Beige[3]	Black
Bermuda Blue[3]	Black
Blue Royale	Black
Dark British Racing Green	Black
Flame Red	Black
Bronze Yellow	Black
Pale Primrose Yellow	Black
Glacier White	Black

Notes
[1] Following GT trim parts in Grey: roof lining, sun visors, header and cant rail covers, rear quarter upper liner and quarterlight rear edge cover.
[2] Black typically only to special order from 1970 model year onwards.
[3] GT model only

COLOUR SCHEMES – MGB ROADSTER AND GT (1971 MODEL YEAR)

Paint	Trim[1]
Black	Black or Autumn Leaf
Bedouin (beige)	Autumn Leaf
Midnight Blue	Black
Teal Blue	Autumn Leaf [2]
New Racing Green	Autumn Leaf [2]
Green Mallard[3]	Autumn Leaf
Mustard[4]	Black
Blaze (orange)	Black
Flame Red	Black
Bronze Yellow	Black
Glacier White	Black

Notes
[1] Certain GT trim parts in Grey, as for 1970 model year. Hood, hood cover, tonneau cover and hard top were all in black only.
[2] A few early cars in these paint colours had Black trim.
[3] Used only on a few cars at the end of the model year.
[4] Used experimentally on a few GTs at the end of the model year.

This MGC roadster is painted Dark British Racing Green, a colour that was available between 1963-70. From the rear, an MGC can be distinguished from an MGB only by its 15in wheels and boot lid badge.

COLOUR SCHEMES, MGB ROADSTER AND GT (1972 MODEL YEAR)

Paint	Trim[1]
Black	Navy or Autumn Leaf
Teal Blue	Autumn Leaf
Harvest Gold	Navy
Green Mallard	Autumn Leaf
Blaze (orange)	Navy
Flame Red	Navy
Aqua (turquoise)	Navy
Bronze Yellow	Navy
Glacier White	Navy

Notes
[1] Certain GT trim parts in Grey as before; console and armrest cover in black for all colour schemes from 1972 model year.

COLOUR SCHEMES, MGB ROADSTER AND GT, MGB GT V8 (1974 AND '1974½' MODEL YEARS)

Paint	Trim[1]
Black	Black or Autumn Leaf
Mirage (mauve)[2]	Black
Teal Blue[3]	Autumn Leaf
Bracken (brown)	Autumn Leaf
Harvest Gold	Black
Tundra (green)	Autumn Leaf
Blaze (orange)[3]	Black
Aconite (purple)[3]	Autumn Leaf
Damask Red	Black
Citron (yellow)	Black
Glacier White	Autumn Leaf

Notes
[1] See note ([1]) for 1972 model year.
[2] Discontinued December 1974.
[3] Discontinued February 1975.

COLOUR SCHEMES, MGB ROADSTER AND GT (1973 MODEL YEAR)[1]

Paint	Trim[2]
Black	Navy or Ochre
Teal Blue	Ochre[3]
Harvest Gold	Navy
Limeflower (green)	Navy
Green Mallard	Ochre[3]
Blaze (orange)	Navy
Black Tulip (purple)	Ochre[3]
Damask Red	Navy
Bronze Yellow	Navy
Glacier White	Navy[4]

Notes
[1] The 1973 colour range was also used for early production of the MGB GT V8 from March 1973, although early V8s were predominantly finished in Damask Red, Glacier White and Harvest Gold (all with Navy trim), or Teal Blue (with Autumn Leaf trim). Only a handful of very early V8s had Ochre trim.
[2] See note ([1]) for 1972 model year.
[3] Ochre trim used to approximately July 1973. Most late 1973 models in Teal Blue, Green Mallard and Black Tulip had Autumn Leaf trim.
[4] Many White roadsters in July-August 1973 had Black trim.

COLOUR SCHEMES, MGB ROADSTER AND GT, MGB GT V8 (1975 AND 1976 MODEL YEARS)

Paint	Trim[1]
Black	Black[3] or Autumn Leaf
Tahiti Blue[2]	Black[3] or Autumn Leaf
Bracken (brown)[3]	Black[2] or Autumn Leaf
Harvest Gold[3]	Black
Sandglow[4]	Autumn Leaf
Tundra (green)[3]	Autumn Leaf
New Racing Green[5]	Black
Brooklands Green[4]	Autumn Leaf
Damask Red	Black
Flamenco (red)[2]	Black
Citron (yellow)[3]	Black
Chartreuse (yellow)[4]	Black
Glacier White	Black[2] or Autum Leaf[3]

Notes
[1] See note ([1]) for 1972 model year.
[2] Introduced February 1975.
[3] Discontinued January/February 1976.
[4] Introduced January 1976.
[5] Used only on the 751 Jubilee GT models in 1975, and one V8 model.

As on roadsters, the main seat colour was found also on liners, mats and carpets, and door seals.

Until 1969, when roadster bodies were made and painted by Bodies Branch in Coventry, it seems that cellulose (or lacquer) paints were used for at least some colours. On the other hand, GT bodies, which were painted at Cowley, were usually finished in synthetic (or enamel) paints. From 1969, all cars were finished in synthetic paints.

The first major redesign of the trim occurred in 1968 for the 1969 model year. This new trim style was available mainly in black, the only exception being that a few beige GTs had a new trim colour called Mushroom (adequately described as beige) which came with brown mats and carpets. Mushroom was used only from March to September 1969. The trim was again changed comprehensively for the 1970 model year on the first GHN5/GHD5 series cars, where for the first time the front seats were Ambla rather than leather, and black was the only trim colour for the 1970 model year.

The paint range was also changed on 1970 models, with some of the old BMC colours being replaced by the first new British Leyland BLVC-coded colours. By 1971, the colour range was composed entirely of BLVC colours, and 1971 was also the first year when

COLOUR SCHEMES, MGB ROADSTER AND GT (1977 MODEL YEAR)

Paint	Seat facings (RHD cars)	Other trim, liners, carpets (RHD cars)	Seats, liners (NA cars)	Carpets (NA cars)
Black[1]	Silver/Grey or Orange/Brown	Black	n/a	n/a
Tahiti Blue	Silver/Grey	Black	Autumn Leaf	Black and Autumn Leaf
Sandglow	Orange/Brown	Black	Autumn Leaf	Black and Autumn Leaf
Brooklands Green	Orange/Brown	Black	Autumn Leaf	Black and Autumn Leaf
Damask Red[2]	Silver/Grey	Black	Black	Black
Carmine (red)[2]	Silver/Grey	Black	Black	Black
Flamenco (red)	Silver/Grey	Black	Black	Black
Chartreuse (yellow)	Orange/Brown	Black	Black	Black
Glacier White[3]	Orange/Brown	Black	Black	Black

Notes
[1] Black not available on North American roadster.
[2] Damask Red discontinued and Carmine introduced in February 1977.
[3] Alternatively Triumph White.

COLOUR SCHEMES, MGB ROADSTER AND GT (1978-80 MODEL YEARS)

Paint	Seat facings (RHD cars)	Other trim, liners, carpets (RHD cars)	Seats, liners (NA cars)	Carpets (NA cars)
Black[1]	Silver/Grey or Orange/Brown	Black	Black or Beige	Black or Black and Chestnut
Pageant Blue	Silver/Grey	Black	Beige	Black and Chestnut
Russet Brown	Orange/Brown	Black	Beige	Black and Chestnut
Brooklands Green	Orange/Brown	Black	Beige	Black and Chestnut
Carmine (red)	Silver/Grey	Black	Beige	Black and Chestnut
Vermilion (red)	Silver/Grey	Black	Black	Black
Inca Yellow[2]	Silver/Grey	Black	Black	Black
Snapdragon[2]	Silver/Grey	Black	Black	Black
Leyland White[3]	Orange/Brown	Black	Black	Black
Bronze Metallic[4]	Orange/Brown	Black	n/a	n/a
Pewter Metallic[5]	Silver/Grey	Black	n/a	n/a

Notes
[1] North American roadster: Black only used on 1979-80 Limited Edition model.
[2] Inca Yellow discontinued and Snapdragon introduced for 1980 model year.
[3] Also known as Ermine and Porcelain White; Triumph White may have been used alternatively.
[4] Used only on 1980 home market roadster LE model.
[5] Used only on 1980 home market GT LE model.

the colour range was exactly the same on both roadster and GT models. Finally, 1971 saw Autumn Leaf (light brown to you or me) arrive as an alternative trim colour to black. Door waist rails were now in the main trim colour, and on the GT the rear quarter waist rails, rear quarterlight seals and centre pillar covers were also in the main trim colours.

From now on there were regular changes to the colour range for every new model year. There were also some variations to the trim colours. For 1972 model year Black was replaced by Navy (a very dark blue), which was featured for two years until Black replaced it again in the summer of 1973. And in August 1972 Autumn Leaf was replaced by Ochre (a sort of yellow-brown colour), which was not popular and gave way to Autumn Leaf again in July 1973.

While the roadster continued with Ambla trim, the GT was given special seat covers with brushed nylon centre panels for the 1972 model year, and a year later the GT had all-nylon seat facings with a new transverse pattern, echoed by new roadster seats with transverse pleats to their Ambla covers.

When the V8 went into production in early 1973, it was finished in the standard paint and trim colour range of the time, although most early V8s were painted Damask Red, Glacier White, Harvest Gold (all with Navy trim) or Teal Blue (Autumn Leaf trim). The trim colour Ochre was used only on a handful of early V8s.

The 1974 colour range was carried over on the early 'rubber-bumper' cars – the '1974½' model cars – and even the early 1975 models, with most changes only occurring in February 1975 when some new colours were introduced. The final 1975 colour range was in turn carried on into 1976, with changes only occurring in January-February 1976. However, these were the only two occasions when most colour changes took place in the middle of a model year, rather than at the start.

The final important redesign of the interior trim took place in June 1976 for the 1977 model year. Even so, the new trim style was confined to RHD roadsters and GTs, which were given new seat facings in striped brushed nylon, in Orange/Brown or Silver/Grey combinations. All other trim parts which had previously been colour-coded to the seats were now uniformly black, including the now standard headrests. North American roadsters, which had hitherto been produced with the same trim schemes as RHD cars, kept the Ambla seat facings for 1977 and subsequent model years, still with liners and other trim parts colour-coded to the seats. For 1977 North American cars had either Autumn Leaf or Black trim, while on 1978 and later models the trim choice was Beige or Black. On these cars with Black trim, carpets were all black. On cars with Autumn Leaf or Beige trim, carpets were black in front of the seats but brown behind the seats (Autumn Leaf on cars with Autumn

PAINT COLOUR CODES

Colour name	BMC/BL code	Ault & Wiborg/ Berger/Gipgloss	ICI	PPG/Ditzler (US)	Dupont (US)	Glasso/Rinshed Mason (US)
Black	BK.1, BLVC 90, PMA*	-	KE 47	9000	99	946
Brown/beige colours						
Antelope (beige)	BLVC 7	28040	7984	32890	8578	6648
Bedouin (beige)	BLVC4	28664	7855	23581	-	6655
Bracken (brown/orange)	BLVC 93	30096	9427	60760	43275	6672
Bronze Metallic (1980 Roadster LE)	BLVC 370, BMC*	34824M, 35269M	6759M	-	-	-
Golden Beige Metallic	BG.19	26930M	3006M, 2496M	22947	8178	6635
Russet Brown	BLVC 205, AAE*	31072, 32592, 33669	DD 51	24378	44848	9251
Sandglow (beige/gold)	BLVC 63	31030	8651, GC 20	24300	44565	8844
Sandy Beige	BG.15	23473	6187	22213	8177	6639
Blue colours						
Aqua (turquoise)	BLVC 60	28002	7932	14075	8821	6651
Bermuda Blue	BU.40	22885	2846	12630	8582	6587, 6650
Blue Royale	BU.38	23322, 28603	5186	12635, 14475	-	6588
Iris Blue	BU.12	20306	3243	12235, 3199	8184	8536
Midnight Blue	BLVC 12	28666	7963	14245	30011	6663
Mineral Blue	BU.9	18921	3130	12115, 15406	8182	6600
Mirage (mauve)	BLVC 11	30097	7960	33135	43277	6668
Pageant Blue	BLVC 224, JNA*	31913	FC 58	15231	45473AH	9733D
Riviera Silver Blue Metallic	BU.47	26554M	3005M	-	-	-
Teal Blue	BLVC 18	28667	7918	14244	30006	6656
Tahiti Blue	BLVC 65	30788, 31692	AF 45	14866, 15096	43907	6674
Green colours						
Brooklands Green	BLVC 169, HMM*	30683	4498, FM45, FD 68	45190	44630	8848
Green Mallard	BLVC 22	28895	7925	44638	30014	6661D
Limeflower	BLVC 20	28668	7968(?)	44448	30010	6658
British Racing Green (1962-63)	GN.25	21677	8120	43342	8193	6607
Dark British Racing Green (1963-70)	GN.29	24499	9767	46446	8194	6606
(New) Racing Green (1970-71, and 1975 GT Jubilee model)	BLVC 25	28670	7985	44446	30012	6659
Tundra (olive drab)	BLVC 94	30094, 32045, 32777	9424	44978	43278	6670
Grey colours						
Chelsea Grey	GR.15	17581	2750	31733	8198	6669
Grampian Grey	GR.12	21175	7087	31934	-	6575
Pewter Metallic (1980 GT LE)	BLVC 377, MMD*	35700M, 34836M	6766M	-	-	-
Red colours						
Aconite (purple)	BLVC 95	30095	9425	14728	43274	6673
Black Tulip (purple)	BLVC 23	28058	7970	14417	30015	9406
Blaze (orange)	BLVC 16	28665, 30545	7864	60637	30007	6654
Damask Red	BLVC 99, (RD.5?)	20921, 30488	4808	72261, 71064	8819	6622R
Carmine Red	BLVC 209, CAA*	29355	9236, FD 32, EE 80	72065	43019	8325R
Flame Red	BLVC 61	28216, 29787	3442	71861	8571	6652R
Flamenco (orange red)	BLVC 133	30789, 32137, 32635	9718, DA 63, DA 90	72144	43661	6675
Tartan Red	RD.9	20817, 32046	3770	71062, 71416	8204	8534R
Vermilion (orange red)	BLVC 118, CML*	32781	FC 57, GE 40	60932	45471	9732R
White colours						
Glacier White	BLVC 59	27962, 30099	4309	8845, 90074	8579	6647
Leyland White (also known as Ermine White or Porcelain White)	BLVC 243, NMC/NME/ NAF/NCG*	32335, 36133	FA 78	90106	H7896	9734
Old English White	WT.3	32043, 24643, 18580	2379, 2122(?)	8177	8207	6642
Police White	WT.2, BLVC 1024	24048	HT 49	-	-	-
Snowberry White	WT.4	19303	3012	8341	8210	6644
Triumph White	BLVC 206, NAB*	24863, 31694(?)	3738	8380	4318	10053
Yellow colours						
Bronze Yellow	BLVC 15	27944	9785, 7861	81827	8581	6649
Chartreuse	BLVC 167	30645	CH 76	45189	44629	8847
Citron	BLVC 73	30083	8653	44947	43276	6669
Inca Yellow	BLVC 207, FAB*	33668, 31073, 32694	DD 50	82309	44880	9252
Pale Primrose Yellow	YL.12	26111	3297	81499	8319	6630
Snapdragon	BLVC 235, FMN*	31939	GJ 80	82462	45475	12115
Harvest Gold	BLVC 19	28894	7919	82018	30013	6662

*These three-letter codes are found stamped on the VIN (car number) plates of 1980 model year RHD cars.

Note
This table lists the BMC/BL paint codes, together with the codes from major UK and US paint manufacturers, to assist restorers who need to order paint in the correct colour. Please note that occasionally there may be more than one shade of the same colour, although differences between such shades are usually small. None of the MGB records specify these shade differences and should it prove difficult to determine which is the correct shade, the best advice would be to try to match existing original paint.

Vermilion, as seen on this 1980 roadster owned by Brian Keates, was introduced in the last significant overhaul of paint colours in 1977.

Leaf trim, or Chestnut on cars with Beige trim).

The last major overhaul of the paint colour range occurred in 1977. The only change after this was that Inca Yellow was replaced by Snapdragon (yellow) on 1980 models, although there is some confusion over the different white paint colours used in the final years. The long-established Glacier White may have given way to Triumph White in 1977, and this may also have been used in 1978 or later, although the standard white colour on 1978-80 models was Leyland White, which is also sometimes known as Ermine White or Porcelain White.

Of the various Limited Edition models, the 1975 Jubilee version of the GT was finished in the 1971 colour of New Racing Green. The North American Limited Edition model of 1979-80 was Black, a colour otherwise not offered on the North American cars after 1976. Black, incidentally, was mostly available only as a special order colour from 1969 onwards. The 1980 home market LE models were available exclusively in Bronze Metallic (roadster) or Pewter Metallic (GT), the first and only metallic colours since 1968, and rather mundanely picked out of the range of colours used on the Princess saloon at the time.

The other important non-standard colour which was used time and again over the years was Police White, as found on MGB police cars. Police White cars usually had Black trim, or failing that the darkest trim colour available – thus Navy in the 1972 and 1973 model years. But if any GTs were ordered in Police White from 1976 onwards (the possibility is not very likely!), they would have been given the Silver and Grey seat facings.

Special colours occurred from time to time, usually for experimental purposes rather than because of customer orders. The only example I have found of a small batch of cars being finished in an experimental colour is for a dozen or so GTs which in mid-1971 were painted Mustard. Otherwise most experiments were one-offs. As late as 1978 there was a one-off Metallic Denim Blue GT with dark blue bumpers to be seen around the styling studio at Longbridge.

While it is known that CKD cars assembled in Australia had their own unique paint colour range, sadly at the time of writing a list was not available – but at least owners of Australian cars can read their cars' original colours direct from the Australian assembly or chassis number plate. Cars assembled in Belgium or Eire are thought to have been painted in the standard colours used in Britain.

The accompanying tables list all known combinations, in greater detail on the early cars – matters became simpler in later years. On the other hand it is necessary to list most model years individually from 1970 because of the changes. There is also a list of BMC/BL paint codes as well as the codes from major UK and US paint manufacturers.

BUYING GUIDE

Buying an MGB or any other classic car is frighteningly easy, bank manager permitting, but selling it again can be worryingly difficult. Because of the number of MGBs built there will at any given time be a large selection available, of almost any year or model. Many are simply bought and sold privately and this can be the cheapest way of buying, but there may not be any easy way of getting things sorted out in the case of misrepresentation. Some MGBs are sold through auctions but these tend to be the cream of the crop.

As the classic car scene has become more professional in recent years most MGBs are undoubtedly handled by dealers. Some of these are very long-standing firms with a sound reputation, and many also offer parts or restoration services. Some will trade primarily in restored cars, re-shelled using Heritage bodyshells, and will if required complete the car to customer requirements. Many have come to specialise almost exclusively in MGBs but may also handle other MGs or other makes of car. For peace of mind and the possibility of some sort of warranty, it can well be worth paying the extra amount that a dealer typically charges compared with a private individual. There are always plenty of MGBs advertised for sale by dealers as well as private vendors in the classic car magazines or the MG club publications.

A decision will have to be made about which model to select. The purist will want a pre-1970 Mark I or Mark II roadster, with the original chrome grille and leather seats. From the point of view of enjoyment, later roadsters – including the 'rubber-bumper' cars – are almost as satisfying. GTs are not so popular, but they are cheaper and much more practical as everyday cars. From later years of production, there are more GTs in the UK than roadsters (disregarding re-imported cars). In North America there are no GTs later than 1974. The 1975 'Jubilee' model and the 1980 LE cars command a premium over comparable ordinary MGBs. In the USA at the time of writing, later cars (1977–80 models) were still regularly attracting higher prices than earlier cars. In the UK the opposite was almost true, always allowing for variations depending on condition and originality.

If you believe price guides, MGCs are more valuable than MGBs, but this seems not always to be born out in practice. While the MGC has a following, it is a rather more specialised car and does not quite have the same instant appeal as an MGB. The ultimate 'lemon' in terms of being difficult to sell must be a North American specification MGC GT with automatic gearbox – not even its rarity can compensate! The MGB GT V8, on the other hand, is considered very desirable, with the accent inevitably on the 'chrome-bumper' cars. While originally this model was only sold in the UK, some examples have since migrated to distant places and a few are now even in the USA.

Some extras are undoubtedly desirable, although wire wheels would not be on my personal list – I'm too lazy to clean them. Overdrive is a blessing as it makes the car much more relaxing as a high-speed cruiser. The automatic gearbox is a genuine rarity and some enthusiasts prize it mainly for this reason, but I would very much question whether one should pay over the odds for an automatic car. Anything else is really down to personal preference. Almost all cars have some form of extra equipment – for instance exterior mirrors and seat belts on the early cars – and many items can still be fitted if the owner wants them.

In later years, an incredible number of cars originally sold in North America have found new homes in the UK, Europe or Australia. Some of these will have been modified, for instance converted to RHD (legally required in Australia, convenient in the UK), and will hopefully be described as converted cars rather than being claimed to be original RHD cars. Others will have had the special emissions equipment removed and the engines brought up to UK standards of tune. In certain European countries, such modifications of later cars may contravene local regulations.

Anyone contemplating buying a car in the USA, or buying an ex-US car in the UK before it has been registered with the DVLA, should ensure that the original American title document is available, that the number on here does match the car number (or engine number) on the vehicle, and that the customs clearance document ('pink slip') is available. A UK importer normally has to pay the current rate of VAT on re-importation, levied on the purchase price of the car plus shipping and insurance costs. Import duty is only payable if the car was assembled outside the EEC – as was the case with CKD cars from Australia. Certain US dealers specialise in selling cars for export, and some shipping firms have become very expert in handling the car as well as the paperwork involved.

Some MGBs have been customised, but such modifications should be obvious to the reader of this book! Items which are available include special all-leather trim kits, various steering wheels, wood cappings for the facia, special hoods with contrast-colour piping, improved full carpet kits and so on. Much more useful are the various suspension modifications which have been introduced to improve the handling, especially of the 'rubber-bumper' cars. There are roadsters which have been converted with V8 engines, or other more modern Rover Group engines such as O-series, M16 or T-series. There has also been a fashion for converting the 'rubber-bumper' models to 'chrome-bumper' looks, with the original pre-1970 grille and – hopefully! – lowered suspension. Nothing wrong with any of these modifications – but they do make the car non-original.

There are other books or magazine articles which cover all aspects of restoring the cars and it would be pointless in the present volume to try to match the

A new MGB roadster bodyshell taking shape in the jig at British Motor Heritage's body factory in Faringdon, Oxfordshire. Although a car with a new bodyshell can no longer be said to be 'original', re-shelling is often more convenient and less expensive than restoring a badly corroded body.

excellence of these works. Most MGB owners who do their own servicing, repairs or restoration will probably benefit more from these books than from the official or proprietary workshop manuals, as the original manuals were never written with a full restoration project in mind, and in the case of the factory publication it is written for the professional mechanic rather than for the amateur. Nevertheless, it is a useful book.

Most of the more common problems with MGBs concern the bodywork, unless the car has been re-shelled. The weakest areas for rust are sills, doors and wings. In severe cases rust will also attack the floor panels and the inner structure of the front wings and dash. Many cars have had poorly-executed body repairs with badly aligned panels or bumpers, or they may be full of filler. Severe corrosion of the structure is a reason for MoT test failure in the UK, apart from being probably dangerous if, for instance, rear spring hangers are affected.

In mechanical terms, the MGB and related models are quite robust. There will be problems, but they are mostly the sort associated with any classic cars. The early 1962-64 three-bearing engines are not as long-lived as the five-bearing engines, and all B-series units will gradually use more oil as they age. On the MGC, the condition of the front suspension should be carefully checked as some parts are difficult to obtain. On the V8, gearbox problems are more likely than on other cars, simply because the 'box is at the limit of its torque transmitting capacity. The V8 final drive gears are also difficult to obtain, while the exhaust manifolds on this model can split or crack if they have been bolted too tightly. The V8 engine is notably robust, but the hydraulic tappets and rocker shafts may need replacing after 50,000 miles. The water pump may also fail.

Parts availability for the MGB and associated models is outstanding, and improving all the time. With the exception of the VW Beetle, no other classic car is likely to have such excellent parts coverage in so many parts of the world.

In 1988, the Rover Group subsidiary British Motor Heritage introduced the re-manufactured MGB roadster bodyshell, and subsequently followed this up with an MGB GT shell. This was a pioneering effort and thousands of these bodies have been manufactured. Re-shelling a car is often more convenient than trying to restore a badly corroded original body, but the end result will be a car that can no longer be said to be 'original'. Whether originality or a perfect new rust-proofed bodyshell is more important at the end of the day comes down to individual preference. The Heritage shells were originally sold without bonnet, front wings, doors and boot lid, but are now complete with all these parts. They are of a rather composite specification, to cater for variations over the production period: they are most closely based on the 1967-74 'chrome-bumper' shells with the larger transmission tunnel, but can be adapted to the earlier specification, as conversion kits to install the smaller tunnel are available from some specialists.

Many enthusiasts have successfully completed re-shelling jobs in their own garages, even if the odds are that it has taken longer and cost more in other new parts than originally bargained for! It has become common practice for professional restorers to offer re-shelled cars for sale, and this is perhaps the most painless way of acquiring an MGB. One slight problem which has occurred concerns original GTs that have been re-shelled as roadsters; the DVLA may consider the resulting car as 'new' or 'assembled from spare parts' and may re-register the vehicle under a new registration mark, possibly with a Q prefix. Another problem is that in some countries it becomes financially prohibitive to re-shell a car as the authorities consider the car to be 'new' and at the very least insist on charging purchase tax again...

The lasting appeal of an MGB, MGC or MGB GT V8 lies in the combination these cars offer of undiluted period sports car appeal, versatility and practicality in everyday use. Long may this continue...

PRODUCTION CHANGES

CHANGES BY ENGINE NUMBER

18G ENGINES

18G-U-H/101 (May 62)
Start of engine number series.

18G-U-H/4385, 18G-U-L/2815 (Dec 62)
Separate valve guide shroud discontinued, valve spring cup replaced by type with integral guide shroud.

18G-U-H/5572, 18G-U-L/2854, 18G-RU-H/5108, 18G-RU-L/?? (Feb 63)
New crankshaft front pulley.

18G-U-H/8822, 18G-U-L/7763, 18G-RU-H/8610, 18G-RU-L/7402 (Mar 63)
New outer valve springs (interchangeable).

18G-U-H/8841, 18G-U-L/7785, 18G-RU-H/8610, 18G-RU-L/7402 (Mar 63)
New con rod assemblies (interchangeable).

18G-U-H/27090, 18G-U-L/24108, 18G-RU-H/25577, 18G-RU-L/10744 (Dec 63)
Engine front mounting plate (interchangeable); cylinder front cover and oil seal changed, probably at this time.

18G-U-H/30470, 18G-U-L/24910, 18G-RU-H/30147, 18G-RU-L/10778 (Jan 64)
New stronger dynamo front pulley (interchangeable).

The cylinder front side cover (tappet cover) with ventilation elbow outlet was also changed at some stage during the 18G engine production run. The change point is not known but the parts are interchangeable.

18GA ENGINES

18GA-U-H/101 (Feb 64)
Introduced with closed circuit breathing system, cylinder front side cover with oil separator, new rocker cover without breather pipe attachment, new inlet manifold. On all bar the first 61 high compression engines without overdrive, carburettor specification was changed from AUD 52 to AUD 135, with standard needle no. 5 instead of MB.

18GA-U-H/12176, 18GA-U-L/8314,
18GA-RU-H/11150, 18GA-RU-L/9710 (Jul 64)
New inlet valve guides (interchangeable); also fitted to engine numbers from 18GA-U-H/11927 to 12000 inclusive.

18GB ENGINES

18GB-U-H/101 (Oct 64)
Introduced with new crankshaft with five main bearings, necessitating substantial redesign of cylinder block, etc. Gudgeon pins now fully floating with circlips, instead of con rod small ends being split with clamp bolt; drivegear for mechanical rev counter deleted from camshaft; standard carburettor needles now FX instead of no. 5; gearbox first motion shaft with larger spigot end and gearbox casing modified.

18GB-U-H/14217, 18GB-U-L/11876,
18GB-RU-H/14625, 18GB-RU-L/13720 (Apr 65)
New rocker cover (interchangeable).

18GB-U-H/18629(?), 18GB-U-L/11851,
18GB-RU-H/14031, 18GB-RU-L/13711 (Apr 65)
New front oil thrower to crankshaft.

18GB-U-H/16418, 18GB-U-L/16509,
18GB-RU-H/15815, 18GB-RU-L/3316 (Jun 65)
New pistons and rings (interchangeable).

18GB-U-H/23538, 18GB-U-L/21980,
18GB-RU-H/22650, 18GB-RU-L/19405 (Sep 65)
New rocker cover (interchangeable); MG nameplate and Weslake patent plate are now self-adhesive instead of rivetted. Coinciding with car number 71122.

18GB-U-H/31472, 18GB-U-L/29123,
18GB-RU-H/31003, 18GB-RU-L/25995 (Dec 65)
New second speed gear baulk ring synchroniser.

18GB-U-H/42716, 18GB-U-L/36742,
18GB-RU-H/43101, 18GB-RU-L/29758 (Jun 66)
New starter motor.

18GB-U-H/44413, 18GB-U-L/36732 (Jun 66)
New water pump assembly (interchangeable); but change points for overdrive engines not quoted.

18GB-U-H/56047, 18GB-U-L/51556,
18GB-RU-H/54406, 18GB-RU-L/29792 (Sep 66)
New clutch cover (interchangeable); new reverse selector plunger and detent plunger in gearbox; reverse light switch added.

18GB-U-L/51565, 18GB-RU-L/29792 (Oct 66)
New low compression pistons and rings (interchangeable).

18GB-U-H/63765, 18GB-U-L/60543,
18GB-RU-H/64060, 18GB-RU-L/58216 (Jan 67)
New thermostat, Weston-Thomson latch-open type, 13H 3585 (part number for standard 82°C thermostat), (interchangeable).

18GB-U-H/65681, 18GB-U-L/60553,
18GB-RU-H/65337, 18GB-RU-L/58216 (Jan 67)
New starter motor, with new armature shaft and drive assembly.

18GB-U-H/67973, 18GB-U-L/60571,
18GB-RU-H/68285, 18GB-RU-L/58224 (Jan 67)
New sump and sump gasket (interchangeable).

18GB-U-H/68675, 18GB-RU-H/68416 (Feb 67)
New high compression pistons and rings (interchangeable).

18GB-U-H/74720, 18GB-U-L/60596,
18GB-RU-H/74529, 18GB-RU-L/58223 (Mar 67)
Gearbox fitted with layshaft of larger diameter as already found in close-ratio gearbox (competition part) and with caged needle roller bearings; gearbox casing and assembly modified to suit.

18GB-U-H/86521, 18GB-U-L/84009 (Aug 67)
New water pump assembly (interchangeable); but change points for overdrive engines not quoted.

Three different types of crankshafts are quoted for the 18GB engines without change points indicated, but they are all interchangeable. Nor are change points recorded for the modification to the closed-circuit breathing system, but the affected parts are interchangeable.

18GD/GF ENGINES

18GD-We-H/101 (not USA), 18GF-We-H/101 (USA) (Nov 67)
From start of Mark II model, car number 138401, new engines with following changes: all-new gearbox with synchromesh on first gear; Borg Warner type 35 automatic gearbox introduced as optional equipment (not for the USA); new overdrive unit and relay; new gearbox mounting plate; new larger flywheel and starter ring gear; new inverted Tecalemit oil filter; modified closed-circuit breathing system; new rear engine mounting crossmember; new thermostat and water outlet elbow; new distributor, with cap where cables exit from top rather than side; modified ignition coil; longer ignition cables, fitted with suppressors for all markets; pre-engaged starter motor type M418G introduced; 16AC alternator introduced, with separate control box and negative earth electrical system; new oil pressure and thermal transmitters; new oil cooler; cylinder block drain tap replaced by a drain plug; carburettor specification changed, now AUD 278 on 18GD engines, AUD 265 on 18GF engines. 18GF engines for the USA have the following differences: inlet manifold; cylinder head with air injectors, air manifold and air pump fitted on bracket from thermostat housing, driven by belt from special fan pulley; six-blade metal fan; gulp valve and check valve fitted; special name and instruction plate to rocker cover. Cars for Canada were initially fitted with the 18GD engine, replaced by the USA-type 18GF engine in August 1968. Cars with automatic gearbox were fitted with the USA-type six-blade fan.

18GD-We-H/836, 18GD-We-L/1046,
18GD-RWe-H/1713, 18GD-RWe-L/1137,
18GD-Rc-H/104, 18GD-Rc-L/107, 18GF-We-H/2159,
18GF-RWe-H/531 (Mar 68)
New inlet and exhaust valves with chrome stems and narrower notch at the top of the valve stem; new valve springs and cups, new valve cotters without circlips.

18GD-We-H/2239, 18GD-We-L/1063,
18GD-RWe-H/2624, 18GD-RWe-L/? (May 68)
New inlet manifold (not on USA-Type engine); but change point not quoted for engine with automatic gearbox.

18GD-We-H/2307, 18GD-RWe-H/2793,
18GD-Rc-H/104, 18GF-We-H/7315, 18GF-RWe-H/7001 (May 68)
New high compression pistons (interchangeable); the new pistons were also fitted to engines with numbers from 18GF-We-H/7116 to 7200 inclusive, and 18GF-RWe-H/6905 to 6920 inclusive.

18GD-We-H/3651, 18GD-We-L/1090,
18GD-RWe-H/3939, 18GD-RWe-L/1137,
18GF-We-H/9258, 18GF-RWe-H/8188 (Jul 68)

New clutch cover assembly (interchangeable); this was also fitted to engines with numbers from 18GF-We-H/8373 to 8400 inclusive.

Not quoted (Aug 68)
From car numbers 153878 (roadster) and 154231 (GT), cars for Canada were fitted with the USA engine type 18GF instead of 18GD.

18GG/GH/GJ/GK ENGINES

18GG-We-H/101 (not NA), 18GH-We-H/101 (NA) (Oct 68)
Introduced on 1969 models from car number 158231, with following changes: carburettor crankcase ventilation instead of closed-circuit breathing system; new dipstick and dip stick tube with dust cover; new inlet manifold, common to both 18GG and 18GH engines; 16ACR alternator with built-in regulator instead of separate control box; new water pump with pressure balance seal (interchangeable with previous types); modified carburettors, specification AUD 325 with needle FX on 18GG engines, AUD 326 with needle AAE on 18GH engines.

18GH-We-H/20289 (Sep 69)
New rocker cover on North American engine.

18GH-We-H/20290 (Sep 69)
Carburettors on North American cars modified, new float chamber lids and levers, carburettor specification becomes AUD 405.

18GJ-We-H/22647 (Oct 69)
With the introduction of the evaporative loss control system on cars for California, engines for these cars are designated 18GJ, with engine numbers allocated in the 18GH series; 18GJ engines have a non-vented oil filler cap; introduced from car number 187701 (roadster) and 188659 (GT).

Not quoted (Mar 70)
BL sticker instead of MG plate to rocker cover, from car number 203093.

18GG-We-H/12300, 18GG-We-L/9143,
18GG-RWe-H/12506, 18GG-RWe-L/7461,
18GG-Rc-H/527, 18GH/GJ-We-H/32763,
18GH/GJ-RWe-H/31824 (Mar 70)
New oil filter of cartridge type with inverted canister introduced; this oil filter was also fitted to engines 18GG-We-H/12013 to 12110 inclusive, 18GG-We-L/7404 to 7410 inclusive and 18GH/GJ-We-H/32590 to 32600 inclusive.

18GG-We-H/16004, 18GG-We-L/???,
18GG-RWe-H/16352, 18GG-RWe-L/7486,
18GG-Rc-H/639, 18GH/GJ-We-H/40754,
18GH/GJ-RWe-H/40392 (Jun 70)
New con rod assemblies, of tapered shape, with horizontally split big ends.

18GK-We-H/101 (Aug 70)
From the start of the 1971 model year (car number 219001) all North American cars are fitted with the evaporative loss control system, and North American engines are now designated 18GK, with a new number series; 18GK engines are fitted with a modified distributor and carburettor needles AAL. Cars for other markets continue with engine 18GG.

18GG-We-H/212689, 18GG-We-L/??,
18GG-RWe-H/22060, 18GG-RWe-L/20208,
18GG-Rc-H/738, 18GK-We-H/10952,
18GK-RWe-H/10073 (Jan71)
New dipstick tube.

18GG-We-H/21285, 18GG-RWe-H/21804,
18GG-Rc-H/758, 18GK-We-H/10280,
18GK-RWe-H/10497 (Jan 71)
Modified type 16ACR alternator; but change points for low compression engines not quoted.

18GG-We-H/22339, 18GG-We-L/???,
18GG-RWe-H/22443, 18GG-RWe-L/20208,
18GG-Rc-H/758, 18GK-We-H/12014,
18GK-RWe-H/10557 (Jan 71)
New crankshaft front pulley and front engine cover.

18GG-We-H/23567, 18GG-RWe-H/23728,
18GG-Rc-H/867, 18GK-We-H/15223,
18GK-RWe-H/13906 (Mar 71)
Cylinder front side cover with separate cylindrical oil separator, instead of oil separator built into cover itself. The new cover was also fitted to engines 18GK-We-H/15034 to 15100 inclusive; but change points for low compression engines not quoted.

18GG-We-H/24249, 18GG-RWe-H/24641,
18GG-Rc-H/847, 18GK-We-H/17433,

18GK-RWe-H/14364 (Mar 71)

New pistons with three rings instead of four; press-fit instead of fully floating gudgeon pins, new con rods; block modified. Also fitted to engines 18GG-We-H/21492 to 21500 inclusive, and 18GK-We-H/17237 to 17300 inclusive; but change points for low compression engines not quoted.

18V ENGINES (1971-74)

18V-581-F/Y-H/L (not NA), 18V-582-F/Y-H/L (not NA), 18V-583-F/Y-H/L (not NA), 18V-584-Z-L (NA), 18V-585-Z-L (NA); all number series start with 101 (Aug 71)

Introduced from the start of the 1972 model year (car number 258001). Engines now painted black; home market cars with F prefix have HS.4 carburettors specification AUD 492 with spring-loaded needles; all export cars have HIF.4 carburettors with horizontal integrated float chambers, specification AUD 434 on non-North American cars with Y prefix, or specification AUD 493 on North American cars with Z prefix. High compression ratio now 9:1, low compression ratio of 8:1 standardised on North American engines; new cylinder head, with larger inlet valves (1.625-1.630in); new bucket type tappets and longer pushrods; blanking plate fitted over aperture for mechanical fuel pump found on other vehicles sharing same basic engine (Marina, Sherpa); new water pump, common to BMC 1800, and new fan pulley; new air cleaners; new distributor on North American cars; new starter motor, Lucas 2M100; sump with less capacity.

18V-581-F/Y-H/1584, 18V-581-F/Y-L/1014, 18V-582-F/Y-H/2593, 18V-582-F/Y-L/1208, 18V-583-F/Y-H/258 (Jan 72)

New straight dipstick on non-North American engines.

18V-584-Z-L/7472, 18V-585-Z-L/805 (Jan 72)

Seat belt inhibitor switch added to gearbox, with attendant changes to remote control shaft and housing, on North American engines only.

18V-581-F/Y-H/1643, 18V-581-F/Y-L/1014, 18V-582-F/Y-H/2914, 18V-582-F/Y-L/1208, 18V-583-F/Y-H/258, 18V-584-Z-L/9449, 18V-585-Z-L/?? (Jan 72)

New gasket for front main bearing cap.

18V-581-F/Y-H/2102, 18V-582-F/Y-H/4230, 18V-583-F/Y-H/304, 18V-584-Z-L/12914, 18V-585-Z-L/1829 (Mar 72)

16ACR alternator fitted with modified regulator and surge protection device; change points for 581/582 series low compression engines not quoted.

18V-581-F/Y-H/3106, 18V-582-F/Y-H/8106, 18V-583-F/Y-H/439, 18V-584-Z-L/16307, 18V-585-Z-L/2119 (Jun 72)

New key holding crankshaft timing gear to crankshaft; change points for 581/582 series low compression engines not quoted.

18V-672-Z-L/101, 18V-673-Z-L/101 (Aug 72)

From start of 1973 model year (car number 294251), North American engines modified and now designated 672/673 series. Specification of HIF.4 carburettors changed to AUD 550 with ABD needles instead of AAU; new distributor; non-North American engines continue without change.

18V-581-F/Y-H/4106, 18V-581-F/Y-L/1029, 18V-582-F/Y-H/11379, 18V-582-F/Y-L/???, 18V-583-F/Y-H/546, 18V-672-Z-L/3024, 18V-673-Z-L/322 (Oct 72)

Single timing chain instead of duplex chain, with new drive gears to crankshaft and camshaft.

18V-581-F/Y-H/4419, 18V-581-F/Y-L/1040, 18V-582-F/Y-H/13178, 18V-582-F/Y-L/1225, 18V-583-F/Y-H/605, 18V-672-Z-L/6184, 18V-673-Z-L/2778 (Feb 73)

17ACR alternator introduced instead of 16ACR.

18V-581-F/Y-H/5266, 18V-581-F/Y-L/1072, 18V-582-F/Y-H/21955, 18V-582-F/Y-L/1249, 18V-583-F/Y-H/871, 18V-672-Z-L/21326, 18V-673-Z-L/3158 (Oct 73)

Alternative cartridge oil filter of spin-on type with modified external oil pipes introduced, but see also change point at car numbers 338568 (GT) and 338791 (roadster) in Dec 73. It appears that the original type of oil filter was reinstated by Feb 74 at car numbers 343303 (roadster) and 343761 (GT); engine number change points not quoted.

18V-581-F/Y-H/5302, 18V-582-F/Y-H/22277, 18V-583-F/Y-H/871, 18V-672-Z-L/21739,

18V-673-Z-L/3178 (Nov 73)

New cylinder head gasket and cylinder head studs; but change points for 581/582 series low compression engines not quoted.

18V-779-F-H/101, 18V-780-F-H/101 (Nov 73)

Modified non-North American engines now designated 779/780 series. HIF.4 carburettors, specification AUD 616 complying with ECE.15 emissions standard, now fitted to all cars including home market models; export-type air filters and fuel filter introduced on home market cars; new distributor, cap and plug leads, complying with ECE.10 ignition suppression standard; low compression option discontinued; automatic gearbox option no longer offered, having been discontinued at the start of the 1974 model year.

18V-779-F-H/275, 18V-780-F-H/2366, 18V-672-Z-L/27270, 18V-673-Z-L/3645 (Jan 74)

New water pump and water pump gasket.

18V ENGINES (1974-80)

18V-846-F-H (not NA), 18V-847-F-H (not NA), 18V-836-Z-L (NA), 18V-837-Z-L (NA); all number series start with 101 (Sep 74)

Modified 18V engines introduced for the '1974½' model year at the start of production of rubber-bumper cars (car number 360301). All engines have new engine front mounting plate and engine mountings. The following changes apply at least to 846/847 series engines but see also note below: new cylinder head with smaller inlet valves (1.562-1.567in as on the 18G series engines); rocker pedestal number four with off-set instead of direct oil feed; new engine front cover; new cylinder front side cover with built-in oil separator; new crankshaft pulley, diameter increased from 5⅛in to 6in; smaller fan pulley, new fan belt and alternator adjusting link; modified sump; new distributor type 45D4 instead of 25D4; gearbox with modified casing, new first gear with altered ratio, new speedometer drive wheel and pinion; modified overdrive unit; 846/847 series engines have new inlet manifold and carburettor specification is now FZX 1001 with ACD needles instead of AAU.

18V-797-AE-L/101, 18V-798-AE-L/101 (Dec 74)

New North American engines introduced for 1975 model year (car number 367901): single Zenith-Stromberg carburettor fitted on new combined inlet/exhaust manifold with induction heater and new air filter; automatic choke; exhaust gas recirculation valve added; new cylinder head BHM 1062, lead-free tolerant design, with the smaller inlet valves; new camshaft CAM 1156; new air pump drive; new remote control shaft and housing. The parts list quotes the following changes, shared with non-North American 846/847 series, as having been introduced from the start of the 797/798 series: rocker pedestal with off-set oil feed; engine front cover; cylinder side cover with oil separator; crankshaft pulley, sump, distributor, gearbox and overdrive modifications. These changes may in fact have been introduced on North American engines from the start of the 836/837 series, which are likely also to have had the smaller inlet valves and the same inlet manifold as the 846/847 series engines. The first engine numbers for non-American engines in the 1975 model year were 18V-846-F-H/212 and 18V-847-F-H/937.

18V-801-AE-L/101, 18V-802-AE-L/101 (Jul 75)

New North American engine introduced at first only for California, and then from Aug 75 (start of 1976 model year, car number 386601) for all of USA (but not Canada): catalyst added to exhaust system; modified carburettor and air filter; electronic ignition and new distributor. Cars for Canada continue with 797/798 series engines in 1976 model year.

18V-846-F-H/553, 18V-847-F-H/7004, 18V-797-AE-L/9864, 18V-798-AE-L/????, 18V-801-AE-L/5959, 18V-802-AE-L/1493 (Dec 75)

New water pump.

18V-846-F-H/914 (Jun 76)

End of 846 series as overdrive becomes standard on all non-North American cars.

18V-883-AE-L (Fed), 18V-884-AE-L (Fed), 18V-890-AE-L (Cal), 18V-891-AE-L (Cal); all number series start with 101 (Jun 76)

Modified engines for the USA to 49-state Federal specifications as well as to Californian specification introduced at the start of the 1977 model year (car number 410001). The following changes appear to have been introduced at this time and are likely also to have been implemented on the 847

series non-North American engine: crankshaft; distributor drive spindle; exhaust valves; cylinder rear side cover; starter ring gear; gearbox mounting plate. On all engines for the 1977 model year, the mechanical fan was discontinued and replaced by an electric fan (two on North American cars), with attendant changes to pulleys, as well as radiator hoses and the water outlet elbow as the radiator moved forward. The 1977 changes appear to have been introduced on 847 series engines intermittently from engine number 10644 and on all engines from 11308. The start of the 1977 model year is likely also to mark the introduction on 847 series engines of the so-called 'tamper-proof' carburettors, specification FZX 1229, with shorter necks to the bellhousings.

18V-892-AE-L/101, 18V-893-AE-L/101 (Aug 76)

Modified engines for Canada, similar to the USA engines introduced in Jun 76 but without catalyst.

18V-847-F-H/15806, 18V-883-AE-L/12545, 18V-884-AE-L/2875 (?), 18V-890-AE-L/3048, 18V-891-AE-L1045, 18V-892-AE-L/920, 18V-893-AE-L/411 (Apr 77)

New cylinder front side cover and oil separator. Also, on 847 series only, new hoses for carburettor ventilation from Y-piece to carburettors.

18V-847-F-H/16941 (Jun 77)

New camshaft gear.

18V-883-AE-L/14675, 18V-884-AE-L/3291, 18V-890-AE-L/3496, 18V-891-AE-L/1187 (Jun 77)

New catalyst.

18V-883-AE-L/14676, 18V-884-AE-L/3293, 18V-890-AE-L/3506, 18V-891-AE-L/1197, 18V-892-AE-L/977, 18V-893-AE-L/429 (Jun 77)

New air manifold.

Not quoted (1978-80)

British Leyland sticker on rocker cover removed, circa 1978; in 1980, rocker cover fitted with sticker with new corporate Austin Morris blue wing logo.

CHANGES BY CAR & BODY NUMBERS

101 (May 62)

Start of production.

368 (Jul 62)

Towing eye added to front suspension crossmember.

619 (Aug 62)

New pattern Armstrong front shock absorbers with built-in reservoir to eliminate damper fade; interchangeable in pairs.

2779 (black trim), 2849 (red trim), 2902 (blue trim) (Nov 62)

Carpet introduced instead of leathercloth for toeboard and air intake box liners.

3189 (Nov 62)

Improved seal for bottom of master cylinder box.

The shield badge used between 1962-69 had a black background surrounding the octagon and red inside the octagon, with silver letters, octagon and border.

3687 (Dec 62)
Additional colour British Racing Green (GN.25) introduced.

4514 (Dec 62)
Improved spare wheel clamp for wire wheel, to prevent damage to luggage.

4961 (Jan 63)
Introduction of pipe clamps instead of retainer rings for carburettor overflow pipes.

5635 (Jan 63)
Screws and washers for trim now finished in 'Florentine Bronze' instead of chrome plating.

5794 (Jan 63)
Windscreen assembly modified with new section to bottom rail, to improve retention and sealing of apron rubber; apron rubber now sits under rather than over frame.

5813 (Jan 63)
Horns relocated from bonnet locking platform (vertical mounting) to wheelarch panels (horizontal mounting); horns fitted with new angled brackets; horn harness modified to suit.

6693 (Feb 63)
Stronger handbrake lever introduced.

6917 (Feb 63)
Heavier wiper arms (13oz) introduced, for increased blade pressure to prevent wipers lifting at high speed; wiper motor and wheelboxes modified.

9043 (Mar 63)
On RHD cars without overdrive, speedometer cable lengthened from 45in to 48in (it remains 45in on LHD cars without overdrive).

9464 (Mar 63)
Improved sealing grommets for windscreen pillars.

10100 (Apr 63)
Longer but thinner rear bonnet seal, 35in by ¼in instead of 18in by ½in.

10205 (Apr 63)
New rear suspension bump rubber to improve ride.

Body 10323 (Apr 63)
Redesigned interior of seat cushion, now produced as a foam moulding, with increased depth.

Body 10466 (Apr 63)
Stiffer aluminium employed for bonnet panel, no change to part number, interchangeable.

10612 (Apr 63)
On RHD cars with overdrive, speedometer cable lengthened from 56in to 60in (always 60in on LHD cars with overdrive).

Not quoted (May 63)
Chrome finisher deleted from inside of instrument hood.

11152 (May 63)
New hood locating sockets which also accommodate hard top locating brackets.

Body 11241 (May 63)
Bonnet prop clip replaced by rubber stop.

11313 (May 63)
New rear springs, slightly softer and fitted with plastic interleaving.

Bodies 13473 (black trim, Jun 63),
15652 (blue trim, Jul 63), 19060 (red trim, Aug 63)
Introduction of new quality leathercloth with a finer grain, to commonise type of leathercloth with Midget and Sprite models; affects seats, liners, trim rolls and trim parts in general.

13681 (Jun 63)
Improved radiator rubber seal with lip section to reduce pressure on bonnet.

14192 (Jun 63)
Improved gear lever grommet.

14864 (red trim), 15031 (blue trim),
16094 (black trim) (Jun 63)
Floor mats modified to allow removal of front mats when seat runners are in their maximum forward position.

15873 (Jun 63)
New fan belt (interchangeable)

15937 (Jul 63)
Longer distance tubes for brake and clutch pedals, to ensure free pedal movement; pedals and spacers modified to suit.

Body 16080 (Jul 63)
New spring for bonnet lock to suit stiffer bonnet panel previously introduced.

17217 (Aug 63)
Harder rubber to front left-hand engine mounting, to compensate for additional overhang on this side of the engine.

17744 (Aug 63)

Black hoods gradually introduced between now and Aug 64 as alternative to coloured hoods for all colour schemes.

Body 19157 (Aug 63)
Introduction of new colour, Dark British Racing Green (GN.29) in place of British Racing Green (GN.25). According to production records, the first car painted in the new colour was GHN3/19127, and the last car painted in the superseded colour was GHN3/19879.

Bodies 19359 (blue hood, Aug 63),
19485 (red hood, Sep 63), 19586 (grey hood, Sep 63)
Improved tailoring of optional folding hood for better fit, affecting hood canopy, frame and header rail.

22538 (LHD, Oct 63), 24908 (RHD, Nov 63)
New wiper motor, reducing angle of wipe to 106°.

23636 (wire wheel), 24812 (disc wheel) (Nov 63)
Bottom lubricators added to swivel pins.

26337 (Nov 63)
Radiator fan modified, distance piece added.

28264 (Jan 64)
Filler pieces between rear bumper and body become smaller and are finished in bright alloy instead of body colour.

28951 (Jan 64)
Knock-ons and octagonal caps for wire wheels strengthened with increased section (interchangeable).

29271 (Jan 64)
Oil cooler ARH 181 replaced by ARH 186 of so-called 'intercalary' construction.

29663 (Jan 64)
Packing felt to rear sidemember in boot introduced for packaway hood stowage, to prevent hood from chafing when stowed.

29696 (Jan 64)
New carburettor overflow pipes (interchangeable).

30283 (disc wheel, Jan 64), 30851 (wire wheel, Feb 64)
Improved seal for lower swivel pin bush, to improve lubrication.

30851 (Feb 64)
Wire wheel hubs front and rear, knock-ons and octagonal nuts, changed from 12 threads per inch to 8 threads per inch, for improved wheel fixing.

Not quoted (Feb 64)
Gauze added to blower intake side of heater or fresh-air unit.

Not quoted (Feb 64)
Horns modified with new 90° Lucar connectors, part numbers become BHA 4463/4.

Not quoted (Feb 64)
Kangol Magnet seat belts (supplied by BMC Service Ltd) introduced as alternative to Britax seat belts.

Not quoted (Feb 64)
New piping for seat cushion and squab, with reduced diameter cord and improved leathercloth covering.

31794 (Feb 64)
Introduction of new engine, type 18GA (see engine number production change list); fitted to all cars from this car number onwards, but also fitted intermittently from car number 28587 onwards.

34662 (Mar 64)
Stop lamp switch type 2SH introduced to commonise with Midget and Sprite models.

38388 (May 64)
New hood fasteners, to improve finger grip and to commonise with Midget and Sprite models.

40578 (LHD, Jun 64), 48787 (RHD, Oct 64)
Steering column cowl of the type previously fitted only on cars with optional headlamp flasher now commonised on all cars.

42285 (Jun 64)
New windscreen washer bottle carrier bracket.

44439 (Aug 64)
New fuel pump, specification AUF 301 instead of AUA 150.

Not quoted (Sep 64)
In addition to standard 82°C thermostat, thermostats of 74°C for hot territories and 88°C for cold territories now available. Soon after, the 74°C thermostat introduced as standard fitting, to increase oil pressure and decrease oil temperature. It appears that cars for cold territories are then fitted with the 82°C thermostat as the 88°C thermostat is not quoted for the 18GB type engine.

Not quoted (Oct 64)
New bonnet prop rod, AHH 7380 (interchangeable).

47112 (intermittent), 48767 (all) (Oct 64)

Introduction of new engine, type 18GB (see engine number production change list). Attendant changes: instruments now labelled Smiths instead of British Jaeger, electronic tachometer instead of rev counter; bi-metal fuel gauge with new tank sender unit; wiring harness modified; oil cooler ARH 186 becomes standard on home market cars; export cars fitted with 13-tube oil cooler, ARO 9809.

49502 (Oct 64)
Construction of radiator grille altered, one-piece pressed grille introduced instead of grille with separate rivetted vertical slats.

53501 (Dec 64)
New seat base diaphragm, seat base frame modified to suit with 10 holes instead of 8 holes.

54700 (Jan 65)
Redesigned support bracket for dynamo control box.

Not quoted (Jan 65)
New thermostats with conical valve seating to improve heater performance (new part numbers: 74°C, 13H 2526; 82°C, 13H 2316; 88°C for service purposes, 13H 2317).

57028 (Feb 65)
Cars for Germany fitted special rear number plate with dual number plate lamps on brackets, and plain rear bumper overriders without number plate lamps; also special flasher unit and direction indicators. Lucas Mark X headlamps introduced for Germany (with built-in sidelamps) but only fitted until car number 59462, then re-introduced from car number 67713 in common with other European cars.

57927 (Feb 65)
Oil cooler ARO 9809 standardised on home market cars.

Body 56743 (Mar 65)
Larger capacity fuel tank (12.7 gallons) of pressed construction introduced with modified fixings, bodyshell modified to suit; fitted to all cars from 22 Mar 65.

Not quoted (Mar 65)
Locking plates added to prevent front brake hoses from twisting, hose brackets modified.

Not quoted (Mar 65)
Option of Dunlop Road Speed tyres deleted, SP.41 radial tyres introduced instead.

Not quoted (Mar 65)
Modified horns introduced, part numbers become BCA 4725/6.

Body 57986 (Apr 65)
Introduction of improved anti-burst door locks similar to Midget and Sprite models, with new push-button exterior door handles, and attendant modifications to bodyshell, doors, door casings and rear wings. Inside locking button on passenger door deleted.

61016 (Apr 65)
New cranked ('shepherd's crook') switch for overdrive, instead of toggle switch.

63148 (overdrive, Apr 65),
64313 (standard, Jun 65)
Introduction of new, lip-sealed prop shaft (interchangeable) on cars with banjo-type axle; fitted on cars with tube-type axle from commencement.

63490 (Apr 65)
New boot lid lock fitted, to commonise locks for roadster and forthcoming GT model.

63692 (France, Jun 65),
67713 (Europe, but not France & Sweden, Aug 65),
85296 (Sweden, Mar 66)
Introduction of Lucas Mark X headlamps on LHD cars except for North America; change point not recorded for non-European LHD cars.

65865 (Jul 65)
Quarterlights to doors with modified frame and capping, felt sealing replaced by rubber, for improved fixing to door and improved appearance of seal, and commonisation of fixings with GT model.

66580 (Jul 65)
Front silencer of twin perforated tube type introduced, for improved exhaust system life.

Body 66808 (Aug 65)
Redesigned door waist rail cappings with 'step' towards the front instead of small 'tab' at the rear. Separate trim roll for waist rail deleted.

67559 (Aug 65)
Pirelli rubber fixing strap for hood stowage bag introduced instead of webbing strap (on cars with pack-away hood).

67567 (Aug 65)
Chelsea Grey paint colour discontinued.

71122 (Sep 65)
Self-adhesive plastic engine name and patent plates introduced instead of rivetted plates (compare engine change point list)

Not quoted (Sep 65)
Leather with HB grain introduced instead of leather with FG 1093 grain. Part numbers for seat assemblies, cushion covers and squab covers are now prefixed AHH instead of AKE.

Not quoted (Sep 65)
Octagonal wheel nuts on cars with wire wheels for Japan.

On early GT models from 1965 to 1969, this style of tailgate badging was used, with the MG badge the same as on the roadster but flanked by letters indicating the model. The MGB GT badging was similar except for the obvious difference!

71933 (GT RHD, Sep 65), 73163 (GT LHD, Nov 65)
Introduction of GT model: tube-type Salisbury rear axle, longer prop shaft, seven-leaf rear springs and 5×14 disc wheels; modifications to brake system to suit; different wiper motor and wiper switch; anti-roll bar standard, stiffer than on roadster; headlamp flasher switch standard (except on cars for North America); door casings, etc, with additional piping line; radial tyre size 165-14, when fitted; wire wheels standard on export GTs; additional colours on GT, Sandy Beige and Grampian Grey; also Mineral Blue instead of Iris Blue; chrome wire wheels optional.

Rdst 73721 approx (Oct 65)
Iris Blue paint discontinued on roadster, together with blue hard-top. Replaced by GT colour of Mineral Blue, with black or white hard-top.

Rdst 73834 (Oct 65)
Headlamp flasher switch standard on roadster, except for North America.

Rdst 74046 (Oct 65)
New direction indicator and headlamp flasher switch, cranked towards steering wheel (fitted on GT from start of this model).

Not quoted (Oct 65)
Chrome wire wheels optional on roadster.

76313 (Nov 65)
New bottom wishbone arm bush (interchangeable).

77832 (Dec 65)
Shade of red floor mats changed, new part numbers (AHH 8165 to 8170), interchangeable in sets.

78545 (N. America) (Dec 65)
New bracket for front number plate to comply with US/Canadian regulations.

Rdst body 77826 (Feb 66)
Two fibre pads added to hood header rail, to improve locking of over-centre hood fasteners.

82656 (Feb 66)
Wiring harness re-arranged to move joint of main harness with body/boot harness clear of universal joint in steering column on RHD cars; headlamp flasher lead now incorporated in main harness; overdrive harness modified to suit.

83540 (Mar 66)
New exhaust system with double end plates in silencer.

Not quoted (Mar 66)

Introduction of improved Trico-Neiman steering lock 13H 2972 instead of ACB 9425/13H 709 (Germany, Sweden).

Rdst body 80091 (Mar 66), GT body 2500 (Apr 66)
Introduction of high impact-resistant laminated windscreen glass with .030in interlayer on roadsters for North America and GTs for all markets.

GT 86216 (Mar 66)
New rear header rail liner AHH 8224/5 in fibreglass instead of fibreboard.

Not quoted (Apr 66)
Cars for Canada now fitted with amber instead of white direction indicator lenses.

Rdst body 83520, GT not quoted (May 66)
Heat fusible insulation pads introduced instead of floor underfelt.

89549 (Jul 66)
Oil pressure gauge modified with sintered plug, to cure 'flutter' on gauge – new part numbers for dual gauge are BHA 4586/7.

90002 (LHD, May 66), 91337 (RHD, Jun 66)
Lighting switch changes from toggle to push/pull knob, changes place with washer pump and so is now found above dual gauge.

90364 (May 66)
Foot dipswitch changed from round to oval section, new bracket for dipswitch on LHD cars, harness modified.

Rdst 91380 (?) (May 66)
Fixings for boot lid motifs changed to push-on type (as found on GT); car number 91380 was actually a GT.

93300 (Jun 66)
New flexible pipes and clips for oil cooler.

93749 (Jun 66)
New type of Lucas battery fitted, BT9E without external busbars, instead of SG9E.

Not quoted (Jun 66)
Cars for Sweden now fitted with headlamps to suit driving on the right (although the Swedes only changed over in Sep 67).

Rdst body 86385, GT body 4307 (Jul 66)
Modified seat belt mounting points on rear wheel arches, inner rear wheel arch panels and carpets modified to suit.

Not quoted (Jul 66)
Modified ashtray with concealed fixings introduced, part number AHH 7061.

Not quoted (Jul 66)
Alloy hammer instead of copper hammer in tool kit of wire wheel cars.

GT body 4463 (Jul 66)
Letter B in tailgate motif with changed peg pattern, to fit in holes common to letter C on forthcoming MGC model.

Not quoted (Jul 66)
Heated rear window available as optional extra on GT.

96263 (Aug 66)
New direction and headlamp flasher switch with longer peg for more positive location.

Not quoted (Aug 66)
Front overriders now fitted as standard to all cars.

97861 (Aug 66)
Heavier gauge material for accelerator pedal stop, new part number AHH 7162 instead of AHH 6503.

GT body 7686 (Oct 66)
Rear seat squab assembly and rear floor board assembly modified to suit seat belt mounting points.

GT body 7762 (beige), GT body 7834 (grey) (Oct 66)
Improved type of sun visor.

Not quoted (Nov 66)
Special accurate speedometers fitted to cars for Germany.

107465 (Nov 66)
Lashing brackets added to rear bumper brackets on export cars.

107703 (Nov 66)
Lashing brackets added to front bumper brackets on export cars, towing eye deleted from front suspension cross member.

Rdst 108039 (Nov 66)
Front anti-roll bar standardised on roadster, with wishbones and front suspension modified to suit.

Rdst 111796 (blue), Rdst 111842 (red), Rdst 112309 (grey) (Dec 66)
Coloured hoods discontinued, black hoods standardised. Coloured hard tops probably discontinued at around the same time, hard top now only black (or supplied in primer).

Rdst 111796 (Dec 66)

Blue trim discontinued on roadster (continues on GT). (Quoted wrongly in parts list as 112464.)

GT body 10476 (Dec 66)
New carpet for folding rear floor, two fasteners (repositioned) instead of four.

Not quoted (Jan 67)
New vehicle identification plates (standard and special German type) showing the British Standard for seat belt anchorages.

Not quoted (Jan 67)
Headlamp flasher deleted on cars for Japan.

117263 (Jan 67)
Introduction of special fixing strap for dual gauge on RHD cars fitted with the optional cigar lighter.

Not quoted (Feb 67)
All cars with wire wheels for the USA now fitted with octagonal wheel nuts; this is extended to cars for Sweden in March.

Rdst 115516, GT 116440 (Feb 67)
Introduction of Pale Primrose Yellow paint colour.

Not quoted (Mar 67)
High impact-resistant laminated windscreen glass now fitted also to non-North American roadsters.

115596 (Mar 67)
Improved handbrake with new lever and handbrake pawl rod (interchangeable).

Rdst body 100016 (intermittent), 100414 (all) (Mar 67), GT body 16928 (Apr 67)
Reversing lamps fitted as standard (with yellow inserts inside lenses on cars for France).

Not quoted (Apr 67)
From 1 Apr 67, new regulations require all cars sold in the UK to be fitted with front seat belts. Seat belt kits (AHH 8366) are now no longer a special order but are supplied by BMC Service Ltd for fitting by distributors.

119500 (Apr 67)
Cars for France and Benelux countries are now fitted with separate, transparent brake fluid reservoir and new brake master cylinder.

123061 (Apr 67)
Moulded polypropylene air demister hoses (AHH 8394) introduced instead of Unitube hoses (interchangeable).

Rdst body 101670 (Apr 67)
New hood locating sockets, AHH 8391, introduced instead of AHH 6524 (interchangeable).

Rdst 123716 (intermittent), 132923 (all) (Jul 67)
Tube-type axle as found on GT introduced on roadster, with lengthened prop shaft to suit.

The boot lid MG badge stayed until the end of the 1969 model year in this form, with separate pieces for the 'M', the 'G' and the octagon, and the paint colour of the body as background. This is an MGC with the appropriate lettering on an extended bar above the MG badge.

Rdst 127525 (May 67)
Wiper switch 13H 1909 (Lucas type 108SA) from GT now fitted also to roadster.
Rdst 123879 (banjo axle, wire wheels, May 67),
GT 125374 (disc wheels, Apr 67),
GT 126834 (wire wheels, Jun 67),
Rdst 127394 (banjo axle, disc wheels, May 67),
Rdst 132463 (tube axle, disc wheels, Jul 67)
Longer handbrake levers to rear brake drums; a change point is not available for the roadster model with tube-type axle and wire wheels.
GT body 19610 (Jul 67),
Rdst body 106604 (Aug 67)
Flock-sprayed glass run channels for door glasses introduced instead of 'silent channel' runs, to prevent door glasses from damaging run channels.
Not quoted (Oct 67)
Cars for Finland now fitted with a steering lock.
Rdst 138401, GT 139471 (Nov 67) MGC Rdst 138, MGC GT 638 (Dec 67)
Introduction of MGB Mark II model, car number prefix becomes GHN4/GHD4. Start of series production of MGC. All cars are now issued with commission numbers. **Changes to MGB models:** new engines, type 18GD except USA, type 18GF with emissions control equipment for USA (see list of engine change points for details); new radiator with central filler at front and foam rubber seal at the top; new gearbox with synchromesh on first gear; new overdrive unit (type LH instead of type D) and relay; automatic gearbox optional (not on MGB for USA); clutch master cylinder assembly modified; prop shaft now 31⅛in (791mm) long on all MGB cars; modified rear axle; 16AC alternator introduced instead of dynamo, with new control box and negative earth electrical system; new two-speed wiper motor, now the same on GT and roadster models; windscreen washer bottle moved to front right-hand corner of engine compartment, behind radiator; wiring harnesses changed; bodyshells modified with bigger transmission tunnel; doors changed, recessed safety-type inside door handles and safety-type window regulators, quarter-light handles changed from curved to straight type; modified windscreen frame assembly on roadster; new bracket for foot dipswitch on RHD cars; new rear bonnet seal, which goes round corners of bonnet aperture flange; modified heater; roof lamp added on GT; GT headlining now made from fibreglass in lieu of Vyweld. MGC cars available in metallic paint finishes, Riviera Silver Blue and Golden Beige; **Changes to cars for the USA:** energy-absorbing steering column fitted; new steering wheel with push-fit centre instead of horn push; two steering column stalks fitted, on the left for direction indicators, horn, headlamp dip and flash, on the right for two-speed windscreen wipers, electric windscreen washer with Trico-Folberth assembly, and overdrive if fitted; new steering column cowl; panel light switch on the left of cowl; Trico side-entry steering lock fitted on the right of cowl for some US states and on US cars delivered in Germany; US cars without steering lock have ignition lock on the right of the cowl; padded safety facia without glovebox but with new console; rocker switches, including hazard warning lights switch; cigar lighter standard; new instruments, 80mm speedometer and tachometer, separate oil and temperature gauges, temperature gauge reads C-N-H instead of °F; map pocket in passenger footwell standard on US roadster (already found on GT); new interior mirrors of breakaway type, roadster has die-cast mirror bracket to windscreen top rail instead of fabricated bracket; roadster fitted with internal sun visors; Kangol lap and diagonal seat belts fitted as standard; US roadsters have seat belt mounting points on tonneau panel instead of wheelarch, with quick-release fastening; driver's door mirror fitted as standard, GT also has wing mirror on right-hand front wing; introduction of dual-circuit braking system, with changes to master cylinder box, pedal, front disc brake pads, rear brake shoes, apart from master cylinder, brake fluid reservoir and brakepipe runs; all-amber lenses to front indicator and side lamps; US cars are fitted with a label on the bonnet locking platform detailing compliance with Federal Motor Vehicles Safety Standards and Environmental Protection Agency standards. **Change to all export cars:** knock-ons on wire wheels replaced by octagonal nuts.
Not quoted (Dec 67)
GT models fitted with improved non-handed seal, for rear quarterlights.

Not quoted (Jan 68)
Cars for Austria fitted with steering lock; cars for the USA fitted with tyre pressure information label; US cars for Puerto Rico and Hawaii now to be without heater; cars for Germany fitted with standard flasher unit type 8FL.
MGB Rdst 139443, MGB GT 139553 (Jan 68)
Snowberry White colour introduced instead of Old English White (on MGC from start of series production, maybe earlier than Jan 68 on MGB).
MGB GT 139881 (Dec 67), MGC GT 665 (Jan 68)
All GTs now fitted with US-type breakaway mirror.
MGC Rdst 548, MGC GT 786 (Jan 68)
Improved rear leaf springs (interchangeable in pairs).
MGC Rdst 570 (Feb 68)
Front shock absorbers with altered settings as found on GT introduced on roadster model.
MGB 140611, MGC 1062 (Feb 68)
Fuel pump specification changed from AUF 301 to AUF 305, breather fitted to end cover in addition to existing breather tube.
MGB GT not USA 141230, MGB GT USA 142355, MGC GT not quoted (Feb 68)
Improved seal for tailgate; change point for MGC GT quoted in parts list as 323, but this cannot be correct.
MGC not USA 1139 (Feb 68)
Brake master cylinder box of the type originally fitted only on cars for the Benelux countries now standardised on all cars except for the USA.
MGC not USA 1154 (Feb 68)
Cars with single-circuit braking system now fitted with servo of USA type, BHA 4700 (one servo unit only).
Not quoted (Feb 68)
USA roadsters with new hood fastener to suit US regulations, necessitating new hood and hard top assemblies; change point is quoted in parts lists as introduction of MGB Mark II and MGC models.
MGC auto 1300 (Feb 68)
Gear selector control now by rod instead of cable.
MGB GT USA 139741, MGB GT not USA 141237, MGC GT not USA 806(?), MGC GT USA 1936 (Feb 68)
Separate chrome-plated finisher at top of windscreen pillar deleted, as the joint here is now solder finished; door seal modified to have better retention to body flange, so spring clips deleted.
MGB USA 141770 (Feb 68)
Facia panel and oil gauge bezel modified, with increased thickness of foam padding under instrument area (found on MGC USA model from start of production).
PED cars for USA (Feb 68)
Radio fitted to Personal Export Delivery cars for the USA is now Ekco Escort type CR.936.
Body numbers (not USA) MGC GT 208 (Feb 68), MGB Rdst 110444 (Mar 68), MGB GT 22889 (Jun 68)
Door handle with simplified two-stud fixing (part number AHH 8885) as found on MGC roadster from start of production now introduced also on other models; change points for US cars not quoted.
All models (Mar 68)
Dunlop SP.68 radial tyres introduced, for some months fitted intermittently alongside SP.41 tyres.
MGC Rdst not USA 1869, MGC GT not USA? (Apr 68)
New stop light switch of dry seal taper thread type without gasket (as already found on MGB), brake pipe connector modified to suit.
Not quoted (May 68)
Improved Trico steering lock 13H 4180 (not USA) with spigot location.
MGB GT 142735, MGB Rdst 147574 (wire wheel cars), MGB GT 148083, MGB Rdst 148833 (disc wheel cars) (May 68)
Front disc brake pads of USA-type, Ferodo 2424FI, and rear brake linings AM8 introduced on non-USA cars; roadster fitted 0.8in rear wheel cylinders, GT fitted new ⅞in rear wheel cylinders; front hub and rear axle assemblies with attendant changes.
Body numbers: MGB GT not USA 22443 (black), 22438 (red), 22496 (blue); MGB GT USA 502009 (black), 502149 (red), 502172 (blue); MGB GT not USA 892 (black), 302(?) (red), 943 (blue); MGC GT USA 500111 (black), 500107 (red), 500606 (blue) (May 68)
Dunlop 'D' carpet quality, as found on MGC roadster from start of production, introduced also on MGC GT and all MGB

models, in place of Rivington carpet; change points are not available for MGB roadster models.
MGB 146104 (Jun 68), MGC 1628 (Jul 68)
New mounting bracket for glass channel in doors.
MGB 146506 (Apr 68)
Radiator modified with repositioned mounting plates.
MGC 1762 (Apr 68)
Improved material for the heater water hose from engine outlet.
MGC USA auto 1936 (Mar 68), MGC not USA auto 2568 (Jun 68)
New oil filler and dipstick tube for automatic gearbox.
MGC Rdst 2064, MGC GT 2604 (May 68)
To commonise heater with MGB, modified heater with water valve repositioned on engine introduced.
MGB USA 147858 (May 68)
New brake pressure failure warning switch, and harness modified.
MGB Rdst not USA 146738 (Jun 68), MGC Rdst not USA 1541 (Jun 68)
New interior mirror with plastic backing and frame.
MGB 151915, MGC 2645 (Jul 68)
New type of lead from battery negative pole to earth introduced, as found on Midget and Sprite models.
MGC 2874 (Aug 68)
Radiator top and bottom hoses of improved material.
MGC USA 3018 (Aug 68)
New brake master cylinder for dual circuit brakes with brake fluid reservoir above cylinder instead of remote plastic reservoir; this was also fitted on approximately 50 cars with car numbers from 1558 to 3017.
MGC 3123 (Aug 68)
Improved rear power unit mountings to gearbox crossmember (interchangeable).
MGB 152455, MGC 3343 (Aug 68)
Stronger Trico steering lock fitted on cars for Germany, Austria, Sweden and Finland (part number 13H 4862).
MGB 153386 (Aug 68)
Improved exhaust system, for longer life and to eliminate rattle.
MGB Rdst 153878, MGB GT 154231, MGC Rdst 3314, MGC GT 3471* (Aug 68)
Cars for Canada now built to USA specification, with all safety features and emissions control equipment, 18GF type engines (MGB) or 29GA type engines (MGC), and USA-type bodies; *quoted wrongly in parts list as 1494.
Not quoted (Aug 68)
Ashtray now standard fitting on all export cars.
Not quoted (Aug 68)
Octagonal wheel nuts instead of knock-ons on home market cars with wire wheels.
MGC NA 3365 (Sep 68)
New brake pressure failure warning switch (not the same as found on MGB), harness modified.
MGB 156090, MGC NA 3667, MGC not NA 4045 (Sep 68)
New seat slides, seat catches with cranked levers.
MGB not NA 156084, MGC NA 4126 (Oct 68)
Water temperature gauge now reads C-N-H (as on North American cars), instead of degrees Fahrenheit/Centigrade.
MGC 4152 (Nov 68)
Modified front/rear brake hoses introduced on all cars, to comply with legal requirements in Pennsylvania, USA.
MGB Rdst 158371 (Sep 68), MGB GT 158231 (Nov 68), MGC Rdst 4266 (Oct 68), MGC 4236 (Nov 68)
Introduction of 1969 models with following changes: new engines on MGB cars, type 18GG except North America, 18GH for North America. On MGC cars, the following engine numbers co-incide with this change point: 29G/3201 (not NA), 29GA/1401 (NA). **Changes to both MGB and MGC:** revised carburettor specifications, carburettor crankcase ventilation system introduced; 16ACR alternator with built-in regulator (compare engine change list); reverse detent mechanism in gearbox changed; new wiper arms and blades on GT model; wiring harnesses changed; all cars have new front wings with sidelamps moved closer to radiator grille; interior trim extensively revised; red trim (roadster and GT) and blue trim (GT only) discontinued; contrast colour piping to seats and trim discontinued; beige headlining and sun visors on GT discontinued; improved quality floor mats and Firth's loop pile carpet introduced; new reclining front seats with transverse pleating, GT rear seat and roadster rear com-

partment cushion redesigned to match; black only trim colour at first. **Changes to North American specification:** new brake check warning light; side reflectors fitted to front and rear wings; roadsters with triple wipers, new front shroud panel to suit; wing mirror on right-hand wing added on roadsters (already fitted to GT models); standard twin-pole headrests introduced, with special tonneau cover to suit. **Changes to MGB only (all markets):** on cars with automatic gearbox, rear axle ratio raised from 3.909:1 to 3.7:1, new speedometers to suit. **Changes to MGC only (all markets):** higher internal gearbox ratios from overdrive cars introduced on non-overdrive cars; rear axle ratios lowered on all manual gearbox cars; new speedometers to suit. The parts lists claim that Rostyle wheels became optional equipment on both MGB and MGC cars at this time, but this is not correct.

MGB 158652, MGC 3596 (Sep 68)
Additional inserts for bulkhead sealing, to prevent fumes from entering passenger compartment.

MGC 4517, MGC Rdst 4651 (Nov 68)
New servo hoses on all cars, to ensure compliance with New Zealand requirements.

MGB GT 160608, MGC GT 4748 (Nov 68)
British Leyland sticker fitted to GT rear window; at the same time, BMC rosette sticker deleted from windscreen of all cars.

MGB 161087, MGC 4680 (Nov 68)
New direction indicator switch with fewer leads, to suit 8FL flasher unit already in use.

MGB Rdst NA 161343, MGC Rdst NA 4353 (Nov 68)
New stowage cover for optional folding hood, to suit seat belt mounting points on tonneau panel.

MGC 4567 (Nov 68)
Protection plate added to forward wiring harness, to prevent bonnet safety catch from fouling harness.

Not quoted (Nov 68)
Heater fitted as standard for all markets, except Australia, Puerto Rico and Hawaii; Australian cars (MGB roadster CKD kits) continue with optional fresh-air unit.

Not quoted (Nov/Dec 68)
Optional metallic paint finishes on GT model discontinued. Following colour schemes re-introduced on GT models: Mineral Blue, with black trim; Sandy Beige, with black (or later Mushroom) trim.

Not quoted, MGB only (Nov 68)
Cars for Sweden now fitted with electric windscreen washer as North American models but with different container, bag type instead of bottle.

Not quoted (Dec 68)
Improved door top sealing rubber AHH 8918 fitted to optional extra hard top.

Body numbers: MGB GT NA 504484, MGC GT NA 501208 (Dec 68)
Sun visor steady brackets modified to comply with US legislation.

Body numbers: MGB GT not NA 25921 (Dec 68), MGB GT NA 504922 (?) (Jan 69)
New rear header rail liner AHH 9462 in fibreboard instead of fibreglass; change points for MGC GT not available; this change point is quoted in parts lists as from the start of the 1969 models.

MGB Rdst NA 164064 (Dec 68), MGB Rdst not NA 167577 (Jan 69), MGC Rdst NA 5152, MGC Rdst not NA 6293 (Dec 68)
Magnatex wiper arms and blades fitted instead of Lucas items.

Not quoted (Jan 69)
North American cars now fitted with an additional car number plate on the top of the dashboard, visible from the outside through the windscreen on the left-hand side.

MGC GT 5325, MGC Rdst 5382 (Jan 69)
Additional insulating pads fitted to gearbox tunnel and speaker panel to reduced heat in car interior.

MGC 5737 (Jan 69)
New heater water valve with nitrile diaphragm (interchangeable with previous type).

Body numbers: MGB GT not NA 26152, MGB GT NA 505124, MGC GT not NA 2212, MGC GT NA 501348 (Jan 69)
New outer seal for tailgate.

MGB GT 165364, MGB Rdst 167129, MGC GT 5495, MGC Rdst 5590 (Feb 69)
New type of tommy bar for plug spanner in tool kit.

MGB 167662, MGC 6388 (Feb 69)
New type of wing mirror common to North American and other cars; standard equipment on NA cars, optional extra in other markets.

Not quoted, NA cars only (Feb 69)
Modified hazard warning light switch.

MGB 167816 (Feb 69)
All MGB cars: new bracket for mounting rear exhaust pipe. NA cars only: new brake pressure failure warning switch.

Body numbers: MGB Rdst NA 15244, (Feb 69), MGC Rdst NA 2173 (Mar 69)
Modified windscreen frame and assembly; change points for non-North American bodies are not available.

Not quoted, roadsters (Mar 69)
Tonneau cover fittings now standardised on heelboards of all roadsters, even when tonneau cover not supplied.

Not quoted, GTs (Mar 69)
GTs in beige paint colours available with the alternative trim colour Mushroom, with brown carpets/mats.

Not quoted, MGB only (Mar 69)
Standard thermostat fitted reverts to 82°C instead of 74°C to improve heater performance; 74°C remains available as optional fitment for hot climates, 88°C for cold climates.

MGC 6731 (Mar 69)
New rubber boots to pistons of front brake caliper units, with attendant change to front hub assemblies.

MGC 7071 (Mar 69)
Longer heater water hoses fitted, to give extra allowance for engine movement.

MGB not NA 170028, MGB NA 170587 (Mar 69), MGC not NA 7335, MGC NA 7316 (Apr 69)
New steering wheels, design not changed but rims now made of polypropylene instead of acetate, to remedy tendency to crack.

MGB 173850 (Mar 69)
Longer fuel pump breather tube, of reduced diameter.

Not quoted (Apr 69)
Heater now included in MGB roadster CKD kits for Australia (and fitted to other Australian cars), fresh-air unit discontinued.

Not quoted (Apr 69)
Corrosion-resistant coating added to brake pipes, to comply with Swedish legislation.

Not quoted (Apr 69)
Dunlop SP.41 now discontinued and all cars with radial tyres fitted with SP.68; Dunlop C.41 cross-ply tyres remain in use.

MGB Rdst NA 175813, MGB GT NA 176783, MGC Rdst NA 7626, MGC GT NA 7824 (May 69)
Ekco radio fitted to Personal Export Delivery cars for North America becomes Ekco Escort Mark II CR.942 instead of CR.936.

MGC 8333 (Jun 69)
Front bumper towing eyes discontinued, replaced by lashing brackets.

MGC 8612 (Jun 69)
Spare wheel clamp for wire wheels of MGB type introduced.

MGB 177601, MGC not quoted (Jun 69)
New Lucas batteries of single-fill type introduced, 9-plate type CA9E on MGB, 11-plate type CA11E on MGC but also available on MGB to special order (police cars, cars exported to cold climates).

MGB 181712, MGC 8718 (Jul 69)
Box spanner (for plugs) and tommy bar deleted from tool kit.

MGC Rdst 9099, MGC GT 9102 (Aug 69)
Last MGC car numbers, model discontinued.

MGB Rdst NA 182755 (Aug 69)
New sun visors with cranked pivot rod.

Not quoted, MGB only (Aug 69)
Alternative makes of tyre now approved (possibly already in use by then), Michelin ZX and Pirelli Cinturato blackwall radial tyres, for both roadster and GT models.

Not quoted, MGB only (Aug 69)
Hard-top now available with Sundym tinted glass rear window and tinted perspex to rear quarterlights as optional extra (possibly only for North America but rarely seen).

MGB Rdst NA 184497 (Aug 69)
New anchor bracket for sun visors, to comply with US legislation.

Not quoted (Sep 69)
Steering lock now mandatory fitment on cars for France.

MGB NA 184865 (Sep 69)
Special type of vehicle identification (car number) plate introduced on North American models: new plate is fitted with pop rivets to the rear pillar to the right-hand side of the left-hand door. It confirms vehicle compliance with US FMVSS and EPA standards in force at the time of manufacture, and quotes month of manufacture.

Not quoted (? 69)
Bonnet panel changed from aluminium to steel. This is thought to have occurred before the end of production of the MGC model, as some of the last MGC cars may have had steel bonnets, and is believed to have been introduced on the MGB at the same time. However, the MGC parts list only quotes part number HZA 1318 for the bonnet panel, while the MGB parts list seems to indicate that the change from aluminium bonnet (HZA 401) to steel bonnet (HZA 4015) occurred at the start of the 1970 models. Some 1970 models may still have had aluminium bonnets.

Rdst 187170* (Oct 69), GT 187841 (Sep 69)
Start of 1970 model year. Car number prefixes changed to GHN5/GHD5. On North American cars, additional letter in prefix to indicate model year, A for 1970 (etc), thus: G-HN5-UA (or G-HD5-UA). **Changes to all cars:** new 15.5in (394mm) steering wheel with simulated leather rim and

This MGB badge, used from the start of production, was in a similar style to the MGC one, but the centre bar did not extend beyond the edge of the letters. The MG octagon became this one-piece plastic style of badge for the 1970 model year.

From late 1969 to 1972, on models with the recessed grille, the MG badge was fixed in the centre of the grille and had red and silver as the dominant colours, but still with a black line in the surround.

three spokes with holes; steering column modified; on non-NA cars, horn push removed from steering wheel centre and foot dipswitch deleted as new steering column stalk switch operating indicators, headlamp flash/dip and horn fitted, with new steering column cowl to suit; revised sealed beam headlamps with new light units on RHD cars; new rear lamps with larger and more angular lenses. Twin Lucas 9H horns standard on all cars; modified fusebox, starter relay and wiring harness; bodyshells modifed in respect of gearbox tunnel, front end assembly and front wings; new recessed radiator grille, separate moulding added to front of bonnet; new one-piece MG plastic badge in black and silver to boot lid/tailgate, with new 'BGT' letters for GT model; British Leyland corporate badge added to each front wing (except for Arab countries where MG badge fitted); sill tread plates added; dipping interior mirror added to all cars, fitted to windscreen top rail on roadster, with roadster windscreen frame modified to suit; new interior trim, black only trim colour, seats modified with new Ambla seat covers; stainless steel exhaust tailpipe fitted on all cars; Rostyle wheels fitted, painted as standard, chromed Rostyle wheels fitted as optional equipment on export cars (except for North America); wheel nuts, spanner and spare wheel clamp to suit; optional extra rear compartment cushion for roadster discontinued. Cars for Sweden, Germany (and later Norway) now to be built using North American bodies, with three wipers on roadster model, and padded safety facias. **Changes to North American cars only**: new Wilmot Breeden steering lock fitted as standard; switchgear revised; rear indicators amber, with indicator lens in the central part of the rear lamps; side marker lamps with reflectors on black plinths introduced instead of simple reflectors, and front side marker lamp in front of wheelarch; audible ignition key warning buzzer fitted; new front bumper overriders with rubber buffers, different on RH and LH sides; new rear quarter bumpers with rubber buffers to overriders and new Lucas L.749 number plate lamps mounted in inner ends of bumper bars; new type of D-section headrest standard, with new tonneau cover to suit; winged or T-shape choke pull instead of round choke pull; Dunlop SP.68 radial tyres standard equipment.

*The Parts List quotes 187211 as the first car number for a 1970 model year roadster; in fact, 187170 to 187210 were also 1970 models, although built later than 187211.

Rdst NA Cal 187701, GT NA Cal 188659 (Oct 69)
Introduction of evaporative loss control system on cars for California; the engine type on these cars becomes series 18GJ (with a number series shared with the 18GH engine, from engine number 22647 upwards); 18GH engines continued for other North American cars.

NA 188684 (Oct 69)
Starter inhibitor deleted from steering lock assembly.

**Rdst not NA 188939, GT not NA 189965,
Rdst NA 190190, GT NA 192164 (Oct 69)**
Optional extra fog and spot lamps, Lucas FT.8 and LR.8 replace WFT.576 and WLR.576.

Rdst 190396, GT 190823 (Oct 69)
Special Swedish export model introduced in production (compare above).

GT NA 191164, Rdst NA 191436 (Nov 69)
Rotary air control with position of cable clamp screw reversed for improved operation.

GT 192016 (Nov 69)
Special German export model introduced in production, as for Sweden but with variations for local requirements (compare above).

GT NA 192390, Rdst NA 193727 (Dec 69)
Radial tyres with narrow whitewalls introduced as optional extra for North American markets (Dunlop SP.68. Michelin ZX and Pirelli Cinturato).

GT NA 193694 (?), Rdst NA 194068 (Dec 69)
Sun visors modified with new standardised grain on covers.

GT 194763, Rdst 195195 (Dec 69)
New ignition switch fitted on cars which are not fitted with steering lock.

Not quoted (Dec 69)
Ashtray now standard equipment on home market cars.

196028 (Jan 70)
LH wing mirror added as standard equipment on cars for Switzerland.

GT 196923 (Jan 70)
Increased radius of rear window channel in door for easier operation.

Not quoted (Jan-Mar 70)
Brake pipes coated in passivated zinc for improved corrosion resistance.

Not quoted (Feb 70)
Brake servo available as optional extra (single-circuit brakes only).

NA 200086 (Feb 70)
On the special North American identification plate, the maker's name now reads 'British Leyland (Austin-Morris) Ltd' instead of 'The British Motor Corporation Ltd'.

Not NA 200679 (Feb 70)
Identification plate (car number plate) now fixed with pop rivets instead of self-tapping screws.

203093 (Mar 70)
MG sticker on engine rocker cover replaced by British Leyland sticker (except for Arab countries).

NA 204983 (Mar 70)
Seat belts modified with straight end fitting to tunnel mounting point plate.

Not quoted (Apr 70)
Optional extra fresh-air unit discontinued.

Not quoted (Apr 70)
Window regulator handles now all-black instead of having bright centres to knobs.

**GT NA 205506, intermittently (Apr 70),
GT NA 208788, all (May 70),
Rdst Na 209421, intermittently (Apr 70),
Rdst NA 210928, all (May 70)**
Magnatex steering lock BHA 5050 fitted as alternative to Wilmot Breeden lock, with alternative steering column cowl.

GT 207650, Rdst 209784 (Apr 70)
Seat frames and seat assemblies modified to suit revised seat belt mounting points. Headrest fittings commonised with Midget/Sprite models and Austin America. Headrests become available as optional extra in the home market.

207818 (May 70)
Improved Lockheed type 6 brake servo (optional extra on cars with single-circuit brake system) with bore increased from 5/8in to 7/8in.

207993 (May 70)
On cars for Sweden, car number is now stamped in boot floor from factory.

GT 212596, Rdst 215215 (Jun 70)
Radiator drain tap deleted, radiator modified to suit.

**Body numbers: Rdst not NA 119382,
Rdst NA not quoted, GT not NA 33625,
GT NA 516753 (Aug 70)**
Revised seat belt mounting points; new sill mats, gearbox cover and tunnel carpet; North American cars also fitted with new type of static seat belt, BHH 419 instead of BHH 368.

Rdst 219001, GT 219002 (Aug 70)

GT models from late 1969 to the end of the 1972 model year had this style of rear badging, with these letters 'BGT' on the left and a one-piece black and silver MG plastic badge on the right.

Start of 1971 model year. **Changes to all cars**: horn push returned to steering wheel centre; improved larger switch for optional extra heated rear window on GT; larger head for stalk switch operating indicators and headlamp flash/dip; door switches for interior lamp added on all roadsters, door switches on roadster and GT operate new courtesy lamp on North American cars, map light on non-NA cars; boot lamp added to all roadsters, with switch operated by boot lid, GT has courtesy switch operated by tailgate for roof lamp; body modifications to front end assembly and gearbox tunnel; bonnet with telescopic strut on LH side instead of prop on RH side; roadster also with telescopic strut to boot lid; new folding hood designed by Michelotti standard on all roadsters, pack-away type hood discontinued; new hood cover; modified bumpers, front overriders with rubber buffers also on non-NA cars, this type of overrider now the same on both sides of the car; gear lever gaiter added; new heater controls on LHD cars, improved heater air ducts, new demister hoses and air outlets; wiring harness modified; Autumn Leaf trim colour introduced. Cars for Sweden now fitted with North American engines (type 18GK) and full evaporative loss control equipment; map pocket fitted as standard on roadsters for Sweden and Germany; radial tyres standard for Sweden. **Changes to North American cars only**: all cars now fitted with evaporative loss control equipment, engine type becomes 18GK; panel light rheostat fitted instead of on/off switch on steering column cowl; courtesy lamp introduced instead of map light; tinted glass standard on GT models; reversion to one-piece rear bumper with number plate lamps again in rear bumper overriders.

GT 219491, Rdst 220129 (Aug 70)
Optional extra servo modified with clamp ring instead of crimped ring.

Rdst NA 220828 (Sep 70)
All North American roadsters now fitted with tonneau cover fasteners on shroud panel (top of facia) as standard.

Rdst 221217, GT 221483 (Sep 70)
Cars for Germany and Japan now fitted with standard rear bumper, rear number plate and number plate lamps.

Rdst 222431, GT 222690 (Oct 70)
New bonnet rear seal, BHH 209 instead of AHH 8934.

225000 approx (Oct 70)
New finisher to seat belt boss, to suit redesigned seat belt fixing, replacing previous washer and cover.

Rdst NA 225567, GT NA 226976 (Nov 70)
Improved choke control with stronger pull, to prevent wings of T-handle breaking (BHH 526 instead of AHH 9640).

Rdst 226006, GT 227793 (Nov 70)
Baffles added to demister ducts to improve defrosting.

Rdst 230617, GT 231339 (Dec 70)
Steering lock becomes universal fitment on all cars; new type of front entry steering lock on non-North American cars.

GT 233393, Rdst 234199 (Jan 71)
Factory-fitted static seat belts now standard (but charged extra) on home market cars; new type of Kangol static seat belt, BHH 525 (instead of BHH 365), with revised fixings common to seat belts used on North American cars; belts repositioned to tonneau panel on roadster, with hood cover and tonneau cover modified to suit; Kangol inertia reel seat belts available as optional extra on home market GTs.

GT 233401, Rdst 235079 (Jan 71)
Headrests available as optional extras for all markets except where already specified as standard; roadster tonneau covers to suit available for all cars.

234492 (Jan 71)
Norwegian specification introduced, as German with NA-style body and facia, and European engine type 18GG.

Rdst 237443, GT 238792 (Feb 71)
New carburettor heat shield (common to Morris Marina 1.8TC) and throttle cable trunnion.

Rdst NA 238408, GT NA 239805 (Feb 71)
New hazard flasher unit (Lucas 9FL) on cars so equipped.

Not quoted (Feb 71)
Crossply tyres now Dunlop D.75 (tubed; black or whitewall), instead of Dunlop C.41.

Not NA 244235 (Apr 71)
New rear brackets for servo when fitted as optional extra (on cars with single-circuit brake system).

GT 245135 (Apr 71)
New Triplex Hotline heated rear window on cars so equipped, including tinted version for North America.

246008 (Apr 71)
German cars only, flasher unit Lucas FL5 instead of 8FL.

Rdst 246077 (Apr 71)
North American-type wiper arms introduced also on RHD cars.

Rdst 246725 (Apr 71)
New hood locating sockets, painted matt black instead of chrome-plated.

Not quoted (Jun 71)
Chrome-plated wire wheels deleted from options list.

NA 252723, not NA 252729 (Jun 71)
New front silencer to exhaust system (on cars for Sweden fitted only from 283886 in May 72).

Rdst 258001, GT 258004 (Aug 71)
Start of 1972 model year. Introduction of 18V series engines, types 18V-581/582/583 on non-North American cars or types 18V-584/585 on North American cars (compare list of engine change points). **Changes to all cars**: new radiator hoses; new horn push to steering wheel, with red MG badge; modified handbrake assembly, cranked away from tunnel console; fresh-air ventilation vents added to centre of facia; tunnel console added between seats, incorporating gear lever surround, ashtray (now painted matt black) and hinged armrest with cubby hole under; Navy (dark blue) trim colour introduced instead of black; new carpet quality, Firth's cut-pile instead of loop-pile; GT has new seat covers with centre panels in brushed nylon; Roadster seat covers modified; door liners now fitted with two chrome trim strips and simple door pulls; map pocket finisher deleted; vanity mirror added to passenger sun visor on cars so equipped; chrome Rostyle wheels now optional in all markets. **Changes to non-North American cars only**: fuel filter added on export cars without evaporative loss control; new choke cable with improved locking device; energy-absorbing steering column fitted; rocker switches introduced; map light deleted from facia, courtesy lamp introduced instead; gear selector illumination lamp deleted on cars with automatic gearbox; combined radio console and switch panel fitted instead of loudspeaker console; tinted glass optional on GT model. 1972 model year cars for Sweden revert to European-type engines (predominantly type 18V-582-Y-H). Cars for Switzerland are now fitted with dual circuit brakes. **Changes to North American cars only**: new steering lock; radio console and switch panel modified; glovebox added to facia; instruments with new bezels; mechanical instead of electrical oil pressure gauge; Arcolectric instead of Lucas warning lights; separate warning light for hazard flashers deleted; new type of Magnatex cigar lighter; two door mirrors fitted to all cars.

258195 (Aug 71)
New courtesy lamp on facia, all-plastic type BHA 5138 instead of AUB 494.

Not quoted (Aug 71)

The first type of British Leyland badge with silver printing on a blue background, found on both sides of the car from 1969 to 1972.

Redesigned Trico washer pump BHA 5146 instead of 13H 3939 on cars with electric windscreen washer.

263625 (Nov 71)
New SAE-type radiator cap (still rated at 10lb) and modified radiator.

NA 266523 (Dec 71)
Marina-type lock for glovebox on North American cars.

Home 266635 (Dec 71)
Modified air cleaners (BHH 548/549) fitted to home market cars to comply with new noise regulations, similar to the air cleaners found on non-North American export models from 258001 onwards.

NA 266647 (Dec 71)
Modified Wilmot Breeden steering lock to commonise shear bolts with those on North American Midgets.

US Rdst 267110, US GT 267333 (Dec 71)
New rocker switches and column stalks with words instead of symbols, to meet new US legislation (cars for Canada, Sweden, Germany and Norway continue with symbol-type switches).

**Rdst NA 267580, intermittently,
GT NA 268281 intermittently,
Rdst NA 268079 all, GT NA 268490 all (Dec 71)**
Introduction of audible seat belt warning system on North American cars; modifications to seats, seat belts, wiring harness, remote control housing, radio console (coinciding with change to intertia reel seat belts, compare below).

267953 (Dec 71)
Revised selection of radio kits available, including new Radiomobile high-output 9 watt models (medium and long wave push-button type 1095, medium wave push-button type 1097); on North American PED cars, Motorola radio replaces Ekco.

Rdst NA 268080, GT NA 268489 (Dec 71)
Inertia reel seat belts introduced on North American cars; on roadster, rear wing inner panel and rear wheelarch carpets modified to suit, also hood cover and tonneau cover as mounting point moved back on wheelarch (coinciding with introduction of audible warning system, compare above).

Not quoted (Jan 72)
On cars with manual windscreen washer, new type pump 13H 6475 introduced instead of ADA 4594 (interchangeable).

268698 (Jan 72)
New reversing lamps with 'diakon' lenses to meet US regulations, fitted on all cars except French export models.

269305 (Jan 72)
GT roof lamp with rim of base in grey ABS instead of aluminised ABS; on all cars, redesigned seat runners and catches to comply with US regulations.

NA 270232 (Jan 72)
New exhaust system (to reduce cost).

273112 (Feb 72)
Cars for Norway now to Swedish specification, with engine type 18V-582-Y-H and overdrive as standard in NA-style body.

273878 (Feb 72)
Clutch and brake pedals re-tooled and re-designed to use a common 'blank'.

273879 (Feb 72)
New seat belt parking cover instead of parking buckle; roadster rear quarter casing and GT lower rear quarter casing modified to suit.

Not NA 275646 (Feb 72)
Lowe and Fletcher steering lock (BHA 5099) instead of Magnatex (BHA 5709).

Not quoted (Mar 72)
Home market GT now has cigar lighter and radial tyres as standard equipment; wire wheels withdrawn from German market as wheel centre nuts protrude beyond body line, contrary to German regulations.

278570 (Mar 72)
New baffles in front wings, with integral seals.

279340 (Apr 72)
Roadster and GT, new door ventilator assemblies with frames made from brushed stainless steel sections instead of chrome-plated brass extrusions.

GT 282420, Rdst 283190 (May 72)
On home market cars: new type of Kangol static seat belt, for one-handed operation. On North American cars: modified glovebox lock; modified speedometers and speedometer cables, angle drive to speedo head discontinued.

282455 (May 72)

In 1972 the colour scheme of the British Leyland emblem was reversed and this revised stick-on badge was fitted only on the passenger side of the car. It is seen in conjunction with the V8 badge, here of the gold type fitted to cars built in 1975.

New type of stick-on British Leyland badge to front wing, only one fitted, always on the passenger side of the car; not fitted for Arab countries.

283886 (May 72)
New front silencer to exhaust system on cars for Sweden (compare change point Jun 71 for non-Swedish cars).

284721 (May 72)
Introduction of cover for starter motor and solenoid.

GT 286062 (May 72)
New rear quarterlights with stainless steel instead of chrome-plated brass frames, two non-handed hinges each side, new catch, B-post modified and B-post finisher also in stainless steel.

287670 (Jun 72)
Alternative wheel nuts for wire wheels introduced.

289875 (Jun 72)
New window winders, new material and method of attaching knob to winder, for improved operation; new under-bonnet insulating pads of rubberised felt instead of fibroleta and felt, for better sound insulation.

Rdst 293446, GT 296196 (Aug 72)
New front springs, to increase height at the front of the car by 0.5in, in order to overcome problem of 'settling' due to export cars being lashed down on board ships.

The 1973 and 1974 model year cars with the plastic grille reverted to the shield badge, but now with all the background in red. On V8 models it was supplemented by this V8 badge sitting on a small plinth on the grille mesh. It may just be possible to see that the ribs in the grille mesh protrude further forward when leading down and towards the centre – in other words the two pieces of plastic grille mesh are 'handed' rather than being the same on both sides.

On 1973 model year GTs, the familiar wing-style one-piece badge was introduced, originally with the 'BGT' letters in blue as seen here.

Rdst 294251, GT 296001 (Aug 72)
Start of 1973 model year. New engines on North American cars, types 18V-672/673. **Changes to all cars**: New gear lever knob, pear-shaped corporate BL design in simulated leather, new gearlever gaiter; new steering wheel, three spokes with long slots; new type of cigar lighter, common to North American and non-NA cars, standard on home market cars; matt black wiper arms and blades; new radiator grille with matt black cross-hatch in anodised aluminium frame, MG shield badge of pre-1970 design but now in red and silver, separate moulding to front of bonnet deleted; two rectangular air intakes in front fairing panel behind front numberplate below bumper; extensive trim changes to ensure trim meets North American requirements for inflammability; thicker carpet of improved quality; door pulls of armrest type; Ochre trim colour introduced instead of Autumn Leaf; new seat patterns with transverse pleats, GT with all-nylon seat facings; new tonneau covers and hood covers, new storage bags for both; tonneau cover now standard on home market roadsters; heated rear window standard on home market GT models; new tailgate badge of 'wing' type on GT; hood instruction label added on roadster windscreen header rail; optional chrome Rostyle wheels withdrawn from North America but standard on European and all other non-NA export cars; radial ply tyres standard on home market roadsters. **Changes to North American cars only**: anti-run-on valve added, carbon canister modified; new Wilmot Breeden steering lock; illuminated rocker switches and heater controls, words on switches on cars for the USA, symbols on other cars with North American-type facias; special anti-burst units fitted to door locks, with attendant changes to doors, roadster B-post panels and GT rear quarter panels; strengthening bars added in doors.

Not quoted (1973?)
Believed introduced during 1973 model year: alternative brake master cylinder for single-circuit system GMC 150 (instead of GMC 122) and alternative clutch master cylinder AAU 7152 (instead of BHA 4667), both identified by two concentric rings.

Rdst 294985 (Sep 72), GT 296001 (Aug 72)
New door seal with plastic carrier, rear quarter liners modified to suit.

296210 (Sep 72)
Alternative Metallifacture jack, BHA 5178 (suitable also for V8 model).

298518 (Oct 72)
Repositioned seat belt parking covers.

Rdst 301867 (Nov 72)
New front springs BHH 1225 instead of BHH 1076 (interchangeable; may simply be part number change).

303704 (Nov 72)
Heater modified with new air control cables (to commonise design with V8 model).

V8 101 (Dec 72)
Pre-production of MGB GT V8 model starts.

NA 306166 (Dec 72)
New seven-blade one-piece plastic fan 12H 4230, instead of six-blade metal fan AHH 6999; this change also applies to non-North American cars fitted with automatic gearbox.

Rdst 306516 (Dec 72)
Modified windscreen pillars and assembly.

NA 307779 (Jan 73)
Windscreen washer bag relocated, now 3 pint rounded type instead of square bag; rear lamps with improved performance, lenses marked SAE class A; reversing lamps with new reflectors, lenses marked SAE class A (both changes made to comply with US legislation, subsequently also introduced on non-North American cars). All cars have new identification (car number) plates, with manufacturer's name now given as 'British Leyland UK Limited'. The new plates may have been used intermittently from Sep 72 onwards.

Not NA 308099 (Jan 73)
Steering lock commonised with Midget, lock now BHA 5215 instead of BHA 5099. On all cars, floor heating insulation pads modified with a cut-out, to clear centre panel and pedal box on V8 model.

V8 124 (Apr 73)
Series production of V8 model starts.

V8 125 (Apr 73)
New front engine mountings.

Rdst 314277 (Apr 73)
New hard top sealing rubber with plastic covered carrier, instead of rubber with moquette-covered carrier.

NA 314935 (Apr 73), V8 111 (Jan 73)
Magnatex steering lock instead of Wilmot Breeden (side entry type).

GT 315950 (Mar 73)
Front anti-roll bar of V8 type (BHH 882) commonised on 4-cyl GT model.

317050 (May 73)
Alternative King Dick jack of stronger design (BHH 1264 instead of AHH 6538); Metallifacture jack BHA 5178 remains in use.

GT 317929 (Apr 73), V8 103 (Jan 73)
New type of intertia reel seat belt when fitted as optional extra on home market GT (standard on V8).

320197 (Jun 73), V8 103 (Jan 73)
New steering wheel, solid spokes without slots but still with indentations.

Rdst 320325, GT 323468, V8 349 (Jun 73)
Door waist rails and covering foams redesigned.

V8 353 (Jun 73)
New sound deadener to rear half of bonnet, with cut-outs for improved carburettor clearance.

Not NA 321699 (Jun 73)
North American type rounded windscreen washer bag introduced instead of Tudor plastic bottle.

322460, V8 302 (Jun 73)
New wiper motor with improved insulation for windings.

323161, V8 444 (Jul 73)
Improved fixing for combined door pull and arm rest.

Rdst NA 323125, GT NA 324828 (Jul 73)
Electronic audible seat belt warning buzzer, instead of electrical-mechanical type.

Rdst 323853, GT 325416, V8 412 (Jul 73)
Ochre trim largely discontinued and replaced by Autumn Leaf on cars painted Teal Blue, Green Mallard and Black Tulip. Black trim fitted on some roadsters.

NA324943 (Aug 73)
Modified steering lock, Wilmot Breeden type (18G 9064) re-introduced.

GT 325750, V8 490 (Aug 73)
Modified switch for heated rear window, for improved fit in facia panel.

NA 325856 (Aug 73)
Modified steering lock, part number now 18G 9118.

Rdst 328101, GT 328801, V8 604 (Aug 73)
Start of 1974 model year. **Changes to all cars**: automatic gearbox option on 4-cyl cars discontinued; external door mirrors now fitted with anti-glare flat glass instead of ordinary flat glass (implemented on V8 only from car number 962, Nov 73); Black and Autumn Leaf trim now found on all cars (compare change point in Jul 73); radial tyres (Dunlop SP.68, Pirelli Cinturato or Michelin ZX) with tubes fitted on all 4-cyl cars; hazard warning lights fitted on home market cars; inertia reel seat belts standard on home market 4-cyl GT; brake servo standard on home market 4-cyl cars; improved steering column stalk switches. **Changes to North Amer-**

ican cars only: sequential seat belt warning system fitted together with new inertia reel seat belts; modified steering lock, part number now 18G 9119.

GT 328975, Rdst 334715 (Aug 73)
New front engine mounting rubbers and longer bolts.

NA 329017, LHD not NA 329453, V8 650 (Sep 73)
On cars with electric windscreen washer, Jideco pump (13H 7553) introduced instead of Trico pump (BHA 5146).

329770 (Sep 73)
Covers added over front seat squab pivot points.

GT 331127, V8 754 (Oct 73)
Boot board in one piece instead of two, rear seat squab and hinges modified.

GT 331127, Rdst 331491 (Oct 73)
Ignition coil terminals now fixed by studs and nuts instead of rivets.

Not NA 332033, (intermittently, approx), Not NA 336650 (all, approx) (Nov 73)
New engines on non-North American cars, series 18V-779/780 (compare list of engine change points); there was some overlap with the previous engines, series 18V-581/582.

V8 926 (Nov 73)
New hose from oil cooler to filter, for improved clearance to horn.

V8 1149 (Dec 73)
New oil filter, new oil gauge pipe running from oil pump cover instead of filter, for improved reading on oil pressure gauge when starting engine.

GT 338568, Rdst 338791 (Dec 73)
Alternative oil filter of spin-on type introduced, with oil cooler pipes modifed to suit.

Not quoted (Dec 73)
GT model withdrawn from Californian market.

Rdst NA 339095, GT NA 339472 (Jan 74)
New front and rear bumpers with big rubber overriders, complying with US legislation. New rear number plate and number plate lamps.

Rdst 339123, GT 339472 (Jan 74)
New improved door lock assemblies with longer operating lever.

Not quoted (Jan 74)
All models (including V8), new fuel tanks without drain plugs.

Not NA 339965, V8 1248 (Jan 74)
Number plate lamps moved from rear overriders to centre part of bumper bar, new number plate lamps Lucas L.780 instead of L.534. Non-handed front overriders fitted also to rear bumper.

Rdst NA 341295, GT NA 341730 (Feb 74)
Engine restraint tube added on North American cars, engine front mountings and rear crossmember modified to comply with US legislation.

GT 342851, Rdst 343042, V8 1424 (Feb 74)
New black Metallifacture jack BHH 5329, common to both 4-cyl and V8 models, introduced instead of previous King Dick and Metallifacture jacks.

Rdst 343303, GT 343767 (Feb 74)
Inverted oil filter re-introduced, oil cooler pipes revert to pre-Dec 73 types.

Rdst 345391, GT 345804 (Mar 74)
Seven-blade plastic fan with metal inserts fitted to cars for all markets.

V8 1661 (May 74)
Additional packing for front engine mountings with longer bolts (used intermittently from car number 954, Nov 73).

V8 1720 (May 74)
Front and rear brake hoses with anti-torsion lines.

Rdst 351869 (Jun 74)
Seat covers modified.

V8 1782 (Jun 74)
New clutch slave cylinder pushrod for improved clutch release.

V8 1825 (Jun 74)
Oil pressure gauge now reading to 100 lb/sq in instead of 60lb/sq in. Later gauges read to 80lb/sq in.

V8 1956 (Sep 74)
Heat shields added to plug leads for four middle cylinders.

Rdst 360301, GT 361001, V8 2101 (Sep 74)
Start of '1974½' model year (rubber bumper cars). Revised 4-cyl engines, series 18V-846/847 (not North America), 18V-836/837 (North America). **Changes to all cars (including V8 unless otherwise specified)**: new oil

The MG badge on 'rubber-bumper' cars was mounted on the bumper. The earliest cars of this type, built in 1974, had a red background and this was also found on the home market LE models in 1980.

cooler, pipes and hoses; V8 radiator modified; fuel pipes modifed, fuel pump mounted in boot and black metal guard added; exhaust systems revised; ballasted ignition coils introduced, Lucas 16C6 on North American cars, 15C6 on all others; overdrive unit on 4-cyl cars changed; steering rack modified; new collapsible steering column, now the same on all cars including North American and V8 models; side-entry steering lock with press-button key release on all cars; new coil springs on 4-cyl GT; new front anti-roll bar on V8 and 4-cyl GT, anti-roll bar deleted on roadster; roadster fitted with GT-type seven-leaf rear springs; V8 rear suspension rebound straps fitted on 4-cyl cars; rear shock absorbers revised; accelerator cable and pedal, and choke cable, modified on 4-cyl cars; all cars fitted with T-handle choke pull; master cylinder box on non-NA LHD cars modified; brake pipes, handbrake assembly and handbrake cables all modified; one 12-volt instead of two six-volt batteries, one battery box only, new access panel, new battery fixings and clamps; wiring harness modified; switchgear revised, V8-type panel light switch on non-NA 4-cyl cars, two V8-type column stalks on non-NA 4-cyl cars, one stalk operating wipers, washer and overdrive, new steering column cowl; electric windscreen washer on non-NA 4-cyl cars; 80mm speedometer and tachometer introduced on non-NA 4-cyl cars, with V8-type instrument binnacle and revised facia panel; uprated semi-sealed beam headlamps with built-in sidelamps on most non-NA cars (cars for France and Germany continue with non-sealed beam headlamps, and cars for North America with sealed beams); new front direction indicator lamps in bumper, with amber lenses (white lenses for Italy), and incorporating sidelamps on North American cars; new rear number plate lamps, Lucas L.467 on non-NA cars; Mixo horns instead of Lucas; major modifications to bodyshells, including front wings, front fairing panel, front sidemembers, front wheelarch panels, rear sidemembers and boot floor, rear valance panel wider and rear wings narrower, with unleaded joints further outboard; new impact-resistant rubber bumpers; new radiator grille behind front bumper; new number plates, and brackets for front number plate; roadster windscreen assembly modified; new tonneau covers on all roadsters; new heater water valve on 4-cyl cars, new heater controls and knobs (illuminated on North American cars), longer North American type demister nozzles introduced on all cars; front mats and rear compartment carpet modified; two door mirrors fitted as standard on all cars; cars with Rostyle wheels now fitted with tubeless tyres; cars for Benelux countries now fitted with dual-circuit brakes. **Changes to North American cars only**: inertia fuel cut-out switch (C.41220) added; service interval counter added; windscreen washer water container now box type instead of bag. **NB**: From the start of production of rubber-bumper cars, all LHD export models were built with North American type bodies and facias.

GT 361016, V8 1955 (Sep 74)
Sun visors modified.

Rdst LHD 361626, GT LHD 363234 (Oct 74)
Cars for Switzerland, original three-blade fan reinstated instead of plastic fan, and new exhaust system with sound deflector shields, to comply with Swiss noise regulations.

GT NA 367803 (Dec 74)
Last GT to North American specification at the end of the '1974½' model year.

Rdst 367901, Rdst NA 368082, GT 368601 (Dec 74)
Start of 1975 model year. **Changes to North American roadsters only**: new engines, series 18V-797/798-AE-L; exhaust system, radiator and heater hoses, oil pipes all modified; oil cooler deleted; direct-acting brake servo introduced as standard (servo not previously available on NA cars); harness altered; new tonneau cover. Non-North American cars continue unchanged.

V8 2146 (Dec 74)
New heater water valve.

Rdst 369259, GT 369697, V8 2199 (Jan 75)
Front bumper badge, boot lid and tailgate badges, and V8 motifs changed from silver to gold colour; horn push badge colour changed from red to gold (yellow); these changes apply during the 'jubilee' year of 1975; MGB letter badge on roadster boot lid discontinued and roadster boot lid MG badge now in metal instead of plastic.

**Rdst NA 371464 (Feb 75), GT 378517,
Rdst RHD 378846, V8 2530 (May 75)**
New lighter front and rear bumper armatures, separate front bumper spings deleted.

Rdst NA 372613 (Feb 75)
Sequential seat belt control deleted, replaced by time delay buzzer; microswitch in passenger seat belt and seat sensors discontinued; harness modified to suit.

V8 2266 (Feb 75)
Additional two heat shields fitted to plug leads for two front cylinders.

Not quoted (Feb 75)
Cigar lighter standard on 4-cyl cars for all markets.

Not quoted (Feb 75)
Heater fitted as standard for all markets, including Hawaii and Puerto Rico (which were the last markets to take cars without a heater).

Rdst LHD 373707, GT LHD 364652 (Mar 75)
New number plate lamps on cars for Germany, two off Lucas L.467/2 (twin bulbs) instead of L.467 (single bulb), new bracket for rear number plate.

GT 374858 (Apr 75)
Special limited edition Jubilee or Anniversary model introduced for the home market; finished in Racing Green with a gold tape stripe; overdrive, headrests, tinted glass and full carpeting standard; steering wheel with black spokes; black door mirrors; fitted V8-style cast-alloy wheels, painted gold and black; cars supplied with special numbered facia plaques (shipped loose with car). Total production, 751 cars (one destroyed in TV stunt).

Rdst 378305, GT 378517 (May 75)
Front and rear brake hoses with anti-torsion lines as found on V8 since May 74.

GT 379495, Rdst 380278 (Jun 75)
Overdrive standard on home market cars, continued as option on all export cars, RHD and North American models.

GT 379554, Rdst 382127 (Jun 75), V8 2600 (Jul 75)
Alternative plastic tool bag introduced (BHH 1808 instead of AHH 6540).

GT LHD 379559, Rdst LHD 380866 (Jun 75)
Special anniversary badge (HZA 5025) fitted on the facia of all LHD cars with North American-type facias to mark the 1975 Jubilee year.

Rdst NA Cal 382135 (Jun 75)
Introduction of special Californian model with lead-free tolerant engine, series 18V-801/802-AE-L, with catalyst to exhaust, electronic ignition, special petrol filler neck, labels on fuel gauge and by petrol filler.

Not quoted (Jul 75)
All models fitted with polyurethane instead of braided metal petrol hoses.

GT 379760, Rdst 384319, V8 2618 (Aug 75)
Front number plate relocated to improve air flow to the radiator.

**Rdst NA 385257 (Aug 75), Rdst LHD 393208,
GT LHD 394579 (Dec 75)**
Oil pressure gauge with dual markings in Imperial and Met-

ric introduced, common to all LHD and North American cars.

Rdst 386601 (Sep 75), GT 391501, V8 2701 (Nov 75)
Start of 1976 model year. All cars for the USA now have engines series 18V-801/802 with catalyst exhausts and other attendant changes, but cars for Canada continue with engines series 18V-797/798 and no catalyst. **Changes to all cars**: new fuel tank hoses and filler neck (special type for unleaded petrol on US cars); handbrake assembly modified; front wheelarch reinforcements added to bodyshells; front fairing and rear valance panels now finished in satin black below bumpers; modified radiator on 4-cyl cars, with cap upgraded to 13lb/sq in. **Changes to all LHD cars, including North American roadsters**: bonnet strut repositioned on RH side on LHD cars, to avoid fouling brake servo; handbrake warning light fitted to all LHD cars; cars with dual-circuit brake systems have a repositioned brake failure switch, incorporating a latching valve to ensure warning light stays on permanently in case of brake pressure failure. **On North American roadsters**, brake system extensively revised, with changes to master cylinder, servo, master cylinder box, and brake and clutch pedals. Wiring harness modified. On cars for Canada, service interval counter deleted.

Rdst 386796 (Sep 75)
Roadster reverts to six-leaf rear springs instead of GT-type seven-leaf springs.

**LHD not NA 391933, Rdst NA 392006,
Rdst/GT RHD 394301, V8 2708 (Dec 75)**
Armoured front brake hoses introduced.

Rdst 392766, GT 394476, V8 2713 (Dec 75)
Fuel filler neck rubber grommet with improved location and sealing introduction.

393600 (Dec 75), V8 2723 (Jan 76)
Gear lever gaiter retainer now finished in black epoxy resin instead of chrome plating.

Rdst 394008, GT 394678, V8 2723 (Jan 76)
Front bumper, boot lid and tailgate badges together with V8 motifs and horn push revert to pre-1975 non-gold types; anniversary badge on facia of LHD cars deleted.

GT 394781, Rdst 395332, V8 2742 (Jan 76)
Lucas starter relay type 26RA with plastic cover and single fixing introduced instead of type 6RA with metal cover and double fixing.

GT 396587, Rdst 397927, V8 2789 (Feb 76)
New hose for oil gauge pressure pipe.

GT LHD 396624, Rdst LHD 397957 (Feb 76)
Modified rear number plate lamp platform bracket on cars for Germany.

GT 396635, Rdst 398486 (Feb 76)
Battery with clamp-on leads instead of screw fixing, new battery cables (not introduced on V8 model).

A gold variation of the familiar wing-style badge was used during 1975 calendar year, with gold as the background colour for the octagon, and 'BGT' now in black. In 1976, the octagon background colour reverted to silver, still with all-black lettering.

On 1975 and later roadster models, a one-piece metal badge was found on the boot lid but the MGB lettering had been deleted.

This GT badge at the top of the rear pillar was introduced in early 1976 to hide the panel joint when it ceased to be leaded. On the other side of the car, the position of the letters relative to the shape of the badge was obviously reversed.

401000, approx (Mar 76)
Roadster: new boot lid seal fitted to lip of boot aperture instead of boot lid. GT: additional GT badges fitted at the top of the rear quarter pillars, to cover a panel joint which was previously lead-loaded. At this time it appears that all lead-loading of bodies was discontinued, and bodies were from now on completed at Swindon without having to be sent to Cowley body plant where lead-loading was carried out.

GT 401338, Rdst 402215, V8 2823 (Mar 76)
Door mirrors of stainless steel introduced instead of chrome-plated mirrors.

Rdst NA 409141 (Jun 76)
New number plate lamp, AAU 2143, made by L E Pirie instead of BHH 5303 made by Lucas.

V8 2903 (Jul 76)
Last V8, model discontinued. Car number 2901 was the last series production car and was built in June. Numbers 2902 and 2903 built in July were partly to 1977 specification, with some body, facia and trim changes.

Rdst 410001, GT 410351 (Jun 76)
Start of 1977 model year. **Changes to all cars, unless otherwise specified**: revised engines on US Federal (49 state) cars, series 18V-883/884, and on Californian cars, series 18V-890/891, with new carburettor specifications; pulleys changes on all engines as mechanical fan deleted; new radiator, mounted further forward and with separate expansion tank; V8-type electric fan adopted, two on North American cars, one on all others; hoses and water outlet elbow modified to suit; mud and acoustic shield added below the gap between radiator and engine; steering rack with reduced ratio, new steering column, 15in (381mm) four-spoke steering wheel; V8-type front hubs introduced on disc wheel cars; front anti-roll bar re-introduced on roadster, both roadster and GT fitted with stiffer anti-roll bars; anti-sway bar fitted to rear suspension, rear axle modified to suit; over-drive standard on all RHD cars, new gear lever with over-drive switch in knob; bodyshells modified, new front wheel-arch panels with revised radiator mountings, new A-post panels and boot floor; tinted glass standard on GT; new striped nylon fabric seat covers on RHD cars, modified Ambla seat covers on LHD cars; new headrests, now standard on RHD cars; new door liners, with built-in radio speakers as standard on LHD cars; LHD cars also fitted with wing-mounted aerial as standard; new rear quarter upper liner and waist liner on GT; sun visors added on RHD roadster, new sun visors on all cars with document pocket on driver's side, vanity mirror on passenger side; all cars fully carpeted, including sill carpets instead of mats; new facias on both RHD and LHD cars; new instruments, similar to Triumph Spit-fire, 4in speedometer and tachometer on LHD cars, still 80mm on RHD cars, all speedometers with dual mph/kph markings; new switches, with illuminated switches also on RHD cars; new Marina-type column stalks, with horn push back on stalk; US cars continue with word descriptions on switchgear etc, all other cars use international ISO symbols; seat belt and handbrake warning lights added on RHD cars; new two-speed fan for heater, new heater controls, illumi-nated also on RHD cars; new courtesy lamps, round on con-sole on RHD cars, rectangular with switch in rocking lens on lower edge of facia on LHD cars; halogen headlamps with built-in sidelamps fitted on RHD cars, LHD NA cars continue with sealed beam headlamps; new wiring harness and fuse-box; roadster windscreen assembly and hood header rail modified, new hood with zip-out rear window; tonneau cov-ers modified to suit new headrests; new accelerator pedal; optional chrome Rostyle wheels deleted, altered paint fin-ish on painted Rostyle wheels. **NB**: From the start of the 1977 model year, production of LHD GTs was discontinued and LHD roadsters were made only for the North American markets.

GT 410390, Rdst NA 410800,
Rdst RHD 411380 (Jun 76)
Unspecified modification to doors (which are interchange-able with the previous type) – probably to accommodate wiring for speakers.

Rdst NA 411635, intermittently (Jul 76),
Rdst NA 429084, all (Feb 77)
Transmission control spark advance system fitted to cure surge problem; system includes a solenoid-activated vac-uum valve mounted on the pedal box lid; pedal box lid and wiring harness modified to suit.

GT 412301, Rdst 415001 (Aug 76)
Start of full fuel integrity system; new fuel tank, incorporat-ing combined fuel feed and gauge unit; short vertical filler neck to tank; fuel pipes altered to suit; additional inertia and roll sensitive fuel cut-off valve (AAU 5050) on NA roadster; new plastic covered handbrake cables of rod-type without compensating lever for better clearance to fuel tank.

Rdst 412871 (Aug 76)
Hard top modified with new liner for improved clearance to sun visor pivot bracket. Hard top when supplied for service purposes now finished in black instead of primer.

Rdst NA Can 414629 (Aug 76)
First 1977 model year car for Canada, with revised engines series 18V-892/893, including new carburettor specification to bring into line with US engines, but no catalyst.

Rdst 416162 (Sep 76)

Luggage rack discontinued as factory-fitted option.
416660 (Sep 76)
Wire wheel BHH 2133 instead of AHH 6487, new wheel has ⁹⁄₁₆in inset to improve tyre clearance to wheelarch.
Rdst NA 417229 (Oct 76)
New Radiomobile loudspeakers, incorporating grille and weathershield in one unit with white plastic deflector over the top half of the diaphragm.
GT 420955, Rdst RHD 421935 (Nov 76)
Probable introduction of alternative black finish instead of chrome plating for number plate lamps.
Rdst NA 423079 (Nov 76), Rdst RHD 435336 (May 77)
Sun visors modified with cranked pivot rod and new grain for the cover material.
Not quoted (Jan 77)
Service interval counter deleted on US roadster (may have happened earlier).
GT 422792, Rdst 425297 (Jan 77)
Fuel pump specification changed from AUF 305 to AZX 1307 for improved contact life and to inhibit buzzing; new pump can be identified by the cover which is not stepped (inter-changeable).
GT 426478, Rdst 429264 (Feb 77)
Strap for front anti-roll bar bearing commonised with strap for rear anti-sway bar bearing.
Rdst US 428511 (Feb 77), Rdst Can 440636 (Jun 77)
Accelerator cable assembly with return spring bracket instead of separate lever.
Rdst NA 428538 (Feb 77)
Optional extra overdrive now operates only on top gear; RHD cars continue with overdrive on third and top gears fitted as standard.
Rdst NA 429589, GT 431464 (Feb 77)
Improved Kangol inertia reel seat belts, series 13 on LHD roadster and series 12 on GT, with new stowing hooks.
Not quoted (Mar 77)
LHD NA roadsters, number plate lamps finished in matt black instead of chrome plating (may have occurred earlier).
GT 431748, Rdst 433038 (Apr 77)
Heat shield added to underside of gearbox tunnel to dissi-pate heat from catalyst exhaust on cars so equipped (heat shield also found on non-catalyst cars).
Rdst 432905 (Apr 77)
New windscreen glass with glazing rubber to suit.
Rdst RHD 435321 (May 77)
Kangol series 13 inertia reel seat belts fitted as standard (already found on LHD roadster) with new stowing hooks and attendant changes to rear inner wing panels; tonneau cover modified to suit, also with new fastening pattern.
GT 436465, Rdst RHD 437181 (May 77)
RHD cars fitted with dual-circuit brakes and direct-acting in-line servo, already found on LHD cars; brake master cylin-der, servo, brake pipes, pedal box, and brake and clutch pedals all changed; attendant changes to bodyshells and wiring harness. NB: 69 cars with higher car numbers were built with single-line brakes to use up old bodies.
GT 436654 (Jun 77), Rdst 437800 (May 77)
Reversing lamps now fitted to body with self-tapping screws, spire nuts and end protectors.
Rdst NA 442350 (Aug 77)
Brake master cylinder, servo and servo vacuum hose modi-fied.
Rdst Jap 443981* (Sep 77)
First roadster to Japanese specification, as 1978 model year NA Californian with engine series 18V-891-AE-L, but with overdrive as standard, km/h speedometer, dip left head-lamps (not halogen type) incorporating sidelamps, rear lamp lenses of RHD type with amber flashers at the top, and switchgear with ISO symbols. Although Japan drives on the left, these cars were left-hand drive. *443981 was the offi-cial starting car number, but one car with a lower number (443383) was actually built after 443981.
Rdst 447001, GT 447036 (Sep 77)
Start of 1978 model year. **Changes to all cars, unless otherwise specified**: MG octagon motif on steering wheel now in hot foiled silver; exhaust system on RHD cars fitted new front silencer of three-pass type, complying with new EEC noise regulations of maximum 82dB; roadster and GT fitted new washer jets of plastic nipple type, two on all cars, with new pipe connections and front shroud panel modified to suit; additional slot in seat rails; convex door mirrors instead of flat glass type on RHD cars, RHD cars now fitted with mirror only on driver's door; dual carbon canisters on

After an interval in the 'Jubilee' year of 1975 when the front badge had a gold (or yellow) background, the better-known silver and black type as seen here was fitted to most cars until the end of production.

North American cars, added on cars for Japan only from 454274 in Dec 77; km/h speedometer on cars for Canada.

Rdst NA 447001 (Sep 77), GT 451053 (Nov 77), Rdst RHD 454203 (Dec 77)
New fuel filler connection hose and rubber neck grommet meeting new Californian requirements, fitted on all cars for North America; found on Japanese cars from start of production, subsequently commonised also on RHD cars.

GT 448388, Rdst NA 449290, Rdst RHD 449607 (Oct 77)
New steering lock, without press button key release.

GT 449493, Rdst RHD 449827, Rdst NA 449834 (Oct 77)
Black carpet material changed to Astrakhan quality, coinciding with introduction of Chestnut colour for carpets (cp. below) which was also in Astrakhan.

Rdst NA 449837* (Oct 77)
Autumn Leaf trim and carpet colour replaced by Beige trim and Chestnut carpet on North American and Japanese roadsters in certain paint colours. *The change point is quoted in the parts list as 449827 but the first North American car in an appropriate paint colour after this was 449837. Either number may be suspect, as the trim colour change may have been introduced from the start of the 1978 model year on cars in Brooklands Green, Carmine Red and Russet Brown, and on cars in Pageant Blue from the start of this colour (possibly roadster car number 453098 in Dec 77).

Rdst 453141, GT 453424 (Dec 77)
Plastic packing strip to battery clamp deleted.

GT 453449, Rdst 453745 (Dec 77)
British Leyland badge on front wing deleted, owing to a change in corporate identity policy as Michael Edwardes had become chairman of BL on 1 November 1977.

Rdst 453786 (Dec 77)
Tonneau cover, already standard on home market cars, becomes standard fitting on North American and RHD export cars.

GT 455131 (Dec 77)
Separate warning light for heated rear window added, relay for heated rear window deleted.

GT 455283, Rdst RHD 455803 (Jan 78), Rdst Can 459665 (Feb 78), Rdst US/Jap 463175 (Mar 78)
Thermal cut-out switch instead of line fuse to eliminate fuse holders overheating; main harness modified to suit.

GT disc 455297, Rdst disc 455768 (Jan 78), Rdst wire 460765, GT wire 461144 (Feb 78)
Steel-braced radial tyres introduced instead of textile reinforced tyres; initial approval for Dunlop SP, Pirelli P3 and Michelin XZX, in tubeless as well as tubed versions.

GT disc 457109 (Jan 78), Rdst disc 457174, Rdst wire 457631, GT wire 458810 (Feb 78)
Repositioned three-way bracket for brake pipes on rear axle, rear brake pipes modified to suit.

Rdst NA 457312 (Jan 78)
Improved material for carburettor heat shield.

Not quoted (Feb 78)
Following alternative tyres approved for fitment: Goodyear G.888+S (tubeless or tubed); Uniroyal Rallye 180 and Firestone S.1 (both tubeless only).

GT 458790, Rdst 459477 (Feb 78)
Front bumper mounting cover plates added.

Rdst US/Jap 459316 (Feb 78)
Modified exhaust system on cars fitted with catalyst, with angle bracket to sump added for increased support.

Rdst 462682, GT 465252 (Mar 78)
New non-return valve for brake servo on inlet manifold, common to both RHD and LHD NA cars.

Rdst NA 464011 (Apr 78)
Tool bag retaining bracket and strap added in boot.

Rdst 467525 (May 78), GT 468233 (Apr 78)
Dual-sensitive Kangol seat belts of GT type now fitted also on roadster, so common type of belt found on all vehicles; seat belt length reduced.

GT wire 469082 (May 78), Rdst wire 471642, Rdst disc 471774, GT disc 473147 (Jun 78)
Rear brakes, back plates and wheel cylinders modified.

Rdst 471001 (May 78), GT 471036 (Jun 78)
Start of 1979 model year **Changes to all cars, unless otherwise specified**: LHD roadster, oil hose from filter to block replaced by pipe; rationalised alternator design with modified fan; horns with earth return instead of insulated return; loudspeakers and radio aerial added on RHD cars (already found on LHD cars), with door liners on RHD cars changed to LHD type to accommodate loudspeakers; front bumper springs re-introduced; wiring harness modified, now also incorporates radiator fan motor wiring in main harness.

Rdst US 472671, Rdst Can 473394 (Jun 78)
Part-aluminised exhaust systems introduced.

Rdst 478946, GT 480032 (Sep 78)
Air intake grille finish changed from black enamel to black epoxy powder coating.

GT 480297, Rdst RHD 481116 (Oct 78)
Speedometer and tachometer graphics altered with figures inside markings instead of outside, speedometer now reads 10/30/50 (etc) instead of 10/20/30/40 (etc).

GT 483819, Rdst NA 485075, Rdst RHD 485400 (Dec 78)
Carpet quality changed from Astrakhan back to Firth's cut-pile (pre-Oct 77 type).

GT 487253, Rdst 488709 (Feb 79)
Fan guard of improved material and finish, and with rear edge extended by 0.56in.

GT 487396, Rdst 489650 (Feb 79)
Loudspeakers with improved watershield.

Rdst 490637, GT 491837 (Mar 79)
Front and rear hubs on disc-wheeled cars changed to ensure compatibility with cast-alloy wheels; rear axle assembly modified to suit.

Rdst Can 492071, Rdst Fed 492107, Rdst Cal 492129 (Mar 79)
First North American roadsters to Limited Edition or 'Special' specification (sometimes referred to at the factory as 'Jubilee' models); fitted with cast-alloy wheels, special leather-covered alloy spoke steering wheel, and tape stripes; front air dam fitted by NA importers; many cars also fitted with luggage rack and floor mats by NA importers; some cars fitted with air conditioning in USA but never in the factory; black paint, black or beige trim; tyre size 185/70SR-14, Dunlop SP4 or Uniroyal Rallye; new spare wheel clamp, wheel nuts and spanner, to suit alloy wheels; available either with or without overdrive.

GT 495182, Rdst 496243 (Apr 79)
Width of air intake grille reduced from 31.40in overall to 30.20in.

GT 496939 (May 79), Rdst RHD 501874 (Jun 79)
Cast-alloy wheel option introduced on RHD cars, with tyre equipment, spare wheel clamp, wheel nuts and spanner as specified for North American LE models (cp. above).

Rdst 501001, GT 501036, Rdst Fed LE 503521, Rdst Cal 498441* (Jun 79)
Start of 1980 model year. Changes: 85mph speedometer on US cars, with six-digit odometer; six-digit odometer on cars for Canada and Japan with km/h speedometers; tachometer graphics altered; new type of distributor on US cars with electronic ignition, now type 45DM4 with separate amplifier; RHD (home market) cars fitted with rear fog guard lamps

Lucas 57320, wiring harness modified to suit; new switch for heated rear window on GT, with built-in warning light, separate warning light discontinued as displaced by rear fog guard lamp switch; new VIN type car number prefixes, new identification plates stamped 'BL Cars Ltd' incorporating colour and trim codes. *Production of Californian cars continued with numbers from 498441 to 500904 to the end of 1979 calendar year as '1979 models', there were officially no 1980 model year Californian cars.

GT 503016 (Jun 79)
Improved wiper blades, Trico series 8 instead of Trico type APC.

Rdst NA 505066 (Sep 79)
New headlamp rim, notched to allow adjustment of lamp without removing rim, headlamp assembly modified in compliance with new US legislation.

Rdst NA 505095 (Sep 79), Rdst/GT RHD 512240 (Jan 80)
Front suspension crossmember altered during re-tooling, in anticipation of O-series engine being fitted for 1981.

GT 505375, Rdst 505820 (Oct 79)
VIN number now stamped in right-hand sidemember of boot floor on all cars.

Rdst 506717, GT 507821 (Nov 79)
Front bumper springs discontinued (again!).

Rdst Cal 500248, Rdst Fed 506953 (Dec 79), GT 512587, Rdst RHD/Can 513006 (Feb 80)
Bottom radiator hose to water pump, shape changed for improved clearance to sidemember.

Rdst FED LE 509502, Rdst US/Jap 511291, Rdst RHD 511250, Rdst Can 511743, GT 512408 (Jan 80)
New thermostatic switch for radiator fan motor, radiator header tank modified to suit; distributor modified on cars for the USA and Japan, with Lucas AB14 amplifier, and Lucas ignition coil 32C5 fitted instead of 16C6, wiring harness modified to suit.

Rdst US/Jap 509268, Rdst Can 511359 (Jan 80)
Improved construction of front silencer with internal pipe in stainless steel.

Rdst 510255, GT 514664 (Mar 80)
Seat belts of modified type, conforming to EEC as well as US regulations.

Rdst 515195, GT 516743 (Apr 80)
New engine earth return wire.

Rdst 516119, GT 516984 (May 80)
Handbrake assembly modified for more accurate assembly during production.

Rdst US/Jap 516374, Rdst Can 517940 (Jun 80)
Fuel cut-out inertia switch changed to type 481, wiring harness modified to suit.

Rdst RHD 518492, GT 519867 (Aug 80)
Production of home market Limited Edition model begins, alongside standard specification home/export cars; fitted cast-alloy or wire wheels, tape stripe, metallic paint, front air dam and special red badges.

Rdst 523001, GT 523002 (Oct 80)
End of production.

The final variation of GT badging was found only on the home market 1980 LE model, the 'MG' letters and octagon surround in red instead of black.

CLUBS

Any MG owner is always well advised to join an appropriate club, in order to obtain the club magazine and other publications, to take part in club activities, to buy spares or other parts which may be available, or to enjoy other privileges available to members such as special insurance schemes. In the UK there are two main clubs:

MG Car Club, Kimber House, PO Box 251, Abingdon, Oxfordshire OX14 1FF (tel 0235 555552). Chairman, Mike Hawke. Administrator, Lyn Jeffrey. This is the oldest MG club, founded in 1930. The club incorporates registers for the MGB, MGC and MGB GT V8, together with smaller registers for limited editions, automatic MGBs and even early models with pull-type door handles. It publishes the monthly *Safety Fast!* magazine and has numerous local centres and affiliated clubs around the world. Readers outside the UK and the USA seeking details of local clubs not listed here are welcome to contact the UK-based MG Car Club headquarters for information.

MG Owners' Club, Freepost, Swavesey, Cambridge CB4 1BR (tel 0954 31125). Secretary, Roche Bentley. Formed in 1973, this club has become one of the biggest organisations of its kind in the world, with 50,000 members. MGB owners are particularly well catered for by its extensive range of services, further improved after the move to impressive new headquarters in 1992. There is also an excellent monthly magazine, *Enjoying MG*. Many local centres operate throughout the UK as well as some abroad. The club shop sells an extensive range of parts and accessories.

MGB Register, PO Box MGB, Akin, IL 62805, USA.

American MGB Association (AMGBA), PO Box 11401, Chicago, IL 60611, USA.

American MGC Register, 34 Park Avenue, Asheville, NC 28803-2056, USA.

There are also numerous local MG clubs throughout the USA and Canada. Apart from the clubs, there are two specialised magazines which will be of interest to MGB owners and enthusiasts, one in the UK and one in the USA:

MG Enthusiast Magazine, PO Box 11, Dewsbury, West Yorkshire WF12 7UZ (tel 0924 499261). Editor: Martyn Wise. Now monthly, available through newsagents or on subscription.

MG Magazine (editors: Henry A. Rippert and Dick L.Knudson), PO Box 321, Otego, NY 13825, USA. Publishes four to six issues per year, available mainly on subscription. Run concurrently with the magazine are the MG Motorists' Group, an informal club, and the Brit Books classic car book service.

Owned by Heather Wood, this is a 1980 GT in Brooklands Green. The car has an A-prefixed number plate because it was mothballed by a garage for four years before being registered, and even today has covered only 6000 miles.